IN THE
MEMORY
HOUSE

∞

HOWARD MANSFIELD

FULCRUM PUBLISHING
Golden, Colorado

For Dr. B. A. Millmoss

The author would like to thank the following for permission to reprint:

Excerpt from *Collected Shorter Poems 1927–1957* by W. H. Auden. Copyright © 1934, copyright renewed 1962 by W. H. Auden. Reprinted by permission of Random House, Inc.

Excerpt from "In Praise of Johnny Appleseed" by Vachel Lindsay. Reprinted with permission of Macmillan Publishing Company from *Collected Poems of Vachel Lindsay* (New York: Macmillan, 1925).

Excerpt from "Monadnock Through the Trees" by Edwin Arlington Robinson. Reprinted with permission of Macmillan Publishing Company from *Collected Poems of Edwin Arlington Robinson*. Copyright © 1921 by Edwin Arlington Robinson, renewed 1949 by Ruth Nivison.

Parts of the following essays have appeared previously:

"On the Eulogy Road: Claiming Jack Kerouac" appeared in the *Washington Post*, the *International Herald Tribune* and *New Letters*.

A small section of "The Forgotten Sorrow of Franklin Pierce, President" appeared in *New England Monthly*.

Sections included in "The Passing of Tall Tree America" appeared in *American Heritage*.

Library of Congress Cataloging-in-Publication Data

Mansfield, Howard.
  In the memory house / Howard Mansfield.
    p.   cm.
  ISBN 1-55591-162-5
  1. Historic sites—New England.   2. New England—Civilization.
  3. United States—History—Philosophy.   I. Title.
  F5.M35   1993
  974—dc20   93-26755
                                     CIP

Jacket Design and Illustrations by Karen Groves
Photograph on Jacket Front © Lorraine Marzilli/MARZ Photo

Printed in the United States of America

0   9   8   7   6   5   4   3   2   1

Fulcrum Publishing
350 Indiana Street, Suite 350
Golden, CO 80401-5093
(800) 992-2908

Contents

In those days before the Great War when the events narrated in this book took place, it had not yet become a matter of indifference whether a man lived or died. When one of the living had been extinguished another did not at once take his place in order to obliterate him: there was a gap where he had been, and both close and distant witnesses of his demise fell silent whenever they became aware of this gap. When fire had eaten away a house from the row of others in a street, the burnt-out space remained long empty. Masons worked slowly and cautiously. Close neighbors and casual passers-by alike, when they saw the empty space, remembered the aspect and walls of the vanished house. That was how things were then. Everything that grew took its time in growing and everything that was destroyed took a long time to be forgotten. And everything that had once existed left its traces so that in those days people lived on memories, just as now they live by the capacity to forget quickly and completely.

—Joseph Roth
The Radetzky March (1932)

Preface

The Cheapest Ornaments of History

I live in a part of New Hampshire that travel writers call "The Currier & Ives Corner." Their stories use the same words in the same order: villages are "charming" and "quaint" and always "nestle" in the valleys. The writers see white picket fences where there aren't any, and all children are "happy children" and sometimes "happy apple-cheeked children."

This is Currier & Ives and Winslow Homer and Norman Rockwell, but not any New England that ever was.

At the height of their popularity, in the 1860s and 1870s, the Currier & Ives prints were already nostalgia. These scenes of rural America hung by city dwellers were advertised as "the cheapest Ornaments in the World." Today, when people travel great distances longing for these scenes, they are longing for a land of never-was, for someone else's nostalgia. This is nostalgia *for* nostalgia. Seizing upon such scenes—barefoot boys, checker games by the woodstove—we have our hands on only the cheapest ornaments of history.

I began looking for a truer sense of the past, attempting to come close to the contours of historical memory itself. I spent hours in little one-room historical museums, the memory houses I talk about in Part I. I started reading town histories, those baggy-pants monsters whose methodology is simplicity itself: naming the world within the precise borders of the town. Every mineral, every bird, sawmill, church, witch and wolf receives a mention. The histories are mystery books, a thousand characters, a ganglion of plots. I attended other people's town meetings, driving miles over frost-heaved roads to sit on hard benches and listen to long soliloquies on dump trucks and dry hydrants.

And I began to stop and read every historical marker I passed (which, around here, can really slow you down). The signs were revealing, not for what they marked, but for when they were so ceremoniously placed. Each is a visible moment of commemoration, the moment we as a society set words into bronze or stone, stake a claim and commit it to the memory house.

At such moments of commemoration, our aspirations are on full view. The doors to the memory house are opened. Each essay in this book deals with commemoration—or failure to commemorate. Who gets to enter the memory house, and who is refused?

Part I is a stroll through some of the little historical societies and museums of New England, many places open only a few hours a day in the warmer months. Each one is a jumble of patriotic relics and thousands of small acts of homage. Part II looks at how we choose our ancestors, who is forgotten and who is remembered. Some are refused entrance. They are not allowed to be part of the story. Part III looks at the rift between "us" and "them."

And some things disappear so totally that we forget that they were ever there. Part IV, "Absences," searches out these losses. The epilogue looks at the character of our modern memory, one so ready to accept a counterfeit history. In the old days "people lived on memories," wrote Joseph Roth in *The Radetzky March,* "just as now they live by the capacity to forget quickly and completely."

Howard Mansfield
Hancock, New Hampshire

Modern Times: A Prologue

A Lost Spring

There was a man I loved to visit. He lived in the house he grew up in—a wonderful, warm, cluttered house that seemed larger inside than out. There were long hallways and rooms, and a barn lined with the things he had collected—antlers and bones, small animal skulls, wood of all sorts. He would carve animals on these or paint scenes of how it used to be. He carved my wife's wedding ring.

I could have listened to him tell me stories for hours. He knew how many turtle eggs it took to make enough mayonnaise to last the summer. In his stories he could remake the land, clear away the woods and bring back the farms he knew in his youth, the trains, the factories making clothespins.

His house is two hundred years old, shaded by a maple tree probably as old—the tree is what you look at first. The house seems to be keeping the tree company. He told me once that it used to get so cold upstairs in his sisters' bedrooms that the nail heads in the wall would frost over. And in summer it would be so hot up there. But they would run down to the swimming hole and come back and slip

1

under the sheets—real cool. The swimming hole was a marvelous place. It was fed by a spring.

Some years back, the state widened the road and built a new bridge. They had to drop a cement slab on that spring. Plugged it right up, he told me. It took quite a load of cement and a bit of engineering, but they stopped the spring and the bridge goes through straight. You wouldn't even notice it.

When I pass his house and that great maple tree, I picture the spring, and the children swimming there in summer twilight.

And when I am away from this corner of New Hampshire, down among the landscape of haste—parking lot and highway, mall and condo—I look into the faces of my countrymen and I think of the plugged spring.

Part I

IN THE
MEMORY HOUSE

In the
Memory House

In Brownington, Vermont, there is a small bottle. The bottle is green, maybe four inches long, and has a label. In fading ink it says, "This barley was grown in 1883 and given by Mrs. Selden Gray." The bottle is filled with barley.

∞

Brownington is a village a dozen miles from the Canadian border, home to 708 souls and the Old Stone House Museum. You can't miss the museum; it is housed in a four-story granite building that was once part of an academy run by Alexander Twilight, said to be the first black to earn a degree from an American college, Middlebury, back in 1823. When the oxen were done hauling the granite slabs for the great dormitory in 1836, the building must have seemed huge. Today it still seems somewhat misplaced, a roaming academic building far from the herd in Dartmouth or Middlebury.

The guidebook says, "The collections are rural and vernacular in scope" (i.e., a mongrel collection) "with many fine examples of local folk art and folk technology" (i.e., bad paintings and old tools, once coveted, now merely curious). In short, the next blockbuster Metropolitan Museum of Art show—tickets by Ticketron, T-shirts, hoopla—will not be stopping in Brownington. But when the museum is open, the director, Reed Cherington, or one of the volunteers will kindly show you through, and in this age of mass tourism, they are ready to accommodate groups of up to forty people.

From the guidebook you wouldn't guess what a feast awaits. There are some five thousand objects in twenty-three rooms, with each of ten rooms devoted to one town in the county. There is "folk technology": the Yankee Flytrap, which, if I understand it, has a rotating gooey wheel to catch flies and a blade to scrape them off into a cage. (Okay, so the world never beat a path to the door of this Brownington inventor.) There are eighteenth-century furniture, needlepoint samplers, children's toys, bells, pitchforks and light bulbs—a three-shelf history of the light bulb, complete with a portrait of Edison himself. There are those unsettling nineteenth-century portraits of children by itinerant painters. The artists would paint a series of bodies first, hit the road, and then do the head in a sitting. The heads and bodies are always a bad fit, making the children seem dwarfish. There is Alexander Twilight's pony-skin-covered wooden trunk with his initials in brass tacks, and his desk and Bible as well. And there is someone's rock collection, gathered on a brave westward trek in the 1880s. There is always a rock collection. Before Kodak and souvenir ashtrays, rocks were what people brought home. They were the proof of the pilgrimage, the moon rocks of their day, and, once donated to the town, part of the "advancement of knowledge for mankind."

The Orleans County Historical Society runs the Old Stone House Museum. This is a populist museum in a way that would set any curator's teeth on edge. For sixty years people have been donating what they thought should be here. Sometimes these treasured objects were on their way to the dump when their owner hesitated, thought, "Oh what the heck, I've got a few minutes before the ball game," and left it to the ages instead. Sometimes a rare eighteenth-century baby cradle is donated and sometimes a bottle filled with barley grain. That bottle is easily overshadowed by the other 4,999 objects in the collection, but it well explains the whole museum.

∞

"This barley was grown in 1883 and given by Mrs. Selden Gray." Why this? Why leave a bottle of grain in the perpetual care of neighbors and their descendants? Who would want to see it? It's not even a rock collection, not a stuffed owl or a wedding dress or a three-shelf history of the light bulb.

Here's my guess: To Mrs. Selden Gray it was the story of 1883 in a bottle: sowing the seed, the rainy spring, the dry summer (or the dry spring and the rainy summer), the blight that threatened, the sickness and health that came along that summer, the day they put aside their work to see the traveling carnival, the harvest, the harvest supper, the meals made from the barley, the animals fed, the barley bartered or sold to neighbors. A harvest corked for one hundred years, a low-tech time capsule. This was life, she was saying.

At least, that is what I presume. Maybe it was just some barley she had around the house. You can read too much into these things. The historical record is distorted by the nasty fact that surviving artifacts are unrepresentative. The Wedding Dress Problem, preservationists sometimes call it. Historical societies and house museums have many wedding dresses, but who saved the workday clothes? Few survive. The same with the houses saved; there are many mansions but few workingman's cottages. You can also call it the Whorehouse Embarrassment: They were there of course, but it's not the kind of thing that makes for a good field trip for Mrs. Wilder's fourth-grade social studies class. Nor would the local garden club want to have their Easter flower show in such a place. The Fort Smith Heritage Foundation in Arkansas is bravely facing these problems: They saved "Miss Laura's House." "Some very prominent people frequented Miss Laura's house," say the restorers.

Still, unless Mrs. Gray was working up to a patent for a bottled

7

barley product, planning to market a high-fiber drink, I think she was very proud of that 1883 harvest.

∞

The Old Stone House Museum is similar to hundreds of little museums throughout New England. Except that the Stone House, with its twenty-three rooms, is something of a mega-museum, a Metropolitan, compared with the others. Almost every town has one, run usually by the historical society. Each is in a house like any other on Main Street, a house inhabited only by artifacts and documents, a house of history, a house of memory.

What is saved and what is discarded, who is remembered and why—all that is significant. Who may enter the memory house is determined by decree and chance and the shared illusions of any society—the "false certainties," as historian Daniel J. Boorstin has called them.

This is what we remember, what we shepherd toward the next generation.

∞

The New Ipswich Historical Society in New Hampshire is one of my favorite museums in the world. It is a close second to the British Museum in London. New Ipswich's holdings can't compare in size. The British Museum covers more than thirteen acres and contains the plunder of the Empire, the Elgin marbles off the Parthenon, medieval illuminated manuscripts and, it seems, almost every Egyptian artifact short of the Pyramids. When I am in London, it is my greatest pleasure just to walk in and visit a favorite item: the page from Lewis Carroll's *Alice's Adventures Under Ground* in his hand, or the crowning procession of man and horse from the Parthenon. Visiting a few objects daily, you come to live with them and think about them in a way that is lost in a prolonged, forced cultural march through the ages, dragging through the Assyrians, praying for a bench in the

Etruscans, looking at Michelangelos and Turners and thinking only of throbbing feet and a pint of bitter.

The New Ipswich museum is in a one-room schoolhouse open only a few hours each summer (there is no heat for the winter, and the curator is in Massachusetts), and since New Ipswich never ruled the waves, the Egyptian collection is lacking. But for a sublime jumble shop of American history, it can't be beat.

The museum is a wonderful musty-cool when you enter; the sweet smell of decay, history hurrying toward dust. Sitting on the floor, in a shoal of dust, is the marble bust of some old Appleton, once the leading family, whose name graced the academy, the mill, and the inn; now off the pedestal, this Appleton, when viewed from above, with handwritten label tottering on his scalp, seems a bit pompous and quite a bit dirty. There is a big, dark oil portrait of an imposing figure. It once hung in the town hall, but now time has caught up with and dethroned the powerful: "A member of the Gibson family" is all the label says. History is like that; you're gone but a hundred, a hundred and fifty years, and someone takes you off your pedestal, or they leave your name off your portrait.

All around the room are items that look like they were dropped off yesterday, like the Civil War rations sitting on a glass shelf:

"Hard Bread or Hard Tack served to John Barnett, 3rd Reg. M.V.M. Dec. 16 1862.

"This was part of a Five-days rations served to each man. Mr. Barnett carried this bread 90 miles, from Goldsboro to Newberne. At this place a friend of his called to see him and he sent some of it home to the north by this man to give his friends an idea of army food.

"Mr. Barnett gave this to the historical society May 18, 1916."

And here it is—a three-inch-square, waffle-like cracker looking as inedible as the day it was baked 130 years ago. (Next to it, a small bug, having tasted of history, lies dead.)

Many of the labels are themselves as old as the century, ink now light brown in proper cursive script. The newer ones are in fading typescript. Unlike its fellow institution, the British Museum, New Ipswich does not hide the pitched debates about authenticity and

9

chronology. Crossouts and emendations of dates and names are in full view of the public. Under a coffee pot, "pewter" is crossed out, "Britannia" is penciled in. On a photo of the Congregational Church burning, "1903" is crossed out for "July 15, 1902." This is as it should be. We are always rewriting the past.

On some matters of authenticity, The New Ipswich (the regal name it should have) maintains a cagey New England silence: "Can't say as 't is, can't say as 't isn't." For example: "Remains of a drum carried in the Revolution. Not known if used as such by Silas Davis or not, but handed down in the Davis Family and given to the historical society by his great grandson. ..." The phrase "Not known if used as such" seems to say, "The family believes this was carried in the Revolution, and we thank them for the gift." This might be another "Wedding Dress" distortion. People believed that their great-great dropped his plow to pick up a—what?—a drum to go face the Redcoats. So many drums have likely been given to historical societies that you could well think the Revolution was a musical engagement, with a few extra muskets in the percussion section.

The curator tells me that when she was growing up, she thought the museum was old-fashioned. She was going to change it, make a proper modern show of things. She went off to college, came back to New Ipswich for summers, and—mercifully she never changed it.

We stand looking at the bottom shelf of a glass display case. There, about ankle level, is a rock collection. Minerals from Nevada, says the label, given to the library in 1901. "We should really do something about that," she says.

The strength of The New Ipswich is its patriotic artifacts. In a glass case (near an "ancient snuff box" and an "ivory back scratcher") are the folded pages of the sermon New Ipswich's Parson Stephen Farrar gave on learning of the death of George Washington. It begins in sure hand: "Know ye not that there is a prince and a great man fallen this day in Israel?" And next to it in the case is "ivy from the tomb of Washington, Oct. 7, 1903" and bark from the Washington Elm, taken in 1923. Across the room is a walking staff made from a branch of the Washington Elm. In another case is a black walnut gathered from the grounds of Mount Vernon.

On a shelf of hats is a "military hat worn by Supply Wilson in the War of 1812." One shelf above the Nevada mineral display is a clump of once-golden braid: "This tassel formed a part of the decorations of the funeral car which carried the remains of the late Abraham Lincoln from Washington to Springfield, April 1865."

In the glass case holding the Washington sermon also resides what is left of the Congregational Church's bell. The bell was made by Paul Revere and brought to New Ipswich, May 2, 1815. It weighed 1,116 pounds. The church was struck by lightning in 1902, and a half-ton bell vanished. There is a spindly, lava-like fragment in the case.

These are relics in the true sense, holy relics, pieces of the true cross of patriotism. Part of the Washington Elm, fringe from the funeral car of Lincoln. Here we see a town mourning Washington, grasping something that was near the *late* Abraham Lincoln. These little museums are our holy reliquaries.

But wait. Does a piece of bark taken in 1923 from a tree Washington may have stood under really tell us anything? Does some faded braid bring us closer to Lincoln? We could just as well be looking at bark taken from a tree outside and braided epaulettes from a Gilbert and Sullivan comic opera. Relics require faith, but history is supposed to be verifiable, true, each event as solid as granite.

If a drum may have never made it to the Revolution, what are we to make of the lesser artifacts, the remnants of daily life: the policeman's rattle, the button collection, the seashell collection, a cigar cutter, a butter churn, old pew cushions from the Fourth Congregational Church, hand-wrought nails, the plates for the one-dollar and five-dollar bills of the New Ipswich Bank. The 1848 Constitution and Bylaws of the Souhegan Division #16, Sons of Temperance. The police regulations from 1904 ("No person shall make any brawls or tumults. ... No person shall use any juggling or unlawful games. ... No person shall within the compact part of town, fire or discharge a cannon").

11

History is a flea market, a jumble shop. What comes down to us from the past? A slice of hardtack, a shard of bell, a few grains of barley. A jumble, suspended in a now-invisible web of family and circumstance, sin and sacrifice.

Of all the objects that ever were, we have these. Of all the Sundays that were, we have a scrap of bell, a few pew cushions, and a chart showing where the families sat.

∞

A flea market: In Ashfield, Massachusetts, the library was faced with a reduced budget. "Somebody said we could sell those old prints over there in the corner," said one of the library's trustees, who fortunately was a history professor. "I walked over and looked at one and it wasn't a print, it was a document and I looked down at the bottom and there was Abraham Lincoln's signature, which was faded a different color from the printed material." The library had one of forty-eight copies of the Emancipation Proclamation that Lincoln had signed in 1864.

∞

In Stoddard, New Hampshire, at the historical society is Zilpha Gould's bread shovel and Dr. Robinson's fire shovel, an old stirrup found at Sumner Knight's house and "pieces of an old kettle found in old cellar hole" and "gloves worn by Minnie M. Barrett. Stoddard N.H., October 29, 1863" (donated by her daughter) and hats and shoes and dresses and hoes and spoons and pieces of Stoddard glass. And just why?

There is a peculiar quality of New England antiquarianism: the ancestor worship, the highly personal nature of the history. Zilpha Gould's bread shovel and someone else's dress and town histories that go house-by-house around the village. This is social history long before the academy had thought to study everyday life.

But the question remains: why herd this collection of objects, gathered by chance and by pride, and give it its own house on Main Street, a house just for memory?

Why not a museum dedicated to just one day of life: August 3, 1854, in Stoddard or July 22, 1973, in Peterborough? And everything, absolutely everything, from that day would be there: all newspapers, broadcasts, advertising, photos of everything that stood on the shelves in stores and pantries and closets; records of everything bought and sold, and everything taken to the dump. Voluntary transcripts—sealed for a generation—of everything said in town that day over dinner, over the fence, over the phone. Copies of all letters written that day, all diaries. And a grand list—to be sealed for two generations: "On this day we do covet": and there would follow thousands of lines of entries of envy and greed, of neighbors' jobs and neighbors' houses. There can be lists for giving thanks and joy, but they will be short lists when, eighty years on, they are opened on Old Home Day and read with the lists of guilt and sorrow, and the longest list, for the injustices, real and perceived, done to the town's residents: "Give us this day our daily grudge."

Or why not just take a flea market or a yard sale and enshrine it in the museum? This is what people were selling, secondhand, in 1969. It would speak volumes, as would a room set aside for a dump display. I am thinking here of a great panoramic picture, like those they used to paint to depict Civil War battles, encircling a large room. Imagine the grandeur of it—a mountain of trash, the cast-off toasters and blenders and refrigerators of 1954 or 1978. In just a few years people will stand at the panorama, point out different objects and laugh at such waste. (They will no doubt be cleaning up after us, as ever more lethal chemical soups are discovered bubbling away at these dumps, our true historical markers.)

∽

Grains of barley, shards of metal, fringe from funeral cars, parts of trees, rocks pulled from the landscape and labeled; everything labeled: Historical marker ahead. ... On this site in 1800. ... On this site in 1776 ... here was ... here stood. ... Towns where each house proclaims over the door, 1777, 1793, 1802, until, heading up the street, you might think these were their addresses. House museums and historical societies, small village histories running to thousands of pages, memory houses all. "Forget Not the Dead"—just one of the hymns sung in a long program of remembrance at Dublin, New Hampshire's Centennial Celebration, June 17, 1852.

Certainly history is important, we say. Children should know history, we say. History is not a flea market or what I throw out today, history is the textbook stuff, history is ... important. "Whereas, New England has a tangible past, not lost to time, but remembered and celebrated by all our people," reads a proclamation by the governor of New Hampshire on the occasion of New England Archives Week.

The little town of Chesterfield, New Hampshire, agrees at its town meetings to spend $4,132 over three years to have its town history volumes rebound. This is no small expenditure in a town that will vote maybe $300 to aid youth services and, after some debate, may set aside a few thousand toward a new police cruiser. The city of Keene, New Hampshire, awakes one morning to find it has a serious municipal problem: a time capsule buried during Keene's bicentennial in 1953, and meant to be opened in the next century, has sprung a leak. A new capsule will be built, and a call goes out to restore the 1953 treasure, to recreate the year 1953 so it can be buried again: city directories, menus, yearbooks, corporate reports, photos are gathered, so the residents of Keene in 2053 won't be deprived. The Peterborough Historical Society announces that the gates of the memory house are opening: any family who has lived in town for fifteen years can be in the official history. (Are standards slipping?)

And the state of New Hampshire, the state that follows all others when it comes to spending (fiftieth in education, fiftieth in health), votes to spend a million dollars to pursue the vest and moosehide britches of Josiah Bartlett, of the Declaration of Independence. A million! That's nearly five times all the money spent on Headstart in the state.

Fortunately for the state, it had to spend only $150,000 of its million-dollar appropriation; $100,000 for an eighteenth-century maple highboy and $14,000 for his vest were the big purchases. (At the same time, Bennington, New Hampshire, ran its library for $13,010.14 for the year, including its state grant of $109.44.) The state was aided by the New Hampshire Historical Society, which spent $50,000 for letters and documents, and $7,000 for a pair of Josiah's moosehide britches.

The bidding was tense. The state was lucky to get the highboy. A private citizen spent $15,000 for Josiah's pocket watch. "You know if anybody likes antiques, it's strictly emotional," said an antiques appraiser who was hired to advise the state. "I mean, this is emotion out there today."

∞

Many New Englanders take up history the way people in other regions take to bowling. They take to their 1777 saltbox and live up to their houses, their patriotism improved by drafty antiquity.

New Englanders think, sometimes, that they invented history. I remember a radio show that discussed the future of town meeting (at which the entire town gathers once a year to discuss and vote directly on all public matters). There was a panel of professors, town moderators and journalists. The public was invited to call in. A professor led off with a discussion of how town meeting was a descendant of ancient Athenian democracy.

No sooner does he say that than the first call comes in. A woman is on the line saying that town meeting government came right out of the Mayflower Compact. She says that she was driving down the interstate and had to pull over and call to correct the professor about the Mayflower Compact. How could the professor overlook the Mayflower Compact?

The professor politely says, Yes, that is a good point, but there are other sources. (This is the academic way of saying: "Thank you for sharing. You're wrong, but class participation is important.") The caller is not to be put off. As I listen to the radio, I can tell she is yelling into the phone at some rest-stop phone booth (and knowing that road, probably right next to one of New Hampshire's state liquor stores).

This is an impassioned debate about a seventeenth-century document written aboard a small wooden ship carrying 102 people, two months at sea, and here the debate is carried out in the twentieth-century manner via telephone, broadcast over the radio, with a woman defending the Pilgrims from an interstate rest stop near a state liquor store. (And one promoting the sin of gambling—Lotto tickets.) Forget not the dead.

∞

The adoration of the moosehide britches of our ancestors is a defining characteristic of New England. Why do we save these things? What do we expect to happen when we herd our children in front of a display that says: "Josiah Bartlett signed the Declaration of Independence. These are his moosehide britches. (We didn't buy the pocket watch.)"

The easy answers lie in artifact and education: This is how they lived, this is what they wore and maybe something of what they thought. But it takes a bit of education, a bit of subtext, to get a story out of one pair of moosehide britches.

No, there is something else at work here, something that historians and preservationists share with people who have basements crammed with old game boards or attics full of old bottles; a blind urge to collect, to gather like the squirrel and the magpie, a big pile of just one thing or every shiny scrap that comes along.

If you look at the history of most respected antiquarian organizations, usually you will find a founder who would not even be hired by his own organization today. The founders are magpies, bower birds who gather everything in sight as a rapturous prayer to the world: Look at this and this and this: so wonderful. They must have it, weave it into their collection before it vanishes from the earth. The world, in their sight, remains always new. Then come the art

16

historians and the skilled art technicians to preserve the hoard and draw up "rationales" for how to present this collection to the public, storylines, actually, a narrative for the jumble. But all that comes later. In the first blush of collecting, it is like love—as the antiques appraiser said, "strictly emotional."

◯◯

There are those steeped in the kinship and folk story of a town who can bring the jumble shop of history to life, animate the objects, make them props in the great show-story of time. But those who dwell in the rising condos, who will know the Turnpike Road and Town Hill and Elm Hill Road only as Route 123/124, may be mystified by these little museums with their labels in fading ink and pieces of hardtack and rock collections. There are no audiovisual shows, no souvenir shops, no interactive exhibits.

We look and see a melted twist of metal and a note saying this was once a church bell. But the townspeople who placed the fragment there saw in that little twist of metal the ruin of their beloved church and the death of fellow townsmen on a summer's day that turned violent.

Sometime around noon, Tuesday, July 15, 1902, during a heavy thunderstorm, the New Ipswich Congregational Church was hit by a bolt of lightning. The church bell was rung to summon the fire company until the rope burned off. Three fire companies swiftly arrived, but it was too late. "The beautiful toned bell that through many long years had given the first note of alarm in case of fire," reported the *Fitchburg Sentinel*, "this time was made to send forth its own requiem." After rescuing the piano and the Bible from the vestry, and some settees, the townspeople could only stand and watch their church burn.

"Hardly had the bell ceased ringing when ... saddening news came from a nearby berry field," reported the newspaper. When the rains came, a party of eight, two adults and six children, had been picking blueberries in the Barrett pasture. They headed for safety

17

"but got no farther than a pine tree under which they all gathered. A terrific-crash stunned the whole party. Mrs. Castonguay was the first to regain consciousness and see the scattered company." Two were dead. A child was hanging over a low limb, unconscious, the others were lying on the ground.

In the adjoining town of Greenville that summer's day a man was killed while haying. He was loading his hay wagon, when his oxen were startled (by the approaching storm?) and threw him to the ground, running him over.

"Three people lying dead in our village over night—all the result of violence—is something that has not before occurred in our history."

They set to gathering fragments of the bell ("No person is allowed to carry away even a tiny bit of it") and by the following day they had over one hundred pounds, which they hoped would be used in a new bell. Only after the fire did the town, consulting the town history, learn that their bell—"so dear to the hearts of all the citizens"—was made by Paul Revere. The bell was never recast.

A shard of metal, or a story—it depends on what you bring to the mute stones to make them speak. And there among the dust and sweet decay of the little museum, one day will open up and reveal itself, sometimes so vividly you can smell the wet hay.

∞

In the Hancock, New Hampshire, historical society is a letter from Horace Greeley, a muskrat-skin stretcher, a ball of lead that was fired at someone at Antietam, muskets and flintlocks, many quilts, a match holder from a hospital for Confederate soldiers, a mite box for church collections with four slots (one for "heathen children"), a lamp-lighter's ladder that cleverly folds out of a single pole, a nineteenth-century penny-farthing bicycle (ridden intrepidly down Main Street each Old Home Day), and the town coffin, once used to bury the poor. (Thrifty Yankees, using the same coffin, and thriftier still—for years it was used as a chicken feeder on a farm.)

So I go from one historical society to the next (when I can; they have quirkier hours than the office hours of a tenured professor). You don't know when you'll see a summer's thunderstorm in a scrap of metal.

∽

Henry Ford—as anyone can tell you—said history is bunk. But he was also among the first to seriously save American history. Magpie-like, he picked up chairs and buggies and houses from the New England countryside. Henry Ford knew something.

The Ford Museum is a warehouse of memory. There are twelve acres under one roof. Twelve acres of cars, ovens, chairs, highboys, typewriters, combines, airplanes, steam engines, a six-hundred-ton locomotive ... if the hand of man made it, Henry Ford collected it in his museum in Dearborn, Michigan. It is such a big place inside that I saw some sparrows flying along—happy, it seemed to me—in the agriculture section.

Ford dedicated this immense collection to his friend and hero, Thomas Alva Edison. The museum's official name is the Edison Institute. Upon entering the museum, one passes the golden shovel Edison used at the dedication and a cement slab with Edison's signature and his footprints. Outside on the grounds of the museum's Greenfield Village are Edison's home and his original Menlo Park lab (moved from New Jersey along with tons of the actual dirt it stood on). There are, as well, Orville and Wilbur Wright's workshop and home, the courthouse Lincoln practiced in, the home of Ford's favorite grade-school teacher and a virtual suburban subdivision of historic houses.

Indoors, at the heart of this twelve-acre bazaar, exactly at the heart, said my guide one morning, is a little exhibit sampler. Under the heading "American Heroes" are the chair Lincoln was sitting in and the shawl he was wearing when he was shot; Washington's folding camp bed; and a test tube, canted to the side, stoppered up and sealed in a display case.

19

"Edison's Last Breath?" asks the label. Sitting across from a nine-hundred-ton steam engine, it seems so fragile. This test tube of breath is the essence of all museums, the motive behind all the crazy collections. The label says, cautiously:

It is alleged that Henry Ford asked Thomas A. Edison's son, Charles, to collect an exhaled breath from the lungs of Ford's dying hero and friend. This test tube was found at Ford's Fair Lane mansion, along with Edison's hat and shoes, after Clara Ford's death in 1950.

The dying breath of yesterday. We want to capture nothing less.

Part II

CHOOSING
OUR ANCESTORS

Choosing
Our Ancestors

On a road I used to travel daily, there is a historical marker, off under the trees, low to the ground, bolted to the front of a granite boulder. I had gone up and down that road a hundred times or more before I noticed it.

The marker stands on Elm Hill Road, a name I have seen only on the map. Most everyone calls it Route 123. The road is just off the Horace Greeley Highway, a bit up from the Twin Elm Farm in Peterborough, New Hampshire. No one calls it the Horace Greeley Highway, and again that is a name I have seen only on the topographical map. I have asked many natives: Why Horace Greeley? What did he have to do with New Hampshire? No one knows. The twin elms at the farm are gone (as is the farming). As are the elms on Elm Hill Road. But you knew that. And I don't tell you this to bring to mind a landscape fallen from grace or to remind you that, as Walt Whitman said, American place names run to contraries, a statement that foreshadowed so many Deer Meadow shopping centers. No, in fact, the landscape is greener and lusher than when it was given these names.

When we name something in the land, we are staking our claim.

And here on a short hill in New England were some expired claims. One day I finally stopped by the marker:

Site of the First Tavern
In This Town Kept in 1775
By
Major Robert Wilson
Was Fifty Feet West of This Spot
From Which on April 19 1775
The Men Marched in Response to
The Lexington Alarm

This is not interesting news in itself. If you read every roadside marker in New England, you would think men were always leaving taverns to go fight a war and coming home to find Washington sleeping there.

I kicked away some leaves and continued to read:

Erected 1914 by Peterborough Chapter
Daughters of the American Revolution

Now, that is the news, the date it was set in place: 1914, the start of the Great War in Europe and an era of great Catholic and Jewish immigration. Our Revolution is a cozy place to visit.

The good ladies of the D.A.R. were anxious to uphold "traditional American values." In our cities, people from strange lands were not speaking English. These "undesirables" had strange customs, cooked odd-smelling foods; who knew what went on in those tenements? Many of those people—frequently referred to as a "wave" or a "flood"—came from lands where "revolution" meant more than the heirlooms and icons of the D.A.R. What was to become of the good Anglo-Saxon stock that built this nation? In a low marker, the ladies were staking their claim.

This marker had been set in place with "appropriate ceremonies," with one hundred in attendance, the ladies in proper hats and white gloves for the afternoon. There was an address of welcome by a regent of the Peterborough D.A.R., a reading of scripture and prayer by a reverend, a poem written for the occasion, and the singing of "The Star Spangled Banner." This was just the opening act. A historical address followed, which was careful to delineate Major Robert Wilson's ancestors as "strong and rugged Scotchmen" who had made a detour through Ireland and "received in history the designation of Scotch-Irish to distinguish them from the kindred branch of the Celtic race. ..." Next came the unveiling. An American flag had been draped over the boulder. The flag was pulled up by Wilson's great-granddaughter ("direct descendant" in D.A.R. talk), and everyone sang "the D.A.R. hymn to the tune of 'John Brown's Body.'" There were three more speeches, including a report by Miss Marie Ware Laughton, principal of the School of English Speech and Expression and regent of the Committee of Safety Chapter of Boston, who "spoke very interestingly" about the Safety Chapter's endeavors in "Patriotic Education among the Italians of Boston." "The exercises concluded with the singing of 'America.'"

An account of the ceremony, the D.A.R.'s first in Peterborough, filled all the front-page news columns of the four-page September 17, 1914, *Peterborough Transcript*, and half of the back page. All this in testimony to the "ancestor and ancestress ... pioneers of sterling character whose influence for truth, honor and righteousness has been handed down to the successive generations of the family which they founded."

Another marker:

N H
Washington
The First Town
Incorporated
Under the Name Of
George Washington
Our First President
December 13, 1776
Erected Nov. 1932

There is a small medallion of Washington on his horse between the letters *N* and *H.* One or two other towns claim to be the first Washington, but that is not important. The key is the last line: "Erected Nov. 1932." Hard times, grim times, a good time to think about Washington on his white horse. The Great Depression was scarcely a time for discretionary spending—surely the dollars for this monument were needed elsewhere. But I look at this large metal plaque as an anchor.

In history, unlike heredity, we choose our ancestors. We choose with monuments, markers and history books. We choose also with bulldozers, by what we remove. One of the saddest losses I know of occurred along the shores of Onondaga Lake in upstate New York.

On a hillside facing the lake, Indians had built an amphitheater. Most historians believe this is where the original five nations of the Iroquois—Seneca, Cayuga, Onondaga, Oneida and Mohawk—formed their confederacy in the closing years of the sixteenth century. The land, about sixteen acres, was known in the town of Liverpool as Thurlow's Lot.

At the time of the Second World War it could have been had for a thousand dollars an acre. It was a cornfield when J. T. Crawford grew up in Liverpool, and he planned to buy the land when he returned from the war and help establish a working Indian village. But on his return he found that the site, which had stood intact since the 1500s, was now a housing subdivision, the amphitheater gone.

In the city of Syracuse, which is on Onondaga Lake and not far from the Onondaga's reservation, there is no mention of the Iroquois. There is a museum for the Erie Canal but not one for the Indians. Crawford wanted to correct this omission. During the Bicentennial in 1976, he unveiled an ambitious plan to have an amphitheater built along the lake at Hiawatha Point, where the story of the Iroquois would be told. Rising behind the amphitheater would be six pine trees, one for each nation. (The Tuscaroras were the sixth, joining later.) Crawford wanted to show "the political unity of the Iroquois law and its similarity to the formation of our Constitution."

He formed the Iroquois Memorial Association of Greater Liverpool, put together a slide show and spoke before every civic group he could find. He gave that slide show about one hundred times. He needed to raise $40,000 for his plan. He raised $800.

People in Syracuse and Liverpool distrust the Onondagas, he says. They do not recognize the sovereignty of the reservation or the claims the Onondagas have on the land of the city. "The people who live in this area say, 'Oh my God, I'm going to lose my house. These bastards, these nasty damn savages are trying to take my land away from me.'" All they know about the Iroquois' history, he says, is Longfellow's poem *Hiawatha*—"By the Shores of Gitchee Gumee"— most of which is a picturesque lie.

The Indians themselves are wary about being joined up in any way with white man's history. After being put off for a year, Crawford was allowed to speak before a council meeting of the Six Nations.

"We got into the longhouse and listened to a lot of Indian language; Iroquois for about an hour and half," said Crawford. He was waiting along with a group that was intent on helping the Iroquois by raising money for them. "But the Iroquois don't want this. These people are just do-gooders," he says. Crawford was tapped on the shoulder; his turn had come. "I was allowed five minutes to explain what I had in mind. All of a sudden I looked around. These people were talking among themselves. It was back to the Indian language again. I never heard another thing out of it." He was later told he had made some progress; those others, the do-gooders, had gotten only a minute's hearing before being turned off.

In the end, Crawford donated the $800 to Liverpool to plant six pine trees in a town park, and the county—Onondaga County—did, at long last, place a sign at Hiawatha Point marking the site of the confederacy. But as might be expected of people in a town bearing the name of an English port, they look elsewhere for their heritage. The Iroquois sit outside the memory house.

∞

We choose with bulldozers. But seldom do we choose our ancestors by a vote: "Resolved that we of this generation stand in awe and in debt and have been forever changed by our venerated ancestor. …" When such a vote does come along, you can expect an impassioned and confused debate that reveals the self-image of a society.

New Hampshire was one of the last two states to recognize the national holiday honoring Reverend Martin Luther King, Jr. Five times in ten years the state legislature resoundingly said no to the "father of the Civil Rights movement."

There is no need here to rehearse in detail a debate that had been as distinguished as a talk-radio shouting match. The *Manchester Union Leader* said King was anti-American, said he abetted the communists by opposing the Vietnam War, said the holiday would "force the people of New Hampshire to kneel before … King's radicalism." In a guest opinion, King was called Hanoi Martin. The *Union Leader* would have none of Reverend King. When the Manchester school board voted for a holiday honoring him, the next morning the *Union Leader* questioned King's patriotism again and printed the home phone numbers of the board members. There was a fuss; the board held another hearing and another vote, narrowly upholding its decision.

Here is an ancestor New Hampshire rejected. He's Hanoi Martin. Martin Luther King is not dead enough. He is, in W. H. Auden's term, not horizontal enough:

> Let us honor if we can
> The vertical man
> Though we value none
> But the horizontal one.

We should honor Booker T. Washington, said others. He's safely dead, the horizontal man. It is the horizontal man that will lie still for the uses of history.

We should look after our own, said several state representatives. We should honor New Hampshire's heroes first: Revolutionary War generals and Christa McAuliffe, the teacher killed in the shuttle explosion. The lists vary, but King is always last. They did not see what King has to do with New Hampshire. "It isn't as much prejudice," they said, "as that black people aren't a part of New Hampshire's culture."

Many representatives said they opposed the holiday because it would result in "lost productivity," but even a proposal to replace a holiday drained of meaning—Fast Day—was stubbornly resisted. Not one in a thousand people in the state could tell you the meaning of Fast Day. The *Union Leader* admitted that, yes, Fast Day "has become virtually meaningless" but said they "don't really care." (For the record: In 1681 when New Hampshire's first colonial governor, John Cutt, fell ill, a day of fasting and prayer was held. Cutt died from the illness, but, I guess, Fast Day is the holiday of good intentions.) When the legislature finally relented in 1991 and dropped Fast Day to adopt the national holiday, it refused to use King's name, giving New Hampshire the only "Civil Rights Day."

Perhaps the resistance to honoring King was best expressed inadvertently by a school librarian. She needed some books on King for a middle school library. She listened to a few of the titles available, dismissing some. *Martin Luther King and Black Identity:* "Oh no, we don't want to go into *that*," she said.

"I think we still don't know what the holiday is about," said King's long-time friend, Andrew Young. That could have been said by anyone in the New Hampshire debate, by the school librarian if she were honest enough, by the editorial writers if they dropped their attack for a moment, by the excuse-making state representatives.

"The holiday has the name of Martin Luther King," continued Young, "but we're not celebrating Martin Luther King demonstrations, which is what much of the white community sees, or his challenge to America on foreign policy. What we are celebrating is that this society did something that no other society has ever done: It took people from completely opposite ethnic and economic backgrounds and brought them together and enabled them to live together and work together almost as a family, without violence."

King, the *Union Leader* said, had a "hate relationship with America." In the same edition as that editorial, the Digital Equipment Corporation has run an advertisement quoting from King's famous "I Have a Dream" oration: "From the prodigious hilltops of New Hampshire … let freedom ring."

The Horace Greeley Highway fades, Washington on his white horse rides through successive Colonial Revivals and Martin Luther King comes knocking on the door of the memory house. We are all the time choosing our ancestors.

Looking for
Johnny Appleseed

In apple blossom time I went looking for Johnny Appleseed. He was born in a town fifty miles west of Boston, Leominster, Massachusetts. Many towns across the country claim him; Leominster has the birth certificate. But does Leominster still have any apple orchards?

∞

Johnny Appleseed belongs to our childhood. He's back there with Winnie-the-Pooh, Peter Pan and Stuart Little, living in a beneficent landscape. Navigating in our adult landscape, eyes keen to note all boundaries—property line, stop sign—Johnny Appleseed, vagabond, wanderer, is not someone we think of for even a waking minute. He is a discarded toy. And so I feel compelled to start in school report fashion: *Johnny Appleseed was a real person.*

I began my search where all school report research begins: *World Book Encyclopedia, A* volume: Apples, Apple Butter, Apple Maggot (or railroad worm), Apple of Discord, Apple of Sodom (an ill-tasting fruit mentioned in the Bible), Apple Tree Borer, Appleseed, Johnny: "(1774–1843) was the name given John Chapman, an

American pioneer who planted large numbers of apple trees. ... His deeds are probably imaginary. ..."

The air is let out of the story so quickly. I wouldn't dare look up Winnie-the-Pooh in the *World Book Encyclopedia.* ("While really just a stuffed animal, Pooh has inspired products supporting a $42.1 million industry. See also Fantasy, the Business of.") After this blow, the *World Book* tells us—if we still care—the story of Johnny Appleseed giving apple trees to everyone he met and acting as a medicine man to the Indians (which sounds backward). And then this deflating comment: "None of the folk stories about Chapman has ever been proved true." Given this statement on the authoritative glossy paper of the *World Book*, it is difficult to look at the drawing of Johnny Appleseed, the woodcut that is reproduced everywhere: tin pot as a hat, coffee sack as a shirt, and no shoes. Peter Pan dressed better than this. He seems so insubstantial, or as the kids say today, he looks like a dork.

Turning next to the *Encyclopedia Britannica,* under Appleseed, Johnny, it says see Chapman, John. Sober up! it tells us.

Again the story, the long trek westward planting apple trees, "his cheerful nature," "gentleness with animals," "flowing hair under an inverted mush pan, bare feet. ..." No one ever asks: Who would wear a mush pan?

I turn to my last reference, the *Encyclopedia Americana.* Three encyclopedias is in-depth research, above and beyond the call for a grade school report. This listing is again under Chapman. (Why do chosen names make people so uncomfortable? Why isn't a name chosen in adult life more "real" than a name given at birth? In one business ledger that survives, his name is entered as John Appleseed.)

The *Americana* is more encouraging. It assures us that he did plant trees, spreading apple orchards from the Allegheny River to the Indiana frontier, and it adds this surprising information: Johnny Appleseed was a religious missionary for Swedenborgism—a word that is surely left out of any grade school report.

Whoever John Chapman was—nothing is known of his child-hood—he was a flypaper for myths: Anything good that Americans might have chosen to think of themselves, that was Johnny Appleseed: gentle, cheerful, generous, a believer in His Works, a good white brother to the Indians and good to the earth, cultivating the wilderness into a rational abundance—rows and rows of apple trees. At apple blossom time, and again at harvest, an orchard is a vision of a rational Eden.

But why wear a mush pan hat?

I do the grown-up thing and check the encyclopedia entries for further references. There is a mention of an article in *Harper's New Monthly Magazine*, 1871, that started the story, and a reference to a book, *Johnny Appleseed, Man and Myth*. But I have had enough myth bashing for one century. I want to go where they still believe. I set out for Leominster, Massachusetts.

Coming into Leominster from the north, the town is a dispiriting sight. In a quarter-mile cluster around the Route 2 highway there are five gas stations, some with rotating signs five stories tall. Traffic lights are closely spaced, and tractor-trailers coming off Route 2 frequently back up into the intersections. A Honeybuddies Waterbed store dominates one intersection. Next door, a white carpenter gothic church bravely holds forth. This quarter-mile strip seems to be telescoped. It looks like those photos taken through a telephoto lens of miles of such development, where the distance is squeezed out of the picture, and the signs and wires have collapsed one on another.

But coming into Leominster's downtown—past Appleseed Personnel—the town presents itself as a small nineteenth-century city. All the civic equipment is clustered around the green known as Monument Square: a columned city hall, a columned library, brick storefronts and many tall churches of stone and brick.

In the library, I look first in the pamphlet file. The Johnny Appleseed file is empty. But under Leominster (pronounced locally as lemon-stir) there are a few reports on the city's history: a population boom from 1900 to 1915 that saw the city double to 20,000—hence the downtown—and then decline in the 1950s and the downtown bypassed—hence the strip; each road out of the city seemed to have one. And now renewal, discovery as a cheap housing market for Boston, a new sewer project, new investment, new malls. And this:

> Leominster is known as the "Pioneer Plastic City." In 1770, Obadiah Hills began making horn combs. By 1800, there were eight comb shops in town and 24 by 1845. Celluloid was invented in 1870 to replace the diminishing supplies of horn, ivory and tortoise shell. In 1925, one of the four largest celluloid manufacturers in the country was located in Leominster. A resident, Joseph Foster, introduced injection molding, which revolutionized the plastics industry in the 1930s. In 1975, 47 percent of the city's 167 industries produced plastics.

Four years before Johnny Appleseed was born on September 26, 1774, Leominster had launched itself on an industrial path. No wonder he left. In Leominster, they never talk about his leaving. Towns that honor native sons—presidents, writers, reformers—never can bring themselves to mention that for the hero to attain his great achievement, he had to leave. No, the focus is always on the town as the cradle of values that nurtured the hero.

But Johnny Appleseed, born in a plastic cradle? (I speak here metaphorically; plastic cradles were still 150 years away.) This is such a typically American tableau that it has been stated hundreds of times: The classic division in our history that pitted Thomas Jefferson's vision for the young republic against Alexander Hamilton's, Jefferson's middle landscape of the independent farmer versus Hamilton's nation of manufacturers. The conflicting urges in the early years of the republic to see ourselves as "nature's nation" and also as "ingenious Yankees" who would "tame the wilderness" and out-produce our English cousins. It is a division that Leo Marx captured well in his book *The Machine in the Garden*. And here we have Leominster, a machine extruding plastics, and its honored native son sowing seeds of gardens. If you are the Chamber of Commerce, which way do you play it? Are you the Pioneer Plastic City? Or the original seed of John Chapman? Do you have an Apple

Blossom Festival? Or do you crown a Miss Injection Molding Queen for the Tournament of Plastics Parade?

You go looking for apple blossoms, and you come up with a handful of celluloid and polystyrene. Disappointing. (The bitter taste of irony in the mouth, like a plastic apple.) I move on to the card catalog and find, under Chapman, many cards, outnumbering by twenty to one the cards for the prior listing, Chaplin, Charlie. To see the books and pamphlets, I have to sign a book and be ushered into the "VC," the Valuable Book Collection, the inner sanctum of true believers.

Here are city reports with Johnny Appleseed on the cover, his image jazzed up from the *World Book Encyclopedia* woodcut; his mush pan hat gone, he is striding out, forcefully, in overalls, looking much like a Tom Sawyer with a pretty big tree planting scheme.

There are all manner of typescript studies by people who had been obsessed with Johnny Appleseed: "An operetta in one act," a play, recollections by people who knew him (one marked "inauthentic"), accounts of the cost of John Chapman's funeral ($9.44) and the settlement of his estate, programs and commemorations by committees—the Johnny Appleseed Week Committee in Mansfield, Ohio, and others in Fort Wayne, Indiana, and Ashland County, Ohio, which had planted stone monuments in his honor—and a few copies of the book *Johnny Appleseed, Man and Myth,* which I refuse to open.

Among the tributes, there is this small play by Henry Bailey Stevens, reportedly performed in 1935 in Durham, New Hampshire:

Johnny Appleseed

A Tree Planting Ceremony at Apple Blossom Time

Cast: Chairman
      Club leader
      Two Boys with spades and pruning shears
      Two Girls
      Johnny Appleseed

The assembled members of the 4–H club. And a hole ready for a tree.

The play is long on the educational lesson, reading like some socialist realism propaganda. It opens with a staged discussion of Johnny Appleseed.

> Chairman: … Who was Johnny Appleseed?
> Club leader: Boys, you tell him, will you?

And so on. Including such lively dialogue as: "Apples have vitamins and mineral salts which are good for our health."

This play is actually a musical:

> First Girl: Another thing I like about apple trees is the blossoms.
> Chairman: You've said something there. Let's sing: (Audience sings "In the Shade of the Old Apple Tree" or "When It's Apple Blossom Time.")

Finally, as the suspense mounts, up walks John Appleseed himself. (Actually he "hobbles.") He is described as a "queer looking sort," and in this incarnation, he's a bit pushy, taking over the planting. "This hole, methinks, ought to be a little deeper to give the roots a better chance. (He starts to dig.)" He makes stunning statements:

> One more thing. The top must be pruned. I'd head the main leader back to this outside bud. (*Gives other directions, in accordance with size and age of tree to be planted. See N.H. Ext. Bull. 47, "Orchard Practice in New Hampshire," pp. 30–32.*)

The play isn't entirely given to such practical matters. One character, the First Girl, quotes a poem:

> Loving every sloshy brake,
> Loving every skunk and snake,
> Loving every leathery weed,
> Johnny Appleseed, Johnny Appleseed,

The poem was written by Vachel Lindsay. In 1928, he published a collection, *Johnny Appleseed and Other Poems,* which started the national interest in commemorating Johnny Appleseed. Lindsay was a mystic who would chant his poems. (Alongside the Johnny Appleseed poems are the instructions "To be read like faint hoof-beats of fawns long gone … " and "To be read like old leaves on the elm tree of Time, Sifting soft winds with sentence and rhyme.") Like Johnny Appleseed, Lindsay had wandered across the country. In exchange for a night's lodging he offered a poem, "The Tree of Laughing Bells." And like Johnny Appleseed he was a Swedenborgian.

Lindsay's poetry was acclaimed in a short season from 1914 to the early 1920s. His books sold well, and audiences enthusiastically attended his poetry "chanting" performances—a "Higher Vaudeville" act of Lindsay's "strutting and flailing and barking and whispering." "The Evangelist of Poetry" was invited to chant at Oxford in 1920—the first American poet ever invited to recite. (Some British critics weren't too keen on all this chanting or on his punctuation and grammar. In the introduction to his collected poems, Lindsay tells them they can take the matter up with his old high school English teacher, who edited his works. "I refer them to the wrath of Susan E. Wilcox. She has a reply, if they care to write to the Springfield High School.")

In one copy of the *Johnny Appleseed* book, Lindsay wrote:

Please my dear friend …, destroy forever
    1. The talk that Johnny Appleseed was a myth.
    2. The talk that he was a fantastic, when every phase of his life can be parallel in the life of William Penn, George Fox, Buddha, or John the Baptist.
    3. Please get the precise record of the history from the cradle to the grave.
Signed, Vachel Lindsay.

A small industry of activity grew up. Commemoration committees like those in Fort Wayne, Indiana, and Ashland County, Ohio, began researching Johnny Appleseed's life. By the Depression years, there were monuments and celebrations, and into the late 1940s photos would appear in *Life* and other magazines of gnarled apple trees, long ago planted by the "vagabond nurseryman," Johnny Appleseed.

The years of interest are telling. At the time of Lindsay's popularity and on through the Depression and the war years, the intellectuals and writers of our country—Van Wyck Brooks, Lewis Mumford and others—worked to discover a "usable past," an American tradition they could build on. F. O. Matthiessen uncovered the American Renaissance—those few fabulous years of the 1850s that saw publication of Thoreau's *Walden*, Whitman's *Leaves of Grass*, Hawthorne's *The Scarlet Letter* and *The House of Seven Gables* and Melville's *Moby Dick*. Melville himself had only recently been resurrected, and *Moby Dick* was raised from obscurity to be crowned one of our great novels. Numerous historical societies started. John D. Rockefeller funded the restoration of Colonial Williamsburg in the 1920s, Henry Ford established his museum and historic village, and many other historic museums followed. The 1930s saw the birth of the American Studies movement in colleges. We choose our ancestors. With Europe in flames we chose America. As we were bombing Dresden, Tokyo and Hiroshima, we chose Johnny Appleseed. Johnny Appleseed would have been 4–F or a conscientious objector. We would have confiscated his mush pan hat and put him to work. All his talk of a "New Jerusalem" would have made him a suspicious character.

It was only in 1935 that Leominster learned it was the birthplace of John Chapman. A researcher from Fort Wayne traced John Chapman back to Leominster, by way of his mother's marriage license in a nearby town. By 1940, at the Leominster bicentennial, a granite marker had been erected to Johnny Appleseed, and the Pioneer Plastic City had itself a certified "pioneer hero."

∞

For all the research by committees and the poetry, Johnny Appleseed plays best in a school report.

The "souvenir booklet of the National Bicentennial, Leominster, Mass." provides the best accounts, "prize winning poems and essays and compositions from 7th, 8th and 9th grade students." Some take in the whole picture, such as this poem by Anne Charpentier, Saint Cecilia's School:

Leominster

Leominster, Leominster when you were a child
What was life all about? Was it harsh, was it mild?

Did you know Johnny Appleseed? That famous man
Who made this country a fruitful land.

Leominster you deserve a hand
For becoming the plastic capital of the land
And so here's a toast to my precious town
"We built you up," let no man put you down.

There is a history of the town by James Fluet, also of Saint Cecilia's, that places Leominster more with the machine than the garden. To the roster of native sons, Mr. Fluet adds, "Alvah Crocker, [who] built the Boston & Maine Railroad ... U.S. Senator David I. Walsh, Father of the U.S. Navy." James Fluet played his hand neatly. You can see why his essay won. He idyllically sets his hometown as as a bustling manufactory in leafy green: "Leominster combines the advantages of both city and country life and is also the pioneer plastic city of the world. There are over 100 industries devoted mostly to plastic yet with wide diversifications in other products."

Beth MacGilvery of Carter Junior High provides the best retelling of Johnny Appleseed that I have read. She doesn't stop to ponder the ambiguities of his life or to question his very existence. And she doesn't feel compelled to go the document and deed route. She wrote:

More than a century ago a man named John Chapman, born in Leominster, was well known to frontier settlers in Pennsylvania, Ohio, Indiana and Illinois. Most of these pioneers did not know him as John Chapman. They called him Johnny Appleseed.

39

Barefoot, dressed in rags, and wearing an old saucepan for a hat, Johnny would appear at a lonely farmhouse carrying a bag of appleseeds. Sometimes he traded the seeds for food. If the people were poor he gave them seeds. He wanted everyone to have the pleasure of seeing apple trees in blossom and of having apples to eat. ...

The lonely settlers were glad to have Johnny Appleseed come to visit. He told the children stories and carved whistles for them. After supper he would lie on the floor and read aloud from the Bible he always carried with him. ...

No harm ever came to Johnny Appleseed in his lonely travels through the wilderness. The Indians knew him and treated him as a friend, and even the wild animals left him alone.

But still Beth misses something essential. Most everything written about him talks about the trees and mentions the Bible as an afterthought. It should be the other way around. He planted trees to spread the word. Swedenborg is the key. Johnny Appleseed is a religious figure. He forsook the wealth of this world and went on a journey, spreading the word. And that is why the mush pan hat and coffee sack.

He read the Bible to all he met; he walked among us. He was of this earth, certainly, planting trees. But not of this earth—he owned nothing. And he left behind trees as the witness of his good work and a series of monuments that could be followed like stations of the cross. That is the Johnny Appleseed seldom mentioned, not the early nurseryman ("the apostle of horticulture"), not the charming vagabond eccentric, but the religious missionary.

Emanuel Swedenborg was an eighteenth-century Swedish scientist and mystic who said he routinely ascended heavens and conversed with the angels. In the spirit world, Swedenborg reported, the spirits lived in cities and carried out a life that closely corresponded to the material, earthly life. Swedenborg's religious teachings influenced many important nineteenth-century writers: Balzac, Baudelaire, Coleridge, the Brownings and Emerson. Swedenborg's teachings were a part of the childhoods of Walt Whitman, William and Henry James,

Robert Frost and Helen Keller (who was a strong believer). "The age is Swedenborg's," wrote Ralph Waldo Emerson in 1854.

Johnny Appleseed traveled with Swedenborg's tracts. Under his tin pot hat he kept a New Testament and a tract from Swedenborg. He would tear the tracts into chapters, leaving different parts of the "news fresh from heaven" at the houses where he stayed. He planted trees, in part, to raise money to buy more tracts.

He didn't merely read the Bible and the works to people, he preached "with a voice rising denunciatory and thrilling—strong and loud as the roar of the wind and the waves, then soft and soothing," recalled one woman who remembered his visits. He was so active a proselytizer that his work was noted in 1817 by the Society for Printing, Publishing and Circulating the Writings of Emanuel Swedenborg in Manchester, England: "There is in the western country a very extraordinary missionary of the New Jerusalem. A man has appeared who seems to be almost independent of corporal wants and sufferings." During his wanderings in central and northern Ohio, at least twelve Swedenborgian societies began.

And here are the parts of his life that his local-historian backers usually soft pedal. He held seances to reach the spirit world. He believed he was regularly in contact with spirits and angels, two of which would be his wives in the next life. He never married but seriously chose a young child of a neighbor to be his bride in the New Jerusalem. John Dawson, who knew him personally in Fort Wayne, wrote in 1871: "On one occasion a gentleman now living, with whom [Johnny] often lodged and ate, and who had a little daughter whom the old man [Johnny] fancied was asked by the old man if he would give him the child for his spiritual wife, and on thoughtlessly giving him his consent, Johnny regarded the bargain as sacred, and treated the child thereafter with much care. This, however was interrupted by an accident. A neighbor's children came over to see this child and others of the family, when the father told a little boy to kiss Johnny's girl, which he did in Johnny's presence. This was considered by Johnny as a violation of faith plighted by the father, and in anger declined to further care for his spiritual wife."

41

One historical paper says that we have a "somewhat lopsided picture" of his life based on his later years when "Johnny became more uncouth of appearance ... and more outspoken in his advocacy of the peaceable kingdom. ..." But his "uncouth" appearance seems to have been the point. He denied himself, suffered deprivations, to assure a comfortable life in the New Jerusalem to come. He went barefoot on ice. He never bought shoes even though he had money to do so. Sometimes he would go about with an ill-fitting boot on one foot—to break a trail through the snow for his bare foot. Once a traveler gave him a pair of shoes—this in the cold of November on the frontier—but a week later he was seen without them. He had given them away, he said, to a family poorer than he. Walking hundreds of miles barefoot, he could endure immense pain—he cauterized his wounds with a red hot iron (as the Indians did). As proof of his endurance, he would thrust pins and needles into his skin.

He had no fear of the venomous rattlesnakes in the area. "This book," he said, referring to a Swedenborg work, "is an infallible protection against all danger here and hereafter." And only once in his whole life did he kill an animal, for which he was ever regretful. While he was clearing land for an orchard, a rattler lashed out at him, biting him. In defense, Johnny killed it. True to his teachings, he believed that every being was endowed with the Divine Essence and that to kill a creature for food was a sin. He was a vegetarian. One time when a hornet flew down his coffee sack, though it repeatedly stung him, he took care to remove it. He put out his campfire when he realized that large numbers of mosquitoes were flying into it. He could not endure to see a beast suffer and regularly bought abused animals from their owners and gave them new homes. Each fall he would search the woods for lame horses that had been let out to die. By barter he would secure them food and shelter for the winter. In spring he would lead them to fresh meadows, and if they recovered, he never sold them but found them good homes. He did not ride horses, though it would have been a help in his hundred-mile hikes through the frontier. And—nurserymen take note—so strong was his belief in the sanctity of life that he refused to ever prune or graft a tree. He thought it was torture. This, at least, is the account given of his life in 1871 in *Harper's New Monthly Magazine.*

As he got older, he seemed to deny himself even more. At his death, aged seventy-two, he was described thus: "Next to his body, a coarse coffee-sack, with a hole cut in the center through which he passed his head. He had on the waists of four pairs of pants. These were cut off at the forks, ripped at the sides and the fronts thrown away, saving the waistband attached to the hinder part. These hinder parts were buttoned around him, lapping like shingles so as to cover the whole lower part of his body, and over all these were drawn a pair of what was once pantaloons."

The rest of the story is facts and legal deeds and footnotes. The more one reads—he bought a pocket knife for seventy-five cents on February 22, 1840; he gave Eben Rice a note good for thirty-eight apple trees on August 12, 1818—the more one wishes to know less and less of Mr. Chapman. Like any great religious figure, the particulars of his life should fade away, as he assumes the more beatific, generalized traits of a minor saint.

I only wish he had a holiday, the way St. Nick has Christmas. A Johnny Appleseed Day, or an observance combined with Arbor Day. We would all go plant trees and bring fruit to the poor. (That's how I see it in my mind. If there was a holiday, Johnny Appleseed would suffer the fate of Lincoln and Washington: to be remembered by sale-day circulars of smudgy red and green ink on cheap newsprint.) Still, in apple blossom time, it does the soul some good to think of a holiday that would honor the land, when we would promise for just one hour of one day of the year to do a good act for the earth.

∽

A question remained: Did Leominster still have any apple orchards? Just one would do. I looked in the yellow pages. There were four orchards listed—none in Leominster. I didn't bother looking under "Plastics."

43

I drove out of Leominster, out of the nineteenth-century downtown, out along the strip past the gas stations and the Honeybuddies Waterbed, out into a shady green neighborhood where the trees towered above the houses, and there I saw a small sign nailed to a telephone pole. "Pick your own apples. Appleseeds."

A few turns, directions asked of a paper boy, the road climbs up, away from the strip development. There as the hill crests are row after row of apple trees in blossom. And in the center of the orchard by the road, a sign from God (via man and plastic letters): "How Great Thou Art." Johnny Appleseed found.

∞

And there I should end—high on a hill, rows of trees in apple blossom, the vision of a rational Eden. But the tree of knowledge was an apple tree, and I know something I wish I didn't. A modern orchard is fruitful, bountiful only because of pesticides. Orchards are some of the most toxic land to be found. People who have bought houses on former orchard land report the disturbing harvest of dead birds fallen on the lawn. It is cruel that what appears to us to be paradise should be so poisonous. You see, an orchard is also fitting for the Pioneer Plastic City. Pesticides are close chemical relatives of plastics. Pesticides may be invisible, but they are the machine that creates the modern orchard.

But on this day I want to believe that it is all a matter of careful husbandry and living the righteous life. I try also to forget that everywhere he went Johnny Appleseed spread dog fennel, a foul-smelling weed and to this day an intractable problem for farmers throughout the Midwest, who sometimes call it Johnny Weed. He believed the weed had "antimalarial virtues" and sowed some near every house he passed. Like any good weed it spread everywhere. Stuart Little did no such wrongs. But after all, Johnny Appleseed was a real person.

On the Eulogy Road:
Claiming Jack Kerouac

1962

"John, I look forward to this visit and I hope you and I do exactly as we did in the old days, i.e., just drink BEER mostly," Jack Kerouac wrote to his friend, John Clellon Holmes. "I've just come off a whiskey drunk (quart or more for seven days) that almost reduced me to a terrified and helpless lump in an insane asylum."

After the visit, Holmes wrote in his journal: "He is a phenomenon, and those who knew him 10 years ago would be shocked & saddened now, to see him so recklessly burning himself up, vanishing in the swirl of his booze-heated mind, still a superb monologist, but almost incapable after 5:00 PM of 'talk.' ...

"Way deep down, I think, he wants to die. ..."

1969

"Jack is dead," Holmes wrote in his journal for October 21. Holmes and his wife met up with Allen Ginsberg and a few others and drove up to Lowell, Massachusetts, for the funeral.

Holmes knew Kerouac when they were young men in the Village. "I remember him when he was something rare, & quick, & burning."

Now he was grave side. "But no ceremonies ease the sight of a coffin poised over a grave's raw hole. … I went up and took a white rose, and put it over the place where Jack's head lay."

Allen Ginsberg was "being set up for a TV interview," wrote Holmes, "(great shot: Ginsberg talking about Kerouac, and behind him the coffin going down into the earth—'So, Mr. Ginsberg, I'll ask you to assess his career briefly, the camera's not rolling yet, but in a minute, and then you make your statement, and just stand a little farther over to the left so that we can get it all in the picture.') I registered all this, but felt nothing. It seemed as meaningless as the commercials that interrupt the disasters on the TV news. The young man from *Rolling Stone* was at my elbow, asking irrelevant questions. Why did Jack drink? Was he, in my opinion, significant? What had he thought of Rock? But I was numb—even to irony.

"I saw Allen and Gregory [Corso] near the coffin that was about to be lowered, and I broke away. I didn't have another word in me. I stood with them, and the funeral-man pressed some sort of button, and, easy as grease, Jack went down into the ground."

⬤

Time Passes.

You are cordially invited to attend the opening ceremonies for
EASTERN CANAL PARK
and
THE JACK KEROUAC COMMEMORATIVE
Saturday, June 25, 1988   1:00 P.M.

The invitation is from the city and state governments and the Lowell Celebrates Kerouac Committee. The mayor has proclaimed it Jack Kerouac Day.

The invitation was just one of the many messages that Lowell had been sending to the outside world in the last decade: "We've survived. We're back. Send tourists."

46

Once Lowell was the world's largest mill town, its many canals powering the textile looms. A mill town is really one big machine: from the locks that guide the water in the canals to the turbines, huge wheels fifteen feet tall, to the belts and gears, to the looms, hundreds to the floor; in mill after mill, all hands joined to one machine. After a long decline, the machine stopped. The mills were abandoned.

First-time visitors have a unanimous reaction: Lowell is an ugly city. To Holmes, on his first visit: "Lowell, of course, turned out to be an ugly, ratchety milltown in unplanned sprawl along the Merrimack; shuttered factories, railyards blown with hapless papers. ..." To Kerouac's first biographer, Ann Charters, Lowell was "ugly, dirty and rundown ... not a town that's easy to feel sentimental about."

When a later Kerouac biographer, Gerald Nicosia, first came to Lowell in 1977, what he found was "pretty close to real horror," more Stephen King than Kerouac. He remembers sitting on his luggage at the bus station looking at the desolate landscape of abandoned factories: a skyline that was a "spider web of guy wires holding up smokestacks." A cab took him to the one hotel he had a listing for: the Kenmore. The cabbie asked him if he was sure he wanted to go there. In his room he was overrun with cockroaches, pouring down the wall, which just seemed to come faster the more he sprayed them. He almost fumigated himself and opened the window. There was no screen. He shared the one bathroom on the entire floor with the other residents: druggies and drunks. After a fitful night's sleep—interrupted by cars without mufflers drag racing—he awoke covered with a gummy black soot. It was Sunday. He tried to get something to eat. Everything was closed. One man chased him from his business.

Today, says Nicosia, the author of *Memory Babe,* Lowell is one of his favorite cities in America. But not because it is now a garden spot. No, he has discovered that "Lowell is an insider's town, a fortress of industrial and tenement ugliness that protects a clean inner world of family love and tenderness and lifelong loyalties."

Nicosia had returned to Lowell as part of the city's celebration of Kerouac. (This time he had a room at the new Hilton.) There was a week of events that culminated in the dedication of the Jack

Kerouac Commemorative, eight triangular columns of red granite inscribed with words from Kerouac's novels and poetry. The sculpture is part of Lowell's revitalization, which has seen the establishment of a national and state historical park commemorating the old mills.

It was an insider's event: a family trying to place value on its native son: a son who caused it quite some grief, a son who made art out of the town's ugliness. They were talking about Lowell's Kerouac: the Franco-American Catholic Kerouac, the author of the five "Lowell Books" as they call them here—*The Town and the City, Visions of Gerard, Maggie Cassidy, Dr. Sax, The Vanity of Duluoz*, and the grander "Duluoz legend"—"Duluoz" being the name he gave himself in some novels. They emphasized a Kerouac who was drunk on words. He had written a million words (two-and-a-half *War and Peace*s) before his first novel. Seldom was *On the Road* mentioned; this was the hometown Kerouac.

For the Kerouacians, the celebration was a triumph: though the commemorative was set in the Eastern Canal Park, everyone was calling it Kerouac Park. They spoke of one day having French Street (which leads to the park) renamed Kerouac Drive. But Lowell is still divided about its native son.

Many in town remember Jack as a rude drunk shouting insults in Nicky's Bar. They think he was a good boy who came back from New York and his travels with his brain scrambled. Drugs—drink— New York City—an unholy trinity of evils that await any hometown voyager.

When the proposal came before the Lowell City Council to place the commemorative in the park, the vote was seven to one. Only one councilor was opposed: Brendan Fleming. It immediately hit the national news wires. The poet Lawrence Ferlinghetti, seeing it as the perfect setup to garner publicity, said to one of the memorial's supporters: "How do you keep him against it? Is he on your side?"

Councilor Fleming is still opposed. He says: "Kerouac's type of living certainly was not a good model for any of my children, or the children of Lowell."

There are other natives more deserving, he says, "who could be used much better: Bette Davis, Ben Butler, Floyd Vandenberg, Cardinal O'Connell—these are just off the top of my head." (Quick cultural literacy note: Butler led northern troops into Baltimore in the Civil War, Vandenberg was a general who has an Air Force base named for him, and Cardinal O'Connell served in Boston; Bette Davis was Bette Davis.)

But without the opposition, Kerouac might be too tame, a Beat generation Longfellow, a counterculture figure no longer counter to anything. As former senator Paul Tsongas observed at the dedication ceremonies, "I felt that Jack Kerouac would have preferred [a] 5 to 4 [vote]."

∞

Over in the Convention and Visitors Bureau, pure numbers won out. They looked at the numbers who attend Kerouac conferences in Canada and, as Michelle Hatem, director of operations, said: "He is a draw. There is a large market out there." And he makes for a good tourism "package": whales, Salem witches and Jack Kerouac.

So they designed an ad campaign using "five characters" affiliated with the Merrimack Valley who would be of interest to "consumers:" city founder Francis Cabot Lowell, a mill girl, James McNeill Whistler (born in Lowell), Thoreau—he spent a week on the Concord and Merrimack rivers, remember?—and the "King of the Beats," Kerouac. The ad has a drawing of Kerouac next to a pack of Lucky Strikes with the quote: "I'm known as the madman, the bum and angel with a naked, endless head of prose." Then it says:

Inside every grown man, there is a young boy. Who likes to play. To imagine. Question. And wander.

Some time ago, up in the Merrimack, there was such a man. Long before the yuppies. The hippies and the yippies. Before Beatles and beatniks. There was Jack Kerouac. The wanderer in every American Soul.

He could up and split town on the quick. Leave without a trace

49

or goodbye. Take to the road and taste everything along the way. Yet, he always returned, if only for a Lucky and a cup of coffee.

(Will Cornish, New Hampshire, do this to J. D. Salinger one day: "He never left his house. Except for a pack of Luckies." ?)

Sam Bregande of Gallagher Advertising, Charlestown, Massachusetts, wrote that ad, and he said he was "careful not to offend any true Kerouac believers or the class of people he might represent." Bregande has not bought the Lowell Kerouac package. "He was basically an itinerant traveler with a reputation for imbibing certain kinds of spirits. We were walking the line between: is he a literary hero or is he a bum? All I ever intended to do was to bring out the romantic and literary side of him. He's Americana, blue collar Americana, if you will."

In the transition from life to granite-bound honors always falls the shadow. After a time, all great figures become comic-book caricatures: Honest Abe, Mad Poe, Noble Jefferson. Sorry, one idea per historical character.

"I thought it was pretty funny that they could be that far out of touch," said Brian Foye, author of *A Guide to Jack Kerouac's Lowell.* "They fell into the trap set by biographers and critics," he said, referring to the standard portrait of Kerouac as the madman on the road, Edgar Allan Poe thumbing for a ride.

The biographers have also underestimated the importance of Lowell, says Foye; they have missed the city for the road. "For example, Ann Charters's biography calls the city 'run down, obstinately bourgeois, belligerently provincial.' Seven pages in, she says he grew up in 'a dirty, run-down town' and two pages later says he lived in 'a quiet residential community.' They just don't know what's going on. Let me be among the first to propose a radical new interpretation—Jack Kerouac actually liked Lowell.

"The Lowell books, a little bit of a French-Canadian angle, those are the best parts of the whole monumental weekend," Foye says.

Lowell was making its claim. At a poetry reading during the weekend, Robert Creeley said his friend "died hating Robert Frost and *Yankee* magazine. This is another New England." He was applauded.

Some feel that the distortion of Kerouac begins at home. "They are promoting a new, clean city, where everything's wonderful, but it's really not the case," said one former park ranger. "People are parochial, bigoted. The National Park is trying to cover over the past: let's not talk about the bad stuff in the past. Now Kerouac is part of this clean-up effort. We'll rehabilitate him and the city can be proud of him."

But Kerouac has resisted being whitewashed, says Foye. "There's worse revisions going on in the city than what's happening with Kerouac. The city renaissance is a whitewash of the mill years. How you want to use history to your advantage: That's what's going on in Lowell."

Kerouac came of age in Lowell and made the city his imaginative universe. But Lowell is assembling a different Kerouac for honors. "One is an honest art form without pretensions or covert aspirations," says Foye. "The other is loaded with all the small politics and game playing and revisions for personal gain that are a part of human life. Each has its own drama."

∞

John Clellon Holmes remembers the many difficulties that fame posed for his close friend: "Once in L.A., alone in a coffee house, he tried to strike up a conversation with the guy behind the counter, saying 'Hey, I'm Jack Kerouac. Let's have a talk or something,' to which the guy replied with hip disdain: 'Sure you are. They all say that.' "

∞

As the dedication ceremonies took place, Bob Pendergast stood leaning on a car in a parking lot. Pendergast is a Lowell native. He runs a video arcade—at a loss, he says, due to the increasing rents.

51

Otherwise, the kids will have nothing to do. Just a few feet away from him were the granite columns and a swirl of people and cameras. Looking on, he said, "Who was he? A guy that grew up in Lowell. Drank a lot. Did drugs. I don't quite understand."

Still, he takes some pride in the monument—it's better than the warehouse that was there. Just the other day he chased away five kids who were skateboarding up and down the granite benches of the memorial.

∞

No wonder writers often end badly: You say it and say it. Write twenty books, have a cavalcade of biographies. Scream it from the rooftops, lay it out line by line in interviews. You turn blue in the face and people say, "Now what was that all about? Drugs? Drink? Do your own thing? Aw, get a job."

"I knew him as a good kid. A real good kid. After he became famous he went cuckoo—did drugs," one native tells me. "After he moved away to New York and came back, he wasn't the same Kerouac I knew. Dope—drink—blew his brains."

I start to write it down, and he pulls my notebook from my hand. "You be careful what you say down here. They all come here. Say he was a drunk. Don't you write that. He was a good guy. Just got drinking." I ask for my notebook back, and in his eyes I see him weighing whether he ought to slug me. He tosses the notebook at me and turns away.

If part of the Lowell spirit is narrow, suspicious, cantankerous, then in his final days Jack Kerouac became as embittered as an old Lowell millhand. In his last days, he had become a right-wing reactionary "going into furies over Jews, Negroes, intellectuals," says his friend Holmes. He appeared on Bill Buckley's "Firing Line" to denounce the war protesters as un-American. He was an embarrassment to his friends from the Beat days. In the summer of 1969, they had gathered to discuss what to do about Kerouac's pronouncements. He had become the worst of Lowell.

Irene R. Desmarais had come straight from Mass to see "Mr. Ginsberg" at the poetry reading. A crowd of eleven hundred showed up for a reading by Allen Ginsberg, Robert Creeley and Lawrence Ferlinghetti. She has lived her seventy-one years in Jack's parish, St. Jean Baptiste. She knows that Jack is still remembered in Lowell for his drinking. She says thoughtfully, "As I listen more to what Kerouac wrote, he did love his city very much. He seemed to flaunt all the principles Franco-Americans stood for. But that does not take away from his being a great poet."

For Father Armand "Spike" Morrissette, Jack can do no wrong. "He was for the beatitude, that was the idea of beat, you know; beatitude, blessed are the merciful, blessed are the peace makers: Sermon on the Mount." Everyone calls him Father Spike (the seventy-eight-year-old priest got the name in the seminary), and he proudly says they also call him "Jack's priest." When Kerouac was a teenager, he came to Father Spike. "He was really upset. He said, 'People think I'm a sissy because I want to be a writer.' 'A writer,' I said, 'that's wonderful,' and I encouraged him right there." Father Spike delivered the eulogy at Jack's funeral in 1969. Outside of the family of Kerouac's wife, he cannot remember anyone else from Lowell attending. There were about seventy-five people at the funeral.

"I was getting into the hearse to ride with the body to the cemetery. An old man stopped me and said, 'Who's that?' And I said, 'Kerouac.' 'Who's Kerouac?' But nowadays they all knew him: 'Oh yes, I knew him. I went to school with him. Oh I had a drink with him. Oh yes, I knew him well,'" says Father Spike, and he laughs.

These days, says Father Spike, "a lot of very prominent people have been telling me that he's going to be rated as one of the greatest writers of all time, with Shakespeare, Victor Hugo, Alexander Dumas, Hemingway—he's that good."

Before the week's events began, Father spoke of how he was hearing from people all over the country who were coming. "And his daughter [Jan] is coming in for the celebration, from Eugene, Oregon.

She wrote two books herself: *Baby Driver* she signed, 'To dear Father Spike who babied my father through his life.' I always sided with him. I always said that man is a generous man, that man is a good man, a compassionate person. He's just like Christ to me. I think he's a modern saint."

∞

The morning before the ceremonies, Jan Kerouac waits with about forty others to board a yellow school bus for a tour of Jack Kerouac's Lowell.

"He was just a shy guy who drank too much. Sure he wrote a lot of great stuff, but he wasn't a god. He would be squirming in his grave. They're building up this pile of illusions," his daughter, thirty-six, says.

This is Jan's second trip to Lowell. She has ridden a Greyhound all the way from Oregon. In 1967, when she was fifteen, she came to see her father for only the second time in her life. He was drinking a fifth of whiskey, watching "The Beverly Hillbillies." She saw him for the first time years earlier in New York City; she was nine-and-a-half years old. Her father had denied that she was his daughter. He had come to New York to take a blood test to settle the question. As she talks, a woman comes up to say how much she looks like her father. Everyone is taking pictures of her. There's a photo of her on the front page of that day's *Lowell Sun*, boarding a train. She has just published her second novel, *Trainsong*.

She says she wouldn't normally take a bus tour, but she's been invited. She's never been on a bus tour of anything, she says, and she tries to slink off to the back of the bus. But the two enthusiastic tour guides, Reginald Ouellette and Roger Brunelle, guide her to the front seat.

It's a long tour, with readings from the Lowell novels at each stop—the yellow brick high school ("When Jack was a senior he played hooky forty-eight days"), the former Bon Marche department store, where he signed his first book, and the many houses—the Kerouacs moved about once a year.

54

A brief unloading at Christian Hill and more pictures of Jan with all of Lowell behind her: spire, dome, spire, smokestack, smoke-stack, smokestack.

At tour's end the bus pulls into Edson Cemetery, where Jack is buried. Everyone on the bus goes to the grave. Jan walks off by herself in the opposite direction. She bends down to feel the letters on the gravestones. It may be too public a moment to approach your father's grave for the first time with forty people around. But she has come all this way, cross-country.

The grave is a stone set flat in the earth. "Ti Jean," it says ("Little John"):

John L. Kerouac
March 12 1922–Oct 21 1969
He Honored Life

There are flowers, a penny and a bottle of wine ("Cheap Red Wine" says the label). It is common to leave offerings. Someone in the group remembers a well-read copy of *On the Road* left on the marker on another visit.

After a reading, there is a moment of silence and some tears among the crowd. The group starts to file back to the bus. Standing over the grave, Reginald Ouellette in a red beret is talking on about how he discovered Kerouac's writings. He is nearly the same age as Kerouac would be, and he attended the same schools. "This was my life," he says, hitting a book for emphasis.

Jan stands at a distance talking with Frankie Edith Parker, Jack's first wife, and Henry Cru, Jack's friend from his Greenwich Village days.

Turning her back on her father's grave, she reboards the bus.

The Forgotten Sorrow of Franklin Pierce, President

Handsome Frank

When at last New Hampshire honored its only native son president, Franklin Pierce was more than fifty years in the grave. In an afternoon of speeches, the main oration concluded: "He was not a traitor, nor an ingrate, nor a coward. ..."

On his day of honor, speakers came forth to say that now at the start of a war in Europe—World War I—"he could be acquitted of unforgivable public acts" committed before and during the War of the Rebellion, the Civil War.

Franklin Pierce was forty-eight years old when he took the oath of office on March 4, 1853. He spoke without notes, a vigorous man, the youngest yet in the White House, an example of the movement called "Young America." "My Countrymen," he began his inaugural address:

"It is a relief to feel that no heart but my own can know the personal regret and bitter sorrow over which I have been borne to a position so suitable for others rather than desirable for myself. ..."

"You have summoned me in my weakness; you must sustain me by your strength," he said.

A record crowd of eighty thousand had gathered on a raw, cold day. It started to snow, and by the time Pierce spoke only fifteen thousand remained.

Pierce was a compromise candidate chosen in a moment of domestic calm, and he vowed to maintain the repose. By the end of his term, the Missouri Compromise allocating slave and free states in the new territories had been overthrown, there was open warfare in the Kansas and Nebraska territories, and Pierce had sent federal troops into Boston, at great expense, to return an escaped slave to bondage in the South. In a few short years the nation had turned a dangerous corner: the abolitionist cause no longer belonged solely to the extremists. His party refused to renominate him. (He was the only elected president ever denied by his party.)

North and South, Franklin Pierce may have been the most hated man in the republic. At age fifty-two, he was finished. His countrymen—his neighbors—were finished with him.

"To Franklin Pierce more than to any other man do we owe the awakening of this evil spirit of sectionalism," wrote the *Boston Weekly Atlas*, a Whig newspaper. "Who but you, Franklin Pierce, have unsealed these bitter waters? Who, but you have kindled the flames of civil war on the desolated plains of Kansas?"

Even by the standards of an age that routinely libeled its public men, Pierce was singularly vilified. Other presidents have been hated, said the opposition *Philadelphia Bulletin*, "but it was reserved for Franklin Pierce to draw upon himself, by a long continued course of weakness, indecision, rashness, ignorance, and an entire and utter absence of dignity, of all great personal qualities, and even common talent, a degree of contempt, or of scornful mocking pity, such as no incumbent of our chief magistery has ever before encountered.

"He was the flatterer of the North and the basest slave of the South ... a convenient tool in shrewd hands. ... They have suffered him to sink to the very bottom of disgrace, and now they leave him there."

His "wretched career," said the newspaper, is over.

∞

Early in life, the sun shines the brightest. People liked Franklin Pierce, liked to hear him talk, wanted to see him get on in this world and wished him well.

At Bowdoin College, his friend Nathaniel Hawthorne said that Pierce possessed what we would call charisma: "He was distinguished by the same fascination of manner that has since proved so magical in winning him an unbounded personal popularity. ... Few men possess any thing like it; so irresistible as it is, so sure to draw forth an undoubting confidence. ..."

"His bright and cheerful aspect made a kind of sunshine," recalled Hawthorne. "This frankness, this democracy of good feeling has not been chilled by the society of politicians nor polished down into mere courtesy. ..."

He rose quickly in the world. His hometown entrusted their town meetings to him at age twenty-three, making him moderator. They sent him to serve two terms in the New Hampshire legislature in Concord. His father, a Revolutionary War veteran and farmer, was governor. By the end of his term, Franklin Pierce was speaker of the legislature, the youngest ever. "Frank Pierce is the most popular man of his age that I know of in N. H.—praises in every one's mouth," a newspaper commented. "Every circumstance connected with him seems to contribute to his popularity." Pierce went on to Congress at age twenty-eight, where he served two terms. In 1837, he became a senator. He was thirty-three, the youngest senator and just three years over the minimum age to serve. And then five years later, he resigned, vowing never again to be separated from his family. He returned to New Hampshire.

Early on in his first term in Congress, at age thirty, Pierce had married Jane Means Appleton, a daughter of the president of Bowdoin College and related to the New England aristocracy of families—the Lawrences of Boston, the Masons of Portsmouth, families who ran the mills that were transforming New England. Pierce had grown up on the New England frontier—he was born in a log cabin. Jane's aristocratic relatives had tried to have the wedding called off.

She joined him in Washington, but after less than a year she returned to New Hampshire. A minister's daughter with a stern Calvinist upbringing, she disdained politics and Washington, a rude, half-made, swampy town, where members of Congress lived in boardinghouses and enjoyed gambling and drinking. Pierce was involved in at least one publically noted "drinking spree" at a Washington theater, the first year his wife was away, and he was ill for weeks after. In life and history, Pierce has been shadowed by implications that he was an alcoholic.

He labored his whole life to master himself, says his sole modern biographer, a "desperate struggle of heroic proportions" with self-doubt and alcohol. At Bowdoin he was last in his sophomore class and was told that he would fail. He studied hard, often sleeping only four hours a night, and was graduated third in his class. In Congress, after a season of carousing, he admonished himself to live a quieter life, "adopted a stern and regular regimen," living with a family as its only boarder, and spent the winter thinking of Divine revelation and trying "harder to think and act in conformity with the precepts and commandments of the New Testament."

Pierce may have been speaking from experience when he advised his sisters: "There seems to be a strange fatality attending the existence of some persons which pushes them forward continuously to take steps that make themselves and those who are about them miserable."

His wife was a woman of constant sorrow; by all contemporary accounts she was sickly, "tubercular" and chronically depressed. She spent most of her time in Washington sick, confined to their boardinghouse rooms. Back in New Hampshire she gave birth to their first son, Franklin Jr. He died three days later. Pierce, in Washington, never saw the child. She wanted her husband out of politics, and with the birth of their second son, Frank Robert, she finally persuaded him to leave the Senate. Frank Robert died at age four of typhus fever, and Jane withdrew more into herself and became very protective of their remaining son, Benjamin.

Pierce stayed by her side, running a successful law practice in Concord. As chairman of the state's Democratic party he helped President Polk carry the state. Polk appointed him district attorney for New Hampshire. After that, Pierce became the great refuser. As it says on his statue, in a stubborn Yankee way: "Declined the office of Attorney General of the United States, that of Secretary of War, the United States Senatorship and the Governorship of his state." An impressive résumé of refusal.

"Although the early years of my manhood were devoted to public life, it was never really suited to my taste," he wrote to President Polk. "I longed, as I am sure you must often have done, for the quiet and independence that belongs only to the private citizen, and now at forty, I feel that desire stronger than ever."

By removing himself from politics, Franklin Pierce became the perfect candidate: a man without a past. Outside New Hampshire, no one really knew much about him. By 1852, he had been out of Washington for ten years. (Even his own party's presidential candidate in the previous election of 1848, General Lewis Cass, who had served with him in the Senate for two or three years, had never met him.)

The Democrats were deadlocked at their convention in 1852, with the leading candidates each refusing to throw their votes to another. New England Democrats had planned before the convention to put Pierce forth as a dark horse candidate late in the voting. Pierce published a letter saying it would be "utterly repugnant to my tastes and wishes," but then he consented. His name was put forth on the thirty-fifth ballot. Supporters of the leading candidates were persuaded to throw their support behind Pierce and other minor candidates for a few ballots. Once the names of these dark horse candidates went down, the convention, in theory, would rally around one of the front-runners. On the forty-ninth ballot, however, there was a "stampede" to Pierce, and he won. The Democrats had surprised themselves. Many of the party's leaders were perplexed.

Pierce's wife fainted at the news. She prayed for his defeat. Their son, Bennie, age eleven, told his mother, "I hope he won't be elected for I should not like to be at Washington and I know you would not either."

The vice-presidential nominee, Southerner William King, dismissed the entire convention with disgust: it was mob rule destined to pick inferior men. (Deathly ill in Cuba at the time of the inauguration, King was sworn into office by a special act of Congress. He died one month later.)

Pierce spent most of the campaign at home in Concord, while his party fashioned him into "Young Hickory of the Granite Hills," a new Andrew Jackson. His friend Hawthorne wrote a campaign biography.

It was a particularly nasty campaign, whose major issue was Pierce's conduct during the Mexican War when he had fallen off his horse and fainted. The Whigs called him the "hero of many a well fought bottle." Pierce's party countered that the brigadier general had been smashed in the groin when his horse fell, but he remounted and rode bravely on. The Whigs, in their last days as a party, were led by General Winfield Scott, a war hero twice over in the War of 1812 and the Mexican War. But the pomposity of "Old Fuss and Feathers" lost him the election. Pierce won an electoral college landslide, carrying all but four states, and 65 percent of the popular vote.

"Grand Result in the Union! Complete Overthrow of Whiggery!" said the headlines of Pittsburgh's *Daily Morning Post*, "Who is Franklin Pierce?"

∞

Two months before his inauguration, Franklin Pierce and his wife and son were in a train wreck. Bennie, age twelve, was crushed to death in front of his parents. The Pierces never recovered from their sorrow.

The following month, with a "fixed expression of sorrow and despondency" Pierce went on to Washington by himself. He did not address any crowds along the way. In New York, his train arrived at midnight. The rear car was detached, and he entered the Astor Hotel at track level, under the street. Relatives shepherded his wife as far as Baltimore, where Pierce pleaded with her to accompany him to Washington. But she could not move: "Gloom engulfed her and she sat for the rest of the day in a stupor," her aunt wrote in her diary. She gave her husband a lock of Bennie's hair to hold onto during the ceremonies.

For days after Bennie's death, the Pierces had sat in seclusion, trying to understand God's will. Mrs. Pierce believed her son had been sacrificed by a stern Calvinist God so that President Pierce would be free from distractions. Pierce believed his son was taken as punishment for seeking the presidency against the best interests of his wife's health.

Pierce rode into Washington in the last car and hopped off as it stopped, evading the mayor and his welcoming reception. When taking the oath of office, he did not swear on the Bible. Following Jesus' Sermon on the Mount, he refused to invoke God's consent on any earthly and imperfect endeavor. There were no inaugural balls. Mrs. Pierce arrived quietly in Washington, and for a year and a half, the First Lady did not come out of her rooms at the White House to make a public appearance. She sat by herself, sometimes tearfully writing notes to her dead son.

Nearly half a year after Benjamin's death, she wrote on mourning stationery to a cousin: "I long to fly away sometimes ... God help my weak soul bear its sorrow. ..."

∽

In the White House, Franklin Pierce failed to govern. He appointed a cabinet of strong personalities from the North and the South and let them rule in his absence. In the interpretation of historian Allan Nevin's landmark work, *Ordeal of the Union*, Pierce acted as a mere moderator of his cabinet. Trying to please all factions, he pleased none. It was the Pierce administration in name only, said one contemporary observer. The small-town country lawyer was out of his league.

By the end of his first year, the president was "regarded by most of the leaders of his own party as incompetent," judged historian James Ford Rhodes in his *History of the United States 1850–1909.* "He would make up his mind in the morning and change it in the afternoon. ... He would receive an applicant for office effusively, put on his most urbane manner, listen to the claim with attention, giving the aspirant for public place every reason to feel that the position was surely his. For Franklin Pierce could not say no. ... In more than one case the same important office was promised to different men, and indirect assurances of executive favor were almost as numerous as visitors at the White House."

But when it came to slavery, Pierce did not vacillate. The abolitionists were "reckless fanatics," he had said in speech after speech since his congressional days. They threatened to wreck the Union and usurp Southerners' Constitutional rights to their property. (He once rushed to Concord on a special train to plead with his brother, who was serving in the legislature, not to vote for abolitionist resolutions. "If you vote for those resolutions ... you are no brother of mine; I'll never speak to you again.") The abolitionists, his attorney general said, must be crushed.

In his campaign biography, Hawthorne wrote that Pierce did not hold with "anti-slavery agitation," and then Hawthorne sought to dispose of the whole slavery issue: A wise view "looks upon slavery as one of those evils which divine Providence does not leave to be remedied by human contrivances, but, which, in its own good time, by some means impossible to be anticipated, but of the simplest and easiest operation, when all its uses shall have been fulfilled, it causes to vanish like a dream."

∞

The country had achieved a precarious peace with the Missouri Compromise, but Pierce undermined it in his first major act, with his strong backing of the Kansas–Nebraska bill—new states would be allowed to vote whether to be slave or free. After months of debate, concluding with a thirty-six-hour session and all the pressure Pierce could bring, the bill passed. Pierce promptly signed his administration's first great measure, as he saw it, putting to rest antislavery agitation.

Reaction in the North was immediate. The Compromise had been breached. Northerners would refuse to honor the Fugitive Slave Law. They would send freedmen on to Canada, not back to slavery.

Two days after the House of Representatives passed the Kansas–Nebraska bill, an escaped slave named Anthony Burns was captured by federal marshals in Boston. A mob of two thousand led by a minister stormed the jail trying to free Burns. A federal marshal was killed, and the mob was held off. Burns was tried and found to be the property of his master in Virginia.

A compromise was offered, allowing Bostonians to buy Burns his freedom and spare the government the embarrassment of having to use force to return a man to slavery. Burns's owner was willing to sell, but the U.S. attorney wouldn't allow it. The South would not be appeased; freeing Burns would encourage more runaways. Pierce was determined that the Constitution be honored. "Incur any expense," he telegrammed the Boston district attorney.

The president sent a revenue cutter north and four platoons of Marines to march out this one slave. They joined twenty-two companies of the Massachusetts militia and a battalion of U.S. artillery, as well as a sheriff's posse and the police. Troops were called in from New Hampshire and Rhode Island. In New York City soldiers were under an alert.

Boston was hung in crepe, stores were shuttered, church bells tolled, flags were flown upside down. Thousands poured in from the countryside and lined the route crying "Shame! Shame!" and in places blocked the way of troops who marched with loaded muskets and had orders to shoot if necessary. One unit came close to firing on a group of men who were throwing bricks; other citizens were beaten, bayoneted, handcuffed. Several were wounded when the cavalry charged a crowd, sabers drawn.

"I saw the cavalry, artillery, marines and police, a thousand strong, escorting with shotted guns one trembling colored man to the vessel which was to carry him to slavery," said one eyewitness. "I heard the curses both loud and deep poured on these soldiers; I saw the red flush in their cheeks as the crowd yelled at them: 'Kidnappers! Kidnappers!'"

Pierce had staged a forceful advertisement of the realities of slavery in a city that considered itself "the cradle of liberty." From a window opposite the old state house, there hung a black coffin with the words "The Funeral of Liberty." Overnight, the cause of the "fanatical extremists," the abolitionists, had been adopted by moderates once content to honor the Compromise.

"Yesterday a fugitive slave was arrested in Boston!" cried Henry Wadsworth Longfellow (another Pierce classmate). "To-day there is an eclipse of the sun. 'Hung be the heavens in black.'" And Thoreau expressed the shock of his fellow countrymen with his most widely published speech, "Slavery in Massachusetts":

> I have lived for the last month—and I think every man in Massachusetts capable of the sentiment of patriotism must have had a similar experience—with the sense of having suffered a vast and indefinite loss. I did not know at first what ailed me. At last it occurred to me that what I had lost was a country.

New Englanders would forever hate Franklin Pierce for this act. A friend of Pierce's was with him in the White House when he opened his mail to read: "To the chief slave-catcher of the United States. You damned, infernal scoundrel, if I only had you here in Boston, I would murder you!" North and South had attained a new level of hostility. "We rejoice at the recapture of Burns," said the *Richmond Enquirer*, "but a few more such victories and the South is undone."

At Pierce's election the Democrats had an overwhelming majority in both houses, and their chief opposition, the Whigs, was a dying party. Two years later, they lost their majority in the House, and a new party, the Republicans, had sprung up, fueled by the hatred of the Nebraska bill and the Fugitive Slave Law.

Pierce had spent his great popularity overturning a compromise he had promised to uphold. "Pierce is a runt miserable dog, and seems bent on destroying his country, as well as himself," a Whig senator from Maine wrote home.

Northerners could not stand a president who ordered troops into Boston but who stood aside as Kansas was in armed revolt and said it was a matter of state's rights. His own state turned against him: The New Hampshire legislature censured a senator and a congressman who had voted for the Nebraska bill. They elected the abolitionist leader John P. Hale to the Senate. For years Pierce had blocked Hale's career at every turn, and now Hale stood in the Senate to say Pierce "defames men whose shoe-latchets he is not worthy to untie." (At a White House reception sometime after that attack, Pierce turned his back on Hale. Washington society was offended.)

In a meeting to plan a homecoming welcome for the soon-to-be-retired president, Concord's citizens decided that the most fitting public reception would be "solemn mournful silence." And the Chief Justice of New Hampshire said of Franklin Pierce that he had "the G-d d—edest blackest heart that was ever placed in mortal bosom."

∞

In the months before taking office, Pierce had written to his wife about the impossibility of balancing the demands of the North and the South. "I can do no right. What am I to do, wife? Stand by me."

When he won his party's nomination, the first thing Hawthorne said to his friend, without any other greeting, was: "Frank, I pity you! Indeed, I do, from the bottom of my heart!"

By the end of his first term, Pierce had lost his appetite for politics. Knowing that his renomination was doubtful, he had written a relative: "You would be surprised with how much indifference I contemplate the result. ... I am weary. ..." Before leaving the White House, he burned almost all of his presidential papers. On inauguration morning, he was left waiting by himself. No carriage came to pick him up. "There is nothing left ... but to get drunk," he is reported to have said. He took his ailing wife to the island of Madeira and on to Europe, hoping the change would help her.

∞

In the years following, he became one of the most hated ex-presidents in our history—he seemed to work at it. He denounced Lincoln, remained loyal to his friend and former cabinet member Jefferson Davis and, above all, remained faithful to "the sacred Constitution.""I will never justify, sustain, or in any way or to any extent uphold this cruel, heartless, aimless unnecessary war. Madness and imbecility are in the ascendant," he wrote his wife. "Come what may the foul schemes of Northern Abolitionism which we have resisted for so many years, are not to be consummated by arms on bloody fields, through any aid of mine."

Pierce was hated by the abolitionists, by the Republicans and by his own party. One could pick almost any newspaper in the Union and read a denunciation of his "wretched career."

"I can not ... bow to the storm," he wrote to his wife. "I have no opinions to retract, no line of action to change."

In his first public appearance after leaving office, he warned his fellow New Englanders in 1857 to preserve the Union and respect the Southern institution of slavery. The South, he believed, was the wronged party.

But with the start of the war, he soft-pedaled his opposition, and when called on to address a rally, he spoke of honoring the flag and the Revolution.

In 1861, after making a three-week tour of the West, Pierce was publicly accused of acting in a secret league to overthrow the government. Lincoln's secretary of state, William H. Seward, had brought the charges. By private mail he requested that Pierce respond to an anonymous letter that he was engaged in treason. The charges were later leaked to the press.

67

The *Detroit Tribune* called Pierce "a prowling traitor spy" and printed a mysterious letter about the conspiracy that was signed in code, *]< Δ z = $\Box$. Republican papers across the country, including the *New York Evening Post* and the *Boston Journal*, reprinted the letter.

The allegations and the letter quickly proved to be a hoax, which Seward had known long before the letter was widely reprinted. But the damage had been done: Pierce had to publicly deny that he was disloyal. He stood before his country a man accused of treason.

He was enraged. He spoke out vehemently against Lincoln. He condemned the Emancipation Proclamation as an attempt to "butcher" the white race while "inflicting" freedom on Negroes who would not benefit.

At a July 4th celebration in Concord he condemned Lincoln's abuse of presidential power: the declaration of martial law and the suppression of free speech and suspension of *habeas corpus*. (In Ohio, a critic of the Lincoln administration had been arrested, tried in a military court without benefit of *habeas corpus* and then exiled to the Confederacy.) "The mere arbitrary will of the President takes the place of the Constitution and the President himself announces to us that it is treasonable to speak or to write otherwise than as he may prescribe. ... True it is, that any of you, that I, may be the next victim of unconstitutional, arbitrary, irresponsible power."

As he spoke against the "fruitless, fatal Civil War" and the futility of "all our efforts to maintain the Union by force of arms," word spread through the crowd about a telegram announcing victory at Gettysburg. Pierce was one of the few men in the country to publicly call Lincoln to task, but it did not win him any garlands: Concord after this was not a hospitable place for him. Nationally, the speech was widely reprinted to show that Pierce was no patriot.

His reputation fell even lower when later in the year, a letter Pierce wrote to Jefferson Davis was discovered in a raid on the Confederate president's house. In 1860, Pierce had written his friend to urge him to run for the presidency. In the letter, Pierce told Davis that if war should come due to "the madness of Northern abolitionists

... the fighting will not be along the Mason and Dixon line merely. It will be within our own borders, in our own streets. ..." Pierce was seen as abetting the enemy; encouraging secession by leading Southerners to think they would face a divided North. The letter was published in newspapers throughout the North. Three weeks later there was, indeed, fighting in the streets: the New York City Draft Riots—the worst riot in American history. Troops just finished fighting at Gettysburg were ordered into the city. Pierce, through his letter, was accused of helping to incite a riot.

Pierce, said one Northern newspaper, and those who stand with him "are Democrats only in name, but in support and action are among the worst enemies of freedom, by their affiliation with the lords of the lash and cradle plunderers at the South." Other Northerners more succinctly called him a Benedict Arnold.

When Lincoln was assassinated, the people of Concord hung out American flags in mourning. Pierce did not do so, and a mob stormed his house demanding to know why. He met them at the door and said: "It is not necessary for me to show my devotion for the Stars and Stripes by any special exhibition upon the demand of any man or body of men." He had served his country for thirty-five years, he said, and if "there is any question of my devotion to the flag, the Constitution and the Union ... it is too late now."

∞

Nathaniel Hawthorne had stood by his oldest friend on the platform during his anti-Lincoln July 4th oration, and he stood by him to the end. Hawthorne dedicated his last book to him in 1864 and included a long open letter to the ex-president. ("No man's loyalty is more steadfast," the letter said.) His publisher, pressured by Boston literary society, discouraged him, telling him that one book dealer had threatened to boycott the book, and others in the trade thought Pierce's name would ruin the book's sales.

"I cannot withdraw that dedication and wound my friend. My loyalty to him is involved," Hawthorne calmly told his publisher. "If

69

he is so exceedingly unpopular that his name is enough to sink the volume, there is so much the more need that an old friend should stand by him."

Annie Fields, the publisher's wife, thought Hawthorne admirable in his "determination at all hazards to dedicate this book to his friend. Mr. P's politics at present shut him away from the faith of patriots, but Hawthorne has loved him since college days and he will not relent."

Ralph Waldo Emerson ripped the dedication and letter from his copy and wrote in his journal:

"Hawthorne unlucky in having for a friend a man who cannot be befriended; whose miserable administration admits but of one excuse, imbecility. Pierce was either the worst, or he was the weakest, of all our Presidents."

Hawthorne's friends argued with him, detailing the evils of Pierce, but he waved off all the criticism and at last said with some sadness in his voice, "It is so hard for Frank to get a new idea!"

☜☞

The two old friends were together to the end. Later the same year, Hawthorne became ill, and Pierce took him to the White Mountains for his health. Hawthorne died there. At his funeral, the New England literary establishment turned out: Emerson, Longfellow, Lowell, Holmes, Whittier, Alcott, Channing and others. Pierce was not allowed to be a pallbearer and was made to sit by himself in the balcony of the church.

Just six months before, Hawthorne had consoled Pierce as they stood at the grave of his long-suffering wife, Jane. Even though Pierce was overcome with grief, he had thought to turn up Hawthorne's coat collar to the cold.

Packing up Hawthorne's valise in the hotel room, Pierce came across one picture by itself in a little compartment. It was a picture of Pierce.

At Hawthorne's funeral, Pierce came forward and scattered flowers into the grave.

∞

In Abraham Lincoln's second year in office, he lost his son, William. Lincoln spent days weeping in his son's room. Mrs. Lincoln turned to seances. In the same season that he was publicly charged with treason, Franklin Pierce wrote to console the Lincolns:

> My dear sir,
> The impulse to write you, the moment I heard of your great domestic affliction was very strong, but it brought back the crushing sorrow which befell me just before I went to Washington in 1853, with such power that I felt your grief to be too sacred for intrusion.
> Even in this hour, so full of danger to our Country, and of trial and anxiety to all good men, your thoughts will be of your cherished boy, who will nestle at your heart, until you meet him in the new life, when tears and toils and conflicts will be unknown.

"There can be but one refuge in such an hour," Pierce concluded, "trust in Him. ..."

∞

Three weeks before Christmas 1865, Franklin Pierce was baptized. He was sixty-one years old. For the first time, he said, he felt religious grace. He would live four more years.

In a tumultuous era filled with striking figures, historians did not stop long to puzzle out his fate. In the years that followed, some school history textbooks omitted him.

In the last months of his life, his health ebbing, he traveled to Baltimore to deliver his final speech. He spoke to a convention of descendants of Revolutionary War soldiers, people like himself, who even after a bloody Civil War remembered the bright promise of the Revolution. Pierce had grown up hearing at "his father's fireside" of the generation that had won the peace and written the Constitution. At the close of his inaugural address, he spoke of how he stood

71

"almost within view of the green slopes of Monticello and ... within reach of the tomb of Washington, with all the cherished memories of the past gathering around me like so many eloquent voices of exhortation from heaven. ..." By his father's generation, Pierce judged himself.

He told the convention: "I do not believe that I ever saw a day when I would not have made any possible personal sacrifice to maintain the Constitution of my country and the Union based upon it."

The "sacred Constitution" was Franklin Pierce's true religion. This was the earliest lesson he had learned, he told Hawthorne, and it was what made it so hard for him to get a new idea. "I can express no better hope for my country than that the kind Providence which smiled upon our fathers may enable their children to preserve the blessings they have inherited," his inaugural address had concluded.

Honor and Welcome

One day late in the twentieth century, in a country that Franklin Pierce would scarcely recognize, David Epstein, a Washington lawyer, was on television jesting with Dick Cavett about Pierce. "Who is the most obscure president?" asked Epstein. Cavett thought it was Millard Fillmore.

Epstein is the sole member of the Friends of Franklin Pierce, whose purpose is to "rescue Pierce from the obscurity he so richly deserves." Epstein's quest began in 1961, when he worked for the National Capital Planning Commission. Living in a city of monuments, with papers for more on his desk, he thought: There must be some president who isn't worthy of a monument. And so he began asking around: Who is the most forgotten president?

Many people answered Millard Fillmore. Indeed, too many did, and Epstein concluded that Fillmore is well known for being forgotten.

Pierce has been good to Epstein. On his second date with a certain woman, he popped the question: Who was the most obscure president? She was enthusiastic; that was a question she herself often asked people, although her own candidate was Chester A. Arthur. Soon the two were married, and on the honeymoon they visited the Pierce Manse in Concord. (Alas, it was closed for restoration.)

On the "Dick Cavett Show" and in the *Washington Post,* the Friends of Franklin Pierce have presented a history of Pierce's life as one long pratfall: he faints in battle; his vice president dies; he spends his first night in the White House on a mattress on the floor; his wife won't come out of her room; he has "an overfondness for alcohol" and when his horse runs down a woman, he is the first president charged with a criminal offense; his party refuses to renominate him; historians credit him with "no great presidential decisions." (Even Fillmore is credited with three.) He burns his papers. Of the last, Epstein says, "It certainly made my job a lot easier, and I'm appreciative for it." The Friends, he says, is "an exercise in whimsy."

∞

As a rule, presidential homes are shrines. Americans make pilgrimages to Mount Vernon, Monticello and Hyde Park. Even Plymouth Notch, Vermont, home of Calvin Coolidge, draws a crowd. Pierce's two houses in New Hampshire have narrowly survived. The Concord Manse was almost bulldozed for urban renewal in the 1960s, but the Pierce Brigade scrambled to raise $38,000 to move it (partially by the sale of a commemorative whiskey bottle in the shape of the state house). The Hillsborough homestead was jettisoned by the state in 1980 when it was facing a $44 million deficit. Pierce's true birthplace, an honest two-room log cabin, lies under a reservoir sometimes called Franklin Pierce Lake.

The good ladies and gentlemen of the Pierce Brigade, and the hard-working members of the Hillsborough Historical Society, however, did save his boyhood home up the road from his birthplace. They are tired of seeing a hometown boy roughly treated. "They still run him down," said a former chairman of the historical society's homestead committee. "He did the best he could. He was a golden boy right till he got to the White House. Too bad it happened to him."

They present a picture of Pierce as a hit-and-run victim of history—it could have happened to anyone; it was a dangerous time; "If you were president, you couldn't have done any better"; "He doesn't deserve obscurity." Leave the poor man alone.

"He was a president that New Hampshire could be proud of," says the former chairman. "I would like to see every child in New Hampshire pass through the house."

Upstairs is a banner from a rally for Pierce:

Honor and Welcome

to

Franklin Pierce

who has been faithful

to the

Constitution

and

True to the Union

Kenneth Kooyman is a great-great-great nephew of Franklin Pierce. When Kooyman grew up, Pierce was not to be mentioned in the house. "It was taboo. You did not bring it up," he says. He does recall a few occasions when "Aunt Mary would mention him and talk about him in passing, but if you asked anything about it, it was always: 'Well, we just don't want to discuss that.'"

Time did not win amnesty for Pierce in the family. When Kooyman was an adult and his aunts quite elderly, he tried again. "Three or four years ago I was talking with my Aunt Genevieve when she was a little clearer of mind and asked her some questions concerning Pierce, and her comment to me was very short and blunt and to the point: there are some things that should be left alone. And that was pertaining to Franklin Pierce."

∽

Thirteen men preceded Franklin Pierce to the presidency. Thirteen more had followed Pierce by the time the state of New Hampshire honored him with a statue in 1914.

On the day of the commemoration, the politicians carefully distanced themselves from Pierce. "This statue is not erected to Franklin Pierce because all agreed in the political views which he held ... it is not necessary to indulge in arguments in respect to his attitude toward the highly irritating public questions of the time," said a judge.

A former U.S. senator said the repeal of the Missouri Compromise was "utterly indefensible," but that other honest men of the era had stumbled, and Pierce should be "acquitted of unforgivable public acts." Several speakers made reference to England honoring Cromwell, after a pause of a couple of hundred years.

A case was made for Pierce's patriotism by way of association; he was a "rugged and sturdy ... product of the New Hampshire soil." "In honoring him," New Hampshire "honors herself." He was born of "worthy and patriotic ancestry." His father had "left the plow to enlist in the army of the Revolution." And young Pierce "learned at his father's knee patriotism and a love of the government under which he lived."

The speakers talked of Pierce's charm and his success as the best jury lawyer in the state. They explained his pro-slavery stand as being pro-Union—a Union he believed would be lost in a war. His proud résumé of refusal was given. The activities of his own administration occupied scarcely more than a paragraph in any of the eight major speeches. One quoted the judgment of Senator Bainbridge Wadleigh: "But for slavery and the questions growing out of it, his administration would have passed into history as one of the most successful in our national life."

Another speaker concluded by quoting Hawthorne: "No man's hopes or apprehensions on behalf of our national existence [are] more deeply heartfelt, or more closely intertwined with his possibilities of personal happiness, than those of Franklin Pierce." A statement worthy of inscription in the statue's granite base. Instead, the statue base says more about what he refused to do, the offices he declined, than what he did as president. Just the dates of his presidency are given.

In remembrance, the compromise president suffered a final compromise. For his political sins, Pierce's statue was not allowed within the "golden rectangle" of the state house grounds. Revolutionary War hero John Stark, Daniel Webster and John P. Hale stand on the grounds. Webster, the great orator who had promoted the Fugitive Slave Law, stands front and center. Hale, the abolitionist leader and Pierce's arch-rival, stands to one side. Once again the president has turned his back to Senator Hale. Pierce stands alone, on a lower pedestal, by the street.

The statue is of a young Pierce. At a glance, this is a standard heroic statue. The lean man in the frock coat, one-and-a-half times bigger than life, up on a pedestal. But up close, the face says something else: The brow is lowered, the lips downturned. There are bags under the eyes—the eyes deep in shadow are focused where?—someplace in the middle distance. And on his forehead a lock of sweeping hair frames his face in youth and throws all sorrow into relief. This is a young face growing old as you look upon it. Honor and welcome to Franklin Pierce, the sad young man in bronze.

Part III

US & THEM
AND THEM & US

Us & Them
and Them & Us

A working town is like a beautiful crystal. Hundreds upon hundreds of blood ties and business ties, crossing, spreading out, meeting at the angles of family, friendship and acquaintance. People admire that. This is such a nice town, they'll say, and they may give it the ultimate benediction: "small—quaint—charming." The eye perceives a glorious unity.

But tap the crystal in just the right way and the crystal will cleave in sixteen directions—neatly, cleanly, along fault lines that were previously invisible. The crystal shears along the weakest bonds; we know that from chemistry. In a town that bond is tolerance; we know that in ourselves. The crystal cleaves into pieces: Us and Them and Them and Us.

Who gets chosen as an Us, and who is cast off as a Them? That is the game, the game of gossip and membership. There are Us who are paying taxes, supporting Them. Us who are the bedrock of this community and Them who want to ruin it. Us who are in the right pews on Sundays and Them with their travesty of our religion. There are Us who know how to behave in public, who have values, who raise our children properly, and there are Them who are just not

79

quality people. There are Us who belong here and Them who should go back to where they came from.

The eye perceives a glorious unity. The crystal does not always shatter, but the fault lines are there, hidden in the dazzling form.

The Museum of Democracy:
Town Meeting

A Garland of Myths

There is a painting, once revered as a cultural icon, that is still known to many Americans. A man has risen to speak. His hands, roughened by work, rest on the bench in front of him. His worn work jacket is open, showing a blue plaid shirt. He is at the annual town meeting, and the town report is rolled in his jacket pocket. His eyes look upward; his mouth is slightly open. He looks almost angelic. With a prominent Adam's apple and thin angular face, he is a smooth-faced Abe Lincoln. Near him, two older men in ties look on, respectful, encouraging. Surely this common man is about to speak the wisdom of Jefferson, about to declaim some democratic truth.

The painting is "Freedom of Speech" by Norman Rockwell, one of the Four Freedoms he portrayed in the war year of 1943. Immediately after publication in the *Saturday Evening Post*, requests came in for millions of reprints. The originals were exhibited during Four Freedoms War Bond Shows, and millions more were sold. Then the Office of War Information printed posters of the Four Freedoms, and they went up on the home front offices, railroad stations and schools, and the Four Freedoms were sent abroad. Wherever the Allies were, that man was rising to speak. Those under fascist rule could raise their voices only at huge outdoor rallies, but an American could rise by himself and be heard. The New England Town Meeting had gone to war.

In the other Freedom paintings, people prayed, rejoiced around a Thanksgiving table, and stood over their sleeping children, the mother tucking them in, the father looking on, a folded newspaper at his side—"Bombings … Horror," the headline.

If there were a Museum of Democracy, that painting of the man rising to speak would be in the main gallery, along with all the parchment deeds, the dark oil portraits and the marble busts.

But where in the Museum of Democracy would be this page one report from the *New York Times*. A few weeks before New York's 1989 mayoral primary, the *Times* reported "Most New Yorkers have yet to see a campaign poster, a button or a bumper sticker, much less a candidate." The campaign comes to New Yorkers through the mail, telephone and television.

"'Doors are triple-locked against crime and the only outside voice allowed in is television,' says former Mayor John V. Lindsay, who complains that politics has been transformed from a participatory process into just another televised sport."

Fifty years on, it is hard to imagine Americans rallying around a painting that beatifies the town meeting. I have sat in numerous town meetings come March and pondered the gulf between Rockwell's idealized moment of free speech and the triple-locked doors of modern life.

The meetings always begin with a pledge to the flag. They are usually old flags, the white stripes gone to ivory. During the slow moments of the meetings, I study these old flags. In small towns throughout New England, many Americans are pledging themselves to a flag of forty-eight stars.

In March we are all alone up here in northern New England. It is a dreary time of thaws and freezes. Winter recedes with the slowness of an ice age, leaving the land flattened and exhausted looking. South of us, flowers bloom, and children sit in classrooms talking of poetry. But up here March is the cruelest month, Mud Season, a purgatory between winter and spring. The roads are muddy or icy or both and heaved up by the frost; even traveling salesman shun us in March. There are no distractions, no guests or fine weather; it's just family, and towns get down to their family business.

I go from town to town to sit for hours on hard benches and harder folding chairs, to watch debates late into the night: impassioned speeches about snowplows, dry hydrants, fire engines, schools, death, taxes and dogs.

It's theater, and the theatrical season is short: in Vermont all towns hold their meetings on the same day; in New Hampshire, the meetings are scattered over a couple of weeks, some during the day, some at night. I go to as many towns as I can schedule; hill towns with populations of five hundred that gather in meeting houses smaller than the garages on some suburban homes; and towns of five thousand that assemble in the high school gym. All those odd little towns. It's like walking into family discussions. Part of me can't help but see town meeting as a ritual family gathering, each town a republic of families.

I go to see, each time, if democracy works. The discussions are sometimes heated and sometimes lethargic, good decisions and bad get made, but it all seems entirely natural. This is the way government should be: you get together with your neighbors, discuss and vote.

But then I leave the town meetings in the 1787 meeting houses, the 1890 town halls, the 1953 elementary school cafeterias and the 1977 high school auditoriums, and I drive south, and it's all malls, condos, interstates. And those rooms of decision seem far away.

In the old meeting houses, looking around at the plain roughness of it all solidified by two hundred years of paint and dust, I can see it as a black-and-white photo. That little oil company calendar with the large block numerals and Sundays in red—the one adrift on a wall high up over the regulator clock, that could say 1953 or 1937; and all those faces, the worn faces above the plaid, the creased faces above the folded arms, I see those in black and white momentarily, too. I think, There's a Walker Evans face, a Dorothea Lange face—faces from the great photos of the 1930s New Deal photographers.

And then I hear the faces. They are talking computers and liability and the inflated dollars of the early 1990s. All the black-and-whiteness washes away. All is in color again.

⟳

In New England, more than twelve hundred towns still govern themselves by gathering to vote each March on all matters of the public weal, from an intricate zoning regulation to installing a toilet at the town garage. Town meeting is a form of direct democracy practically unchanged since 1629; the Pilgrims certainly spent less time discussing sewerage, but the structure is the same—only more democratic: back then to vote you had to be a property-holding male in good standing with the church.

Town meeting is a part of our democracy seldom seen. Often celebrated and derided, lauded by Jefferson and Emerson and dismissed by political scientists as a quaint holdover outmatched by today's complex problems, town meeting is viewed through a fog of aspirations. It is seldom seen plain.

The Four Freedoms painting represents what can be called the Olympian view. The gods look down and praise the people (as in the People, Yes!).

Thomas Jefferson wrote that town meetings "have proved themselves the wisest invention ever devised by the wit of man for the perfect exercise of self-government and for its preservation."

Foreign observers, who often saw our republic clearer than we did, have approved. Alexis de Tocqueville, in *Democracy in America*, wrote: "Town meetings are to liberty what primary schools are to science; they bring it within the people's reach." James Bryce, later in the nineteenth century, wrote in *The American Common-wealth* that it was the "most perfect school of self-government in any modern country."

Modern social critics hold up the town meeting as a democratic ideal. Lewis Mumford said: "I believe the greatest defect of the United States Constitution was its original failure, despite the example of the New England township and the town meeting, to make this democratic local unit the basic cell of our whole system of government."

Ralph Waldo Emerson provides the ultimate benediction:

> For the first time, the ideal social compact was real. In a town-meeting the great secret of political science was uncovered, and the problem solved, how to give every individual his fair weight in government, without any disorder from numbers. ...
>
> It is the consequence of this institution, that not a school house, a public pew, a bridge, a pound, a mill-dam, hath been set up, or pulled down, or altered, or bought, or sold, without the whole population of this town having a voice in the affair. A general contentment is the result. And the people truly feel that they are the lords of the soil. In every winding road, in every stone fence, in the smokes of the poor-house chimney, in the clock on the church, they read their own power, and consider, at leisure, the wisdom and error of their judgment.

Schooled in these comments, many people expect town meeting to be a farmers' aristocracy, Socrates in a denim toga, marble busts in animated debate. One quick example: An article in *The Rotarian* for October 1942 describes town meeting in a fictional "Platosburg" that is "any small New England town ... it has an elm lined village green. ..." The article begins by quoting Emerson.

New England has always liked to regard itself as Platosburg, its town assemblies sanctified by the praise of the Olympians. And sometimes the rest of the country assents to this view. In 1980, when the Vermont town meetings passed nuclear freeze resolutions, the freeze movement gained its great momentum. Commentators debated the wisdom of a freeze, but no one questioned the importance of the Vermont vote. The vote of the small towns of a state with one-fourth of 1 percent of the U.S. population carried great authority. (By comparison, the city of Tulsa, Oklahoma, has a population equal to Vermont's, but if Tulsa had voted for a freeze, it would not have set the nation thinking.)

The Olympian view enjoyed its great currency in the late 1930s and 1940s, with the Four Freedoms painting. Town meeting was "No Place for Dictators," as the *New York Times* magazine headlined a story in 1940; it was the "Safeguard of Democracy," as the subtitle said on John Gould's fine little 1940 book *New England Town Meeting.*

But before we started rummaging around for images of national purpose, the popular image of the town meeting was one of quaint irrelevance, a show put on by fools full of regional dialect and fury, signifying nothing but good magazine copy.

In a period ranging roughly from the 1890s to the 1920s magazines visited the town meeting to have sport with the country mice, those quaint Yankees and their funny talk. If Jefferson and Emerson were quoted, it was only to show how far the fall from Olympus had been.

Collier's, in December 1924, offered an account of a town meeting that was a "flood of venom," as Walrus Rowbottom shouted down the selectmen and Frozen-Face Buttonwood rose to "cackle out the eternal grievance" about taxes and education. All was "chaos," as "false election returns, old hates, grudges, family feuds boiled out into pandemonium.

"The newcomers to the town sat there convulsed at the incred-ible farce of it. They hadn't dreamed that anything like this existed outside of books. And in the midst of it, pink-faced Axel Engstrom was on his feet, blazing with anger, his voice trembling."

The editors no doubt told the writer to get lots of local color. It's the 1920s, the jazz age; everyone wants to be cosmopolitan, sophisticated, part of the smart set. New England is a backwater of hicks whose sole purpose in these stories is to entertain the city slickers. Oh, cute country mice, perform for us, confirm our prejudices.

"Town Meeting Day" by Sidney M. Chase from *Scribner's Monthly*, November 1910, is a classic. It begins:

> A shaggy gray horse, drawing an old farmer in a mud-splashed Democrat wagon, ploughed through the depths of a New England country road. A March chill was in the air, and the dark hemlocks still held ragged patches of snow and ice. Presently he came abreast of a white-painted farm-house. In the barn-yard, busy about his chores, was a grim-visaged man in overalls. The driver steered his horse to the roadside, and pulled on the reins.
>
> "Whoa!" he called.
>
> "Ready fer town meetin', Aaron?"
>
> The man in overalls looked up, slowly straightened his rusty length, and spat scornfully at the wood-pile.
>
> "I dunno's I be, Hiram," he said.
>
> "Sho! Riled ye some, Joel's beatin' ye fer dog officer last year, I cal'late!"

"Whoa!" he called. Whoa! indeed.

The old local color approach was pervasive. Apparently most towns in New England were just crammed to the haylofts with quaint and curious characters. The *Woman's Home Companion* of July 1941 in "Town Meeting, A Story" updates Hiram's Democrat wagon to a car. It begins:

> Miss Malvena Avery drew a breath of relief into her flat blue-percale-covered chest as a battered old sedan shuddered to an explosive halt beside her and her nephew Bud inquired, "Hi, Aunt Mal. Want a lift?" She got thankfully in beside him and relaxed. It was a long hot uphill walk from home to the crossroads center of the village of Upright, Maine, and she was late.
>
> Bud grinned. "Hippering right along, wan't you?" he commented.

To which we can only say: *Whoa!* Whoa! to all ye local color writers, all ye TV news simpletons who point a camera at a white church steeple or an old grist mill and say: *Ayuph!* and go home and think you've done your job.

87

In wartime, many transformations take place, and the Hirams and Frozen-Face Buttonwoods, drafted for propaganda and newly shorn, became the standard bearers of common sense democracy. But after the war, town meeting, like so much other war materiel, was retired. The Norman Rockwell icon was mothballed. In the 1950s everyone was talking about the new suburbs. New England slept. There were a few stories saying those quaint Yankees are still at it. But a change was taking place. The word "quaint" was gradually replaced by "anachronistic" and into the mid-sixties came the word "obsolete." We were a long way from Platosburg. In the eyes of political scientists and other academics, now called on regularly for their opinions, town meeting had become a suspect undertaking.

"Is the town meeting finished?" asked the *American Mercury* in 1949, rising early to the attack. Town meeting was all myth, they said, a sentimental self-deception. The town's power had been eclipsed by the state and federal governments, and locally representative government had made direct democracy obsolete. The authors, two young academics from Columbia, drew their conclusions from visits to three town meetings and damned the entire enterprise. "Town meeting is a sacred cow that deserves to be laid to rest." (And when was the last time the postman left a copy of the *American Mercury* in your mailbox?)

Apathy is killing the old town meeting, reported the *Nation* in 1958. A few Massachusetts towns were resorting to desperate measures; the selectmen in one town conducted "round-ups" to flush out warm bodies to reach a quorum of 150 voters in a town of eighteen thousand, and in another town the fire department staged a fake fire at the town hall—sirens and lights—in an attempt to trap the curious into a night of government.

A Bowdoin College study in 1962 reported, "Town meetings are poorly attended, manipulated by minorities, unrepresentative of the community, and cumbersome to the point of rendering town government unresponsive." "Farce Down East" was how *Newsweek* reported it. Town meeting may have been as "sacred as the flag on the Fourth of July" to "granite-ribbed New Englanders" and "starry-eyed artists like Norman Rockwell," but "modern complexities" were forcing towns to leave the important decisions to elected officials. "This evolution is inevitable," said *Newsweek*.

The consensus was growing; towns were too big, the meetings were unrepresentative: "It still lingers on as an instrument of control by small groups of self-seekers," reported the *National Civic Review* in 1965. "It is gratifying to note that there is a steady and inevitable drift away from this precious but outdated and outgrown memory of the past."

There were a few lukewarm endorsements for nonprofessional government. The *American City* magazine, with a readership of town and city managers and planners and an index crowded with articles on refuse collection, street cleaning, traffic control and urban development, ran an article on "Government by the People" in July 1950. The city of Portland, Maine (population 77,634), faced with a disappointing voter turnout, experimented with "a wide-open public meeting" (in which many questions were submitted beforehand) and commissioned a study by a "consultant advertising psychologist." The conclusion: "The public *is* capable of analyzing and understanding problems of local government. ..." (The italics are theirs.)

Town meeting never exported well, one reason it is so often misunderstood. Even when it came to a city on its home ground of Maine, it ended up as a neutered question-and-answer session. It fared worse in Miami, when that city tried a version of town meetings in 1962. At the time, a city of just three hundred thousand, its officials were "feeling a lack of contact" with residents. There is a picture in the *American City* magazine of the proceedings. The vice mayor and other representatives sit up front behind a table and behind a rope fence. (The mayor was out of town.) Above are large posters: "Your Civic Associations," "Your City's Finances." Not: "Our City's. ..." No voting was done at this meeting, but the "crowd," it was reported, "applauded vigorously." (This is the studio audience version of government. And for being a guest on

our show today you will get new streetlights for your block!) Leave
the decisions to the professional managers. That, we were told, was
the modern way. Government had moved behind the ropes.

∞

These three basic portrayals still haunt the town meeting:
Emerson's praise, old Hiram in his Democrat wagon and the political
scientists saying it is all futile. Take old Hiram declaiming on how he's
just a simple farmer and add a few (misapplied) quotes from
Jefferson and Lincoln, and you have New England's version of the
log cabin myth: We're the good simple folks, our common wit
praised by Jefferson.

Town meeting has always suffered under the burden of expectations: *"the wisest invention ever devised by the wit of man for the
perfect exercise of self-government," "the ideal social compact,"* the
*"most perfect school of self-government," "pure democracy," "the most
representative democracy since the Athenians."*

But Platosburg was never a real place, and we can't be Aaron and
Hiram anymore. We don't come up to meeting in a "mud-splashed
Democrat wagon." Cockeyed Yankee pragmatism is admirable, but
democracy isn't about being laconic. Visitors come and newcomers
arrive and find no wise Platosburg and no crackerbarrel philosophers, and they say town meeting is a myth.

Town meeting when it works is really ordinary. Neighbors on
hard chairs, figuring things out. Democracy is in the details. We must
forget Hiram and Jefferson and see for ourselves.

All the Little Republics

A man has risen to speak; in his hand is the town report. He looks
nervous. He is new in town, he says. The eyes of the town are on
him; the women who sit knitting pause. You can almost hear them
thinking, hear the gears falling into place, like on the old adding

machines. Is this bravery or foolishness? The discussion has been about maintaining the dirt roads in town, buying a new road grader. "What's a grader?" he asks. "Is it a snow plow?" The women resume knitting; people shift slightly in their chairs. The adding machine numbers hit the tape: No threat here.

Norman Rockwell had it partially right when he chose to portray the moment of free speech. But it is not a holy moment, it is more like the anxious interval of suspended time at a sports event when they put the ball or puck into play.

One person, one vote—well, almost. Really the town meeting is the stock exchange for reputations. A good joke will be remembered for a generation, long after the issue is forgotten. A silver tongue and a quick wit will confer honor on slow-witted descendants.

When you rise to speak, your townsmen weigh you—what you've done and what they think you've done and who your friends are. If you're found wanting, debate moves on. Like a jury, the assembled town judges character, sometimes at the expense of the issues. But they say that's the way the Senate works as well, the votes of a handful of senators leading the way.

The geography of every town's meeting is similar. The tough guys always stand in the back, usually at the doorway: the police chief, the road agent and his crew (who are also in the volunteer fire department), the rescue squad, and the guy in town who owns the backhoe (or failing that, the largest dump truck). Five or six guys with muscular forearms and beer guts, crowding the door, reviewing all who enter.

Then, still in tough-guy territory, are the back rows where the folded-armed dissenters sit. They are the great refusers. They sit and bellow *No!* at any expenditure. They're quick to their feet to remind the town of the particular municipal apocalypse they have been forecasting since 1953, and the town knows the speech and will miss them when they are gone.

Newcomers to town, professionals, usually sit in the upper third of the hall and give themselves away by their eager-student demeanor and their failure to dress down for the meeting. I know a man who wears Italian leather jackets and linen shirts with zippers and buttons at all rakish angles, but come town meeting, he puts on his most stained gray sweatshirt and dirty jeans. He has dressed for success; people will listen.

Around the room, usually so they block the row, are the ladies who knit throughout the meeting. They camp out with a big bag of yarn and food. I study these ladies carefully, the way you might study squirrels or wooly caterpillars to see if it's going to be a long winter: the more knitters and the larger the balls of yarn, the longer the meeting is likely to last. Sometimes they bring seat cushions, and then you know you are in for a long session.

The chatter index also tells you if it is going to be a good meeting; a town that is all festive and noisy with people mingling before the meeting starts is a healthy town. Where people don't know each other, town meeting is a legalistic proceeding, about as nourishing as watery soup.

Up front sit the selectmen and the town moderator, usually partaking of the New England cult of discomfort. The moderator is never at a lectern of the right height. If he is six-foot-five, the lectern is for someone five-foot. He may serve as moderator for a decade or more; no adjustment is ever made. The selectmen usually sit on the most ill-matching collection of chairs and tables to be found; the shortest people end up in the lowest chairs, so they are all elbows at the table, like grade-school children. If there is a microphone, the wires will be draping everywhere like party decorations, and there will be only one mike that the selectmen can fumble among themselves. New Englanders celebrate discomfort. Like dressing down, it confers the necessary plain-folks atmosphere.

The men get to be the selectmen and moderators; the women are the supervisors of the voter checklist and keep the minutes. They sit and write and write; the men talk. In more liberal climes, however, things are reportedly changing. (Back in 1967, a lone woman moderator was worth a footnote in *The Massachusetts Town Meeting*.)

Sometimes there is a microphone in the middle of the assembly. People are supposed to walk up and actually talk into it. The microphone is as welcome as a pit viper. New Englanders suffer from severe acoustic shyness: they are always so quiet in public. At a Starksboro, Vermont, meeting, there was this exchange:

"Use the mike."

"I'll shout."

"Just use the mike."

He stood a few feet away and spoke his mind.

In Ashby, Massachusetts, the traditional way to deal with a microphone, by citizens and selectmen alike, was to get up close and mumble. The question on the floor had to do with a complicated financial formula, and the leaders and the led, adults all, proceeded to mumble at each other.

The same indecision at confronting a microphone shows itself in towns that give in and concede that there are newcomers in town and everyone doesn't know everyone else, and so they have name tags: tiny tags the size of a return address sticker. You would have to be dancing with the person to read the name. More mumbling.

The moderator is the key figure; he sets the tone. By procedure, all comments are directed to the moderator. He controls the flow of the meeting. He knows everyone in small towns. This is first-name democracy. Familiarity breeds consensus and contempt—but that contempt is a solid fact, hard like a granite curb. Everyone knows how to step over it, and if anyone stumbles, the moderator is there as a crossing guard. Some moderators are wry, others authoritarian, and some see themselves as the civil engineers of discourse confronted with a river: they are looking to channel, dam and regulate the flow, to make the meeting more efficient.

In Nelson, New Hampshire (population 535), the moderator runs a four-minute mile of a meeting. He rushes the town along. The implication is: don't slow things down. Eleven items are approved before the first question is asked, and only at the twenty-fifth article is there a single no vote. This is drive-thru democracy.

In Washington, New Hampshire, they take all day for their meetings and sometimes adjourn to an extra session. The moderator conveys a good nature, scanning the room, looking to include more citizens: "We've got people sleeping all over this room," he says with a smile, as he tries to nudge some comments from people who are silent.

Some moderators think they are refereeing a prize fight. ("I want a good clean fight. … ") "I don't want name calling or vulgarity," the moderator in Bennington, New Hampshire, announces. "We're here to discuss business." He continues: don't stray from the point; carry on and you'll be expelled. …

A good moderator is a delight to watch. There is the moderator cutting off debate, moving along motions and making the town sing. All those in favor: a chorus of yeas! Opposed: a chorus of nays!

At times, watching a particularly deft moderator, I imagine the meeting as a cross between a congregation's responsive reading and a chorus (somewhere between the Greek chorus in the *Oresteia* and the *H.M.S. Pinafore*). The moderator (or a wandering bard) intones:

> O, Sing me a song of road graders and snow plows
> Sing me a song of septic and landfill
> Read me the tax rate, read me the warrant
> Sing me the budget, line by line,
> Salaries, cemeteries and contingencies,
> Sing me the life of a town in one evening.

And the town answers him: The town meeting speaks in a voice that authorizes, directs and spends. It sings the woes of taxes. It says over and over again: this is a small town, not a city. This is Antrim not Peterborough. This is our business. Not Concord's. Not Washington's. It's our business, and we'll do nothing if we so damn please. It resents the entangling vines of state regulations and the word *mandatory*: a flare in the night sky, warning, warning. It laments: the town is growing, the town is growing. It goes line by line: line … by … line. It lives by the poetry of the bottom line: "What it boils down to … in a nutshell … what's it going to cost? I don't want to keep spending my money on such foolishness."

It dissents with folded arms. It says no, it just says no. Says you're taxing us out of town. It's a voice that speaks carelessly: "affirmative yes," "in my own personal case," "viable alternative," "vote my conscious." It speaks in a wise-guy voice, it feigns old-time Yankee horse sense: "Abe Lincoln got a good education in a little school, who needs this fancy plan?"

It cries Make do! Make do! The Harrisville, New Hampshire, meeting studies a request by the crew at the town garage. For seventeen years they have been without an indoor toilet or an outhouse, and, well, it gets cold in the winter up here. … The meeting debates whether these men who have worked faithfully should get plumbing. (No.) The town of Nelson has a fire engine that is twenty-three years old. They have plowed with a 1952 army truck/ambulance until, in 1989, that was replaced with a used truck bought from the state.

Washington has a forty-two-year-old fire engine. It served twenty years in Concord before coming to Washington. Twenty-two years ago its transmission failed. They have kept it going; recently they shimmed in a salvaged transmission. The water tank has rusted and can't be replaced. The truck can only be used as a pumper. Yankee thrift lives.

But the town meeting has only so much fight in it, only stomach for one or two hard-fought debates.

It's a gathering that gobbles: table it, table it.

It spends dollars only when it is worn down, like a mall shopper looking for an exit. It approves $300,000 as it puts its coat on. It votes to approve the town budget—the whole ball of yarn in a nutshell—at ten minutes to midnight.

It's late-night democracy—eye on the clock, 10 P.M., 11 P.M., midnight, good-night. Democracy adjourned until next year.

It is like the spring peepers, the song of the town meeting.

∽

After Emerson had pronounced town meeting the "ideal social compact" he went on to say something that is not often quoted: "In these assemblies, the public weal, the call of interest, duty, religion, were heard; and every local feeling, every private grudge, every suggestion of petulance and ignorance, were not less faithfully produced. Wrath and love come up to town-meeting in company."

Small, passionate battles break out in unexpected places. In Bennington, New Hampshire, there is a call to the barricades: "Bennington is being taken to the coals!" a man shouts. "It's time that the people of Bennington wake up to what it's going to cost! It's costing too much!" What is this speech about? Replacing the bathroom fixtures downstairs.

A man rises in reply. "I don't know if you've been in there lately, but it's scary." People laugh, and somewhere a light goes on: people warm to the longest debate of the evening. Moments before, they passed the town's $575,000 budget with a shrug and nineteen articles with hardly a comment, but here is an issue: Is this bathroom job being put out to bid? Is the shower stall being taken out? and so on. Fortunately, samples of the new tile weren't brought out and put to a vote. (A division of the house for taupe.)

In the town of Washington, a man speaks with passion: "I spent twenty-one years defending this country so you can speak your mind. We keep giving away our freedoms. This is one article we should dismiss without hesitation." He makes Patrick Henry look like a Zen Buddhist. What is this about? The right to elect the town road agent. A short-lived article had proposed that the selectmen appoint the road agent. This speech followed a heated, one-and-a-half-hour debate on the highway budget that had just taken place.

The debate on the roads in Washington lasts as long as the entire town meeting in Nelson, a town with a similar year-round population. Washington, it appears, is a town of six hundred road agents. There is an intense, fervent discussion of wing plows, culverts, gravel, farmers mix, sand, salt, frost heaves, drainage, class one to class six roads, scenic roads and "throwing it up" (closing roads). This must have been what the rough-and-tumble sectarian religious infighting was like one hundred years ago. Now it's roads. Roads are the military budgets of town meeting: expensive, complicated and you can never do enough.

"You've put a teaspoon of sand on my road all winter," says a woman who had an accident on that road. She is still suffering, she says. "Why didn't you come down my road with a wing plow out?" asks another citizen. "The ice is damming up." "Why are we trucking in sand, when we just bought a gravel pit?" a man demands. And so it goes until I feel as if I have traveled over every culvert and frost heave in the forty-seven-square-mile town. Why does the moderator let the debate go on? Probably best just to get it all out in the open.

From different parts of the room, three former road agents rise, in turn, to debate the budget. The meeting is adrift in numbers, caught in the crossfire of a sectarian debate. The three road agents might as well be deacons from feuding churches: each believes differently.

There is a lot of visiting going on in the room; papers are shuffling. The moderator catches this: "Anyone here confused?" A doctor rises and says: "I thought medical school was tough. But I'm confused." Everyone laughs with relief. The moderator calls a ten-minute recess, and a hastily formed ad hoc committee of old agents and the current agent go caucus.

At times like these, town meeting resembles a many-headed blind monster trying to distinguish between different plaid fabrics. The man sitting next to me explains why the debate has taken so long. The road agent has departed with tradition. Usually they come in with a figure higher than they need. The town lops off $30,000, and everyone is happy.

After an hour and a half, Washington has its road budget, and the road agent knows just where he'd better dump some sand and where salt will fall in old wounds.

"Wrath and love come up to town-meeting in company." One year Harrisville's meeting was snarled in a dog fight. Dogs were running deer, a sickening scene if you've ever witnessed it; some in town wanted the dogs tied up, and others stood to defend the liberty of their curs. This was an hour-and-a-half argument—a family argument. These towns are crossed by more bloodlines than roads. Then, disgusted with their neighbors and anxious to go home, the

97

townspeople approved a $50,000 dump truck in two minutes, but they were so shaken up they forgot to vote the money for it. The dump truck had to wait until the next year. Families.

But these are disputes within limits. At the Washington meeting, a man addresses a request by the town's small secretarial staff for a health plan. A few questions show that this proposal has not been well thought out, and he rises to curtail any more discussion. "I feel I should speak against the plan, not the people. The selectmen shouldn't have let them come into town and be cut off at the knees." He could see the frustration in his neighbor's eyes as she stood up front.

When they vote down the police chief's request for a new Ford Bronco, everyone in the room can see he's saddened, much as he tries to hide it. In Bennington, when the fire chief gets his new fire engine, he jumps with boyish joy, though his wife tries to calm him: "Hey! I'm flying. … I get to order a fire truck!" In New Ipswich, New Hampshire, the police chief asks to add an additional officer. Faced with voting against the chief—standing up and being counted—a good number of men find it's time for a cigarette in the hallway.

The feuds obscure the more orderly discussions, the ones that work toward consensus. The town of Washington takes up Article #8, to see if the town will purchase a $25,000 computer system to maintain the tax records.

A representative from the computer company faces the town and talks in the quick jargon of his techno-tribe. The townspeople are not put off and rise gamely to the subject. The town wants to show that it is in on this discussion of megabytes, compatibility and multi-use data bases. They stand and ask about work stations, about the systems being used by similar-size towns. "Is it user interface menu driven?" asks one. Admirable. "Is it compatible?" Yes. A citizen comes forward with an honest question: "It's nice to have compatibility—but to what?"

A farmer in the back of the room doesn't like it. "I'm a down-to-earth fellow," he says. "I know farms with sophisticated equipment that went out of business." It's too expensive, he says—"What do you folks want to do, tax us out of town?"—There's no need, he says, "to go, hey ho, supermodern."

The town seems divided, with the debate running against the computer. A motion is made to dismiss the item. The moderator scans the room and says, "The difference between discussion and a motion for dismissal is that it flushes the support out of the woodwork." The debate picks up.

A man replies to the farmer. His neighbor, he says, "would like us to go out there with a hay rake rather than a baler." But he doesn't see his neighbor out there with a hay rake anymore. No, like all smart farmers, he upgrades his equipment, and so should the town.

This is a debate about change.

The women who prepare the tax lists say this computer will simplify their work. When a property is transferred, they have to record the transaction in eight separate places. Researching tax records is difficult, and they have even lost track of properties. "The day has gone for handwriting each property."

There are more questions about leasing and owning and maintenance. The town is not about to adopt a child with expensive tastes.

"It's like everything. We can all go home tonight with a horse and buggy. But I can't see no horse and buggies out there. Let's move along," says a man.

Having successfully negotiated techno-tribe talk and weighed the impact of modernization in terms of the hay rake and the horse and buggy, the town votes, the motion carries, and they break for a one-hour lunch.

When the meeting slows down, you can read the town reports, a year in the life of the town: who was married (Nelson, New Hampshire, marriage licenses, 3; dog licenses, 60), who was born and who died. (Enter the Caitlyns and Brittanies, the Joshs and Justins; exit the Selmas and Gertrudes, the Everetts and the Floyds.) And make way: "This year's class of first graders will be graduating in the twenty-first century," writes the superintendent of schools in the Washington, New Hampshire, report.

It's all there, from how many books the library loaned to every dollar in the town's budget. I study the pattern of scholarship in the town of Halifax, Vermont. The Hank Wonsey Memorial Fund is endowed to the sum of $77.65, a significant portion of which—$10—it has awarded to Krista Sumner. Miss Sumner also captured the Mary P. Butterfield Scholarship, $5 (out of the fund's total $67.65). But Krista didn't carry away all the glittering prizes. Justin Corey won the Elizabeth Stott Willingness Award of $5. (The following year a Sumner—Andrea—did win the Willingness award, but at a much diminished $1 it was a hardly a victory for free willingness over determinism or just plain sloth.)

The Greenfield, New Hampshire, police's year can be read in a letter of a few terse paragraphs from the police chief: 70 criminal complaints, 20 arrests. There were 306 motor vehicles stopped; of those, 182 got summonses and 132 were given warnings, 6 resulted in arrests. There were 96 dog complaints. (Complaints from dogs?)

Greenfield's Overseer of Public Welfare helped four families, comprising ten people, with food and fuel and other assistance. There were fifty building permits issued, including fifteen for new homes.

There are pages listing arcane offices: fence viewer, clock warden, tree warden, pound warden, inspector of lumber and weigher of coal. There are committees for the annual Old Home Day, to look after various ponds and beaches, to study cable TV, housing for the elderly, recreation, historic districts, landfills. (The recreation committee in Bennington has forged a new word: "craftsreation.")

A quick survey of the committees in Hancock, New Hampshire, shows some one hundred people involved. In a town of about twelve hundred voters, nearly 10 percent of the adult population is directly involved. If you figure in the families of the committee members and then their friends, the majority of the town is close to someone who is active in town affairs.

The section that everyone peruses without fail is inventory of taxable property; every acre in town and who owns it and what it's worth (and who has not paid their taxes). But I enjoy the purely literary endeavors. The poetry by an honored resident in the report of Starksboro, Vermont, and the town journal that many reports include—a narrative of the year, taking pains to mention absolutely everyone who made a tuna casserole for a charitable cause, like this one in Greenfield, New Hampshire:

> 1987 was a year of change and excitement. ...
> It was exciting when Selectwoman Sharon Gordon presented Florence Lee, Greenfield's "most senior" resident, with the Boston Post cane.
> It was exciting when the contributions of Greenfield folk put the fund for the Jaws of Life over the top. ...
> The Annual Harvest Fair of the Woman's Club was a financial and artistic success. ...
> Changes came to Greenfield in 1987. ... Gardner Glover resigned as Custodian of the Meeting House after over thirty years of devoted service.
> The Vice-President of the United States, George Bush, visited Greenfield. It was exciting!

These town reports tell you something remarkable in this age of bigness, something that the critics of town meeting fail, or refuse, to see: these towns do govern themselves.

At the Nelson town meeting, the fire alarm sounds, and one-third of the meeting, thirty people race for the door. The next items are to fund improvements at the fire station and to rebuild a pumper truck. Someone rises to congratulate the fire department on its timing. The item passes, and the moderator has a few words of praise about the volunteer spirit.

∞

The longer I live up here and the more I watch these meetings deal with "modern complexities," paradoxically, the more I find these meetings in black and white (not the sepia of early photos, but black and white).

This is so far from crack and assault rifles, from fear and not caring, from the noise of the media and the freeway hustle of the rest of America.

I am not suggesting it's all Norman Rockwell—it isn't. The world is here: some of these towns are growing rapidly; one town, Hillsborough, faced the threat of being cemented over from border to border to be a nuclear waste dump. There are drugs in the regional high schools. Some of these people are uplinked to the world by satellite dish. A few commute to big cities. And there is the bomb—we know that flesh is flammable and houses will blow down like a stack of cards.

But then here we are sitting on folding chairs, discussing things. And at no time—no time at any of the town meetings I've been to—does someone say: It's Catch-22. It's insolvable. A conundrum. Just a plain mess. Beyond hope. At no time do people feel overwhelmed. They may joke about the number of items on the warrant and they are frustrated that they cannot control the regional school district budget as closely as town spending. But no one is ever the wronged party petitioning on high, beseeching the selectmen. No, when they're mad, they stand up and let their neighbor have it—usually in a circumspect manner. Such equality—it's antique, like a black-and-white photo album. (The old kind with the black pages and the photos held in with those little black corners. Can you still get those?)

Even the most fog-bound discussions, the most wrong-headed assumptions and bull-headed opinions are all so confident. A wide stride toward the future. The tax rate revolts even seem to be part of the script. Someone has to stand up and say: "You're taxing us out of the town. ... "

So, yes it is mythic, and it does work. It is an antique and an anachronism.

But the antique is democracy.

And the anachronism is the word *citizen*.

Seeing Town Meeting Plain

"The reason the whole country is going down the tubes in the center is that we're not raising citizens at the periphery," says Frank

Bryan, a professor of political science at the University of Vermont. "And you can only raise citizens in small open democracies like we used to have in the nineteenth century."

For the last twenty years, Bryan has been studying the town meeting. He has tracked one thousand town meetings, gathering data on thirty-two thousand decisions.

Bryan can see town meeting plain, its achievements and its shortcomings. "Town meeting is a democratic technology," he says. It works well in small towns. Once a town hits about seven thousand, first-name democracy falters. Some changes are in order. He finds "bothersome" those who "believe town meeting can do anything." But he is also tired of hearing town meeting dismissed by critics who visit one meeting in a town of twenty-five thousand. A basic sampling flaw. The critic, usually an academic, just hasn't done his homework and hit those rough March back roads.

But nearly thirty years of criticism has had its effect. Bryan has watched the state cut down on the town's "field of action." The widely reported nuclear freeze vote "camouflaged the fact that while we could give our advice on nuclear war, the state was taking away our power to bury our garbage or have a leash law or educate our kids. You know, the basic things that really ought to be done.

"It leads one to wonder about elites that are willing to take your advice on nuclear war but not willing to give you the capacity to decide whether or not to have a kindergarten. An awful lot of people come into towns and say we really want your advice on this, but on the other hand they really don't want to give you any power.

"Democracy can't survive without power," says Bryan—like a person can't survive without oxygen. "The town meeting can exist on a small amount of oxygen. You don't have to decide everything at the town level—that's crazy. But if you turn the oxygen down too low, the town meeting kind of drifts off to sleep."

After talking with Bryan, I see a classic example at the Ashby, Massachusetts, Town Meeting.

A man asks: "Is it a fact the town has to vote for the school budget?"

A selectman answers: "They don't have to vote for it—they have to pay for it."

This school budget has already been passed by the larger towns in their district, Townsend and Pepperell—what's the little town of Ashby to do? They have to pay their share, even though they haven't voted on the budget yet. The town can raise taxes or cut almost all its services. A selectman says if they refuse to raise their taxes, the courts will intervene and rule that the town is not "financially desperate." (The courts are rarely discussed in town meeting. Voters do not worry that some judge may overturn their law.) Whether they vote yes or no, Ashby will have to pay. In other words, comrades, the party's central committee has spoken. Back to the shoe factory. A little perestroika is needed here. (Or as one man addressed the meeting: "Now, come on, folks, something is wrong … little Ashby up on the hill is the back end of the cow.")

"Let the people decide," says Bryan, "but remember that the results will not be perfect. Each town gets the government it deserves; that is the unsettling truth of town meeting." Just as in school there are bright kids and "slow learners," some towns excel, some fail.

"Failure," he says, "is the price of democracy. One of the great testaments to town meeting is that what you see is what you get. If democracy is really power of the people, then you're going to have the good with the bad ones. Democracy without risk is impossible. You've got to decide which issues in the modern world you let townspeople decide on and then let them decide. If they go down the tubes, that's their business. That's hard to do in the modern world because we search for perfection. We can't put up with things that aren't perfect. And so we accept a mediocrity. At the central level nothing works well, but nothing fails either."

Town meeting shows us the true math of democracy: one ignorant vote equals one informed vote. The village idiot and the woman who manages a million-dollar company can each only vote once. Town meeting is amateur hour. A working definition of a citizen (or a parent) could be an amateur entrusted with great responsibilities. A republic is government by the amateurs for the amateurs.

Political scientists and people who talk of "broad-based public policy initiatives" and the need to "educate the public" have a great distrust of people with dirty fingernails, *those people*, outvoting the people who really do know, the people with the college educations and all the right opinions. They have never taken town meeting seriously. Their questions have framed the debate for the last thirty years: Should town meeting exist at all? they've asked. And it is the wrong question.

These critics would never visit one state legislature and, finding it petty and inefficient, dismiss all state legislatures with the question: Should the states govern themselves?

The time has passed for blanket criticism of the country mice assemblies. There are many questions that need to be asked: What is the quality of the decisions being made? Who is making them? Who really speaks up? What adjustments, what reforms would help to make the meetings more representative?

Just as we are continually adjusting our representative government, we can fine-tune town meeting. But we don't need wholesale surgery—our national political speciality—rather just something small and decentralized. We need a small team of town meeting doctors to analyze and fix sagging town meetings. After all, what you see is what you get: if the meeting isn't working, the town isn't. Town meeting takes the measure of the town, takes the measure of us all as citizens.

The Museum of Democracy

Think of town meeting as a question: How did we, as a nation, get here? We started out in small citizen assemblies, and now three hundred years down the road we are a long way from direct action. From these New England meeting houses to the triple-locked doors of modern life is one measure of the American journey.

We have a mass democracy too big for direct participation, a democracy in which half don't vote. Town meeting unmasks the deception, and by contrast our system seems lacking.

People find town meeting unnerving the way we find children difficult who ask too many questions: Why? Why? Why? When I describe town meeting to friends in distant cities, they are often annoyed and dismissive. It is similar to the annoyance many people have with Thoreau and his account of life at Walden; its concentrated light throws troubling shadows.

So we tell ourselves the textbook story of government and know the truth is something other, something hidden behind the Fourth of July patriotism—but we don't dare look. Town meeting is one of the few places we confront democracy outside the civics textbook. If town meeting is an anachronism, then so is democracy.

Town meeting is the Museum of Democracy. Democracy is a process, after all, a political habit of being. The Museum of Democracy preserves that.

We are used to a different order of preservation, a preservation closer to embalming. We preserve buildings, not the habit of being they sheltered. We save a grist mill building, but not the milling process. That is lost. The mill becomes a gift shop, and we call it preservation. We preserve a farm's buildings, but let the husbandry methods fall away. The Japanese at Ise preserve the great temple by rebuilding it, since A.D. 685, over and over again, every twenty years. They don't attempt to arrest time and hold the building against decay. They preserve the process of temple building, not just the tools in glass cases, but the hands and the hearts to use them. Nothing democratic can ever be that pure. But in town meeting each year we labor to rebuild the temple. Democracy is a process. We make it anew each day. Historically speaking, it is an experiment, and we should regard it that way.

We have many museums in New England, the little historical societies, entire reconstructed villages, stonewalls and cellar holes, but the town meeting is our finest museum, one continuous showing since 1629—the memory house of democracy.

∞

The moderator of Warren, New Hampshire, was asked if town meeting was obsolete. "I suppose it's as obsolete as eating supper at the kitchen table with your family," he said. "If you do, it's great. If you don't, it's your loss."

On a typical weeknight, reports the Gallup Poll, 22 percent of the population eats alone. And of those who eat with their families, 42 percent are also watching television. Sitting down to dinner with your family has gone the way of forty-eight-star flags.

The Chippendale Leg

We are standing outside the Washington, New Hampshire, meeting house, while the ballots are counted on a close vote. In Washington, just one citizen can call for a paper ballot instead of a voice vote. I am talking with a man who has recently returned home after twenty-five years away. When he left, the town had 225 people year-round, now it's 600. He was the only one in his graduating class in the small white schoolhouse next to the meeting house. Next to the school is a church. The three tall white buildings have the sharp lines and the exaggerated height of a child's drawing. These three buildings are Washington, its pride and identity; they appear on the town's letterhead and on the town's bicentennial quilt. For Carroll Farnsworth's one hundredth birthday, the town gathered to have its picture taken in front of the meeting house.

The man I am talking with tells me that the scene of these three buildings is always on New England calendars and in fancy picture books. People stop to photograph them, and the other day he came along and there was an entire photography class. He tells me the exact spot to stand to get the best photo. The meeting house, he tells me, is the oldest meeting house in use on the East Coast.

I turn as if to study the meeting house and listen to parts of the conversations in the groups around me. They are discussing town business. "That goes back to 1956 ... ," says one man. "In '41 we knew ... ," says another man. "When TR was president, I remember ... ," another says. Towns remember—remember deeply—and that, too, is uncharacteristic of modern American life.

Another group is discussing the idea of moving town meeting to a nearby school. "They think they have to sit in this old building," one man says in exasperation.

I turn back toward the man I have been talking with. "We just fixed the belfry last year," he tells me. "The structural members were crumbling. They injected some kind of epoxy stuff in there to save the wood," he says. I look at the building with renewed interest. At the top of this eighteenth-century structure is a late twentieth-century technology.

Furniture restorers use the same technique. Save as much original material as possible. That is the credo of the preservationist. Save the artifact. Wood, as we know from grade-school science, is composed of empty cells. A restorer injects a crumbling Chippendale table leg with a plastic-epoxy substance, the epoxy invades the empty chambers of the wood and becomes a new structure.

Now, preservationists and furniture restorers are great worriers. They worry constantly about authenticity. Like old-time philosophers, they must ask: What is real? And the question applies to the Chippendale leg: What do you now have? Not the original leg and not a copy. You have a third object, something that never before existed. A plasticized Chippendale leg. A disturbing hybrid.

In a sense, that modified Chippendale leg represents the state of American democracy. We have this marvelous handcrafted Chippendale leg—the fruit of the Enlightenment, the Declaration of Independence, the world's oldest working Constitution. We all admire the Chippendale leg, our holidays celebrate it. But the world has seen tremendous changes since the leg was crafted—we can be at war in seconds, we have an undreamed of aggregate of wealth and power. This spindly antique leg is shot through with epoxy, the modern corporate state, the glue we often pretend is not there.

The flip side is that epoxy is toxic. ("Do not ingest. Do not induce vomiting. Consult physician immediately.") So, is our republic held together with ingenuity—the chemistry to produce strong bonds— or is it a crumbling artifact preserved by a poisonous glue?

From a distance this old/new leg looks the same—you can't tell. Even in examining the leg, you can't tell where the new begins and the old leaves off. In America we are confronted everywhere with a confusion between what is real and what is a prop. At town meeting we come close to the real artifact, the unrestored Chippendale leg. But then, even the belfry on the oldest meeting house in use on the East Coast is epoxied in place.

∞

Washington, New Hampshire, is a perfect Museum of Democracy: the 1787 meeting house and the town report listing the citizens committee on nuclear waste and, proudly, high up over the roof on this sunny day, the restored belfry, the plasticized wooden belfry.

Eighteenth-century devices; twentieth-century and twenty-first-century problems. We'll get by.

On an uncommonly soft March afternoon, as the lemony late afternoon light filters into the room, I listen as the road debate takes more turns than a switchback road up a mountain. I indulge in optimism. And I think of what the town moderator did at the meeting's start. He opened up the ballot box, a wooden box all of two feet high, tilted it forward and showed the empty box to the assembled citizens. This is the essential gesture.

In the history of the world, in this time now on the globe, the exception has always been democracy. The empty ballot box opened in front of the people of the town before voting—that would have been revolution enough in Panama, in the Philippines … in perhaps one hundred more countries containing most of humanity.

One can sit back and feel a patriotic pride, the smugness of inherited wealth, any struggle long-time passed. Hurray for us! We are still the nation of Norman Rockwell's Four Freedoms paintings. Hurray! and again hurray! But I have only to think of American life beyond these old meeting houses, outside the Museum of Democracy.

While you are in New England, town meeting is no anachronism. People expect to voice their opinions. But increasingly when

109

I travel, I visit people who live in condominium complexes policed by hired guards, and who shop in malls patrolled by a private security force, scanned by security cameras and observed from behind two-way mirrors. At work, too, they are often under the watchful eyes of a private police force. Even their urine may have been tested, policed. In this setting, the very idea of democracy at all begins to seem like an anachronism, the words *republic* and *inalienable rights*, pricey antiques.

Everywhere there is the rise of a rent-a-cop feudalism. Private security guards now outnumber public police. The public realm is rapidly shrinking. In the last two decades, we have traded in common ground, as it was once known, for a climate-controlled safetyland. We are not free to picket or leaflet at a mall, now the nation's Main Street. (Do the shoppers care? No. They want convenience. Leaflets, opinions, debate, that's all inconvenient.) There are few places to congregate, few places we come together. At these large condo enclaves, the streets are not public, behavior is circumscribed by long lists of restrictions and obligations reinforced with fees.

Oh, but we are free. In a good year, 55 percent of all eligible voters turn out to vote in national elections, and in off-year elections, such as in 1990, only 36.4 percent. We have the plasticized Chippendale leg—the not-real/not-fake antique.

But here is the town of Washington, New Hampshire, ready to take on thirty-four articles on a warm, breezy day. It's what we want to believe about ourselves. Lolling in the warm sun, accepting it as a promise of winter's end, I look out on the meeting.

In my mind I see the townspeople rising up, row by row, town reports in hand, all open to the same page. They sing forth like a boys' choir at Oxford, like the Vienna Boys' Choir: The Washington Town Meeting (draped in red-and-black hunter's plaid robes), angelic voices all, eyes heavenward, singing the dog warden's report, singing the budget line by line, singing the marriages, the births and the deaths. They start asking questions, start asking all the questions beyond capital reserve, questions about life, religion and true meanings. They sing, each voice adding to the next, in unison, and their voices go upward, up past the epoxied eighteenth-century belfry, up through the hole in the ozone layer and out into space. We'll be all right.

Won't we?

The Murder That
Never Really Happened

The broom: When I first arrived in this small corner of New Hampshire, I was struck with how orderly everything seemed to be. I remember this picture in particular: There had been a small auto accident. A car pulling out of a parking lot onto the road had hit the side of another car. A classic tableau of guilt was presented to the passerby. A long-haired young man had dented the driver's side of a car carrying two elderly ladies. As I drove by, a police officer was bending down to talk with the woman behind the wheel. She had her gloved hand to her mouth—as if she was saying "Oh, my"—and a stunned look. But here's the important part. There was some glass on the road from the accident. And out from a store, an auto dealership, came a man with a large broom to sweep the road clean. He was smiling. It was all so tidy up here.

The sign coming into town said "Welcome to Peterborough: A Good Town to Live In." It read without any irony. Here was a town of unlocked doors, unlocked cars, a place where trust was not an abstract verity. In Jaffrey, a neighboring town, the police chief had been campaigning to get people not to leave their keys in their parked cars.

But then, that is already a few years ago.

∞

Craig Lane was working in the Texaco station, one of those lone attendants in a booth. It was late on a slow Sunday afternoon in January 1989, after five o'clock, a gray winter day when most folks just hole up at home after church and visiting with relatives and Sunday dinner. There was football on TV and homework awaiting children. Craig himself may have had some homework to do. He was seventeen, a high school student with two part-time jobs. He called home; he was closing up early, and he needed a ride. Fifteen minutes before his ride came, he was dead, stabbed repeatedly in the neck. He was brutally murdered in a gas station holdup. The robber made off with maybe more than one hundred dollars.

An hour before the funeral that Thursday, people lined up to get in the small church. Four hundred attended, packing the sanctuary with a moist, hot humanity. Mourners spilled out the front door. They stood in the snow, trying to listen as strains of "Onward Christian Soldiers" and "A Mighty Fortress Is Our God" drifted out. The police stood nearby, as did the news cameras down from Concord.

Craig Lane was a hard worker who had known some troubles. His parents had divorced. He lived with his mother until the sixth grade. When she remarried and left New Hampshire, he chose to stay, living first with his father, then with his grandparents in Peterborough, to be closer to his work, he said.

Peterborough's police chief, Butch Estey, had known Craig since he was an infant. Craig's father was also a police officer. Estey, then a new state trooper, had been invited to the Lanes for Thanksgiving. "Craig threw a glass of milk at me from his high chair." Over the years Estey would kid Craig about that, and Craig, a Red Sox fan, would kid Estey about his allegiance to the Yankees. The baseball schedule was posted at the gas station, and the only time he ever argued with his employer was over batting averages. That January he already had tickets for opening day at Fenway.

113

Lane was remembered as an achiever, someone eager to help out, eager to please. He was an honor student, a Boy Scout and a founder of a railroad club. He wanted to work for a railroad after graduation and had his guidance counselor write letters inquiring about jobs. His other part-time job was as a bank teller, and he impressed the bank's president with his willingness to learn, always asking questions. Another former employer remembered the same attitude: "The one big thing about him was that he did everything he could to please people." He was working two jobs to save up to buy a pickup truck.

Others in town remembered small discussions, some of the dozens and hundreds of conversations that make up one person's orbit through a town on a given day. The sum of all of these encounters was identity, was the town itself, far beyond the beloved churches and monuments, the laws and tax collections.

Standing in front of the church, a friend faced the TV camera: "He helped me get through school. I was always a bad reader. I doubt if I could have gotten through school without him." Another mourner said: "One murder can wipe out a thousand kindnesses."

For three years, during his study periods, Craig had worked in the school's office helping the principal. Marge Whitney had been a secretary to the principal. She thought of herself as Craig's "mother at school" and had a picture of him over her desk. "His life was bittersweet," she said. "He had a sense of responsibility beyond his years." And she added: "Of all the things to happen in Peterborough. I can't believe we've gotten so uncivilized."

The *Monadnock Ledger,* a weekly, came out a day early with pages of grief, shock and recollection. That same week, in a neighboring town, another teen had been killed, shot by a friend while they were fooling with guns. Never in anyone's memory had two violent deaths occurred in one week. "Teen Deaths Stun Monadnock Region" was the headline. Both of the local papers were filled with the refrain: "How can this happen here?"

The town's two newspapers groped for an explanation. The word *senseless* was used a lot—a word that cuts hard. These are not people who view life as an absurd, meaningless, shadow-puppet game. Another word was used—*fear*—a word seldom seen in print here.

Under the headline "Senseless," the *Peterborough Transcript* said: "We've tried for two days to come up with the words to adequately deal with the tragedy, anger and feelings of helplessness that pervade the town and region this week."

This murder struck "a chord of fear. Fear that makes kids scared to go out after dark. Fear that makes us not want to be alone. Fear that reminds us all that violence isn't confined to the streets of the inner city. And fear that makes us take a second look at the last customer of the night before we switch off the lights to go home to our comfortable lives."

There is a "physical ache" in the community, the *Transcript* said. "We all find a way to cope, to go through the motions of daily life. But the hole in our lives and in our hearts just never, ever goes away."

The editor of the *Monadnock Ledger* wrote: "The stabbing of Craig Lane, especially, has struck home. This didn't involve a troubled youth, estranged lovers, or a distraught young mother. ... This seems to be a first in recent times—a killing which seems so random that Peterborough area residents are left wondering whether the same thing could happen to them."

"It's so scary," said one of Craig's friends. "Nobody thinks something like this can happen here."

The high school convened a crisis team, sent letters home, offered counseling. Teachers and staff were called the Sunday night of the murder on the school's emergency phone chain—each distressed person in turn dialing the next person. Monday at 7 A.M. guidance counselors met with a psychologist and in twenty minutes drafted a statement issued to teachers at a special early morning meeting. The teachers read the statement in homeroom. The guidance counselors set up two places in the school where students and staff could come and talk.

There were letters to the editor of the *Peterborough Transcript*: Sara Smull, a junior at the high school, wrote: "Besides the incredible feeling of shock that has overcome me since learning of Craig's death, there is also a strong feeling of pity and disdain for a society in which something like this could happen.

"I would really like to know how a human being could do this to another human. What could possibly be so important that someone should have to die ... especially someone so young?"

Michael Hart, in the fourth grade at Peterborough Elementary School, wrote: "Look what's happening to our world. It's falling apart. People are being killed, planes are being hijacked. Something is dying everywhere I look."

∞

The murder occasioned a review of all crime and violent incidents in the last decade. Police chiefs were quoted, statistics noted. Behind every paragraph was the question: "What's going on?"

In the last ten years there had been seven homicides in the surrounding towns—all but one had occurred in the last three years. In each case the victim knew the attacker. They were murders of passion and greed among family and friends. Crimes against persons and property were up; for the first time the police had established new categories for drug-related arrests.

"Longtime Peterborough residents have watched the town change from a place where you could go into the store and leave your keys in the car and your house unlocked, to a place where the doors should be locked if there is anything of any value in the car, and where home burglar alarms are becoming more and more common," the *Ledger* reported. "The Lane murder has some locals even discussing moves to northern New England in search of communities where city-type crime has not yet arrived."

"The police used to go home at six o'clock," recalled one native. That was when he was growing up. "The doctor came to your house. You seemed to know everyone in town." Now his teenage daughter had a part-time job out at the shopping plaza: "I went to her employer and said, 'You know, I'd really rather she wasn't alone in the store.' And I don't think I would have said that six months ago."

116

That week, each evening over dinner, all around town, people worked their variations of one conversation:

"That's not supposed to happen here."

"Do you remember ... two years ago in Dublin, or was it three?... A knife ... never found the murderer. ... the police here, really. ... Two years ago, or was it three? In Troy. ... And down in New Ipswich—four years ago, or was it three?"

"It's all around us."

"You don't even have to turn on the news."

"And just what is the world coming to?"

The world is coming to Peterborough.

∞

"I went to Steele's and got some sympathy cards," said one town resident. "But what can you say to the parents? I know one thing. I'll be sure to tell my kids I love them before I put them to bed tonight."

∞

Deaths come one at a time in small towns. The city dweller may have no idea of how one death will linger in a small town.

This one at a time, this pause at the death of a loved one, neighbor, landsman, this is the last thing left to cling to, the last thing to go before you find yourself behind locks and bars and on sodium-lighted streets, keys clutched between the knuckles ready to gouge any attacker. It takes the collective mourning of a community to hold back the tide, to say this loss is more than a news item. This is not a video death.

In the last thirty years, as America has become more violent, the angel of death has moved through small towns producing the same story of small-town tragedy and loss of innocence. This has become a set piece in journalism, books, television and movies: The peaceful town (Peterborough was listed in *Safe Places for the Eighties*) disrupted by a gruesome murder, sometimes of a young innocent.

117

Then the grief, sorrow and shock and the feeling that nothing is granite-sure anymore.

It is this that reporters come to witness: betrayal, shock, mourning, refusal to forget, belief in justice. So the story of murder comes to a small town is a story of "Look, they still believed." And many others look in on the story with a zoological interest: yes, that is a familiar behavior. Endearing.

The ability to quickly forget, that is the modern memory.

In his great novel of the decline of the Austro-Hungarian empire, Joseph Roth wrote of one death as an absence that would be felt for a long time to come:

> In those days before the Great War … it had not yet become a matter of indifference whether a man lived or died. When one of the living had been extinguished another did not at once take his place in order to obliterate him: there was a gap where he had been, and both close and distant witnesses of his demise fell silent whenever they became aware of this gap. When fire had eaten away a house from the row of others in a street, the burnt-out space remained long empty. Masons worked slowly and cautiously. Close neighbors and casual passers-by alike, when they saw the empty space, remembered the aspect and walls of the vanished house. That was how things were then. Everything that grew took its time in growing and everything that was destroyed took a long time to be forgotten. And everything that had once existed left its traces so that in those days people lived on memories, just as now they live by the capacity to forget quickly and completely.

There is a story my father told me when I was quite young. We were driving on a curving, hilly road that ran through woods and along a pond. And he said that many years ago—this would have to be when they first moved out to Long Island—a young couple about to be married had been killed one night at a bend in the road. Their car was found in the morning smashed into a stone wall. People were quite shaken up by the accident, he said.

At least that's how I remember the story, and I thought of it often along that stretch of the road. I guess it's significant that he thought to tell me. My family does not traffic in tragic tales, so it must have been on his mind. In stories told in small towns, the living carry the dead with them and many times a day commemorate their passing.

Today, where my parents live is much more built up. Where once there were thousands, there are more than a million people. That road now is very busy and is also built up some. The death of a young couple would still upset—but probably only for a day or two before the sheer push of a million daily routines swept away all memory.

∞

The people of Peterborough found the jolt of Craig Lane's murder hard to explain to outsiders. City dwellers, consumers of ghastly murders, require ever more bizarre, intricate and elaborate murders to hold their attention. A gas station robbery would be beneath notice. But look at the other deaths reported locally that week, the week that the lives of two young men ended:

> Mary Parker, 91. She was the oldest living member of the Wilton Gold Star Mothers of World War II. She left behind one brother, seven sons, three daughters, thirty-five grandchildren, forty-five great-grandchildren and seventeen great-great-grand-children.
>
> Ernest McClure, 96. Born June 5, 1892. He served in the U.S. Navy in World War I. Survivors include four grandchildren and six great-grandchildren.
>
> Roland Renshaw, 78. Left behind two daughters, four sons and seventeen grandchildren.
>
> Dr. Robert MacCready, 86. Served as a major in the Army Medical Corps in World War II. Left behind his wife, one daughter, two sons and three grandchildren.

Two of the dead were men who had gone to war and come home to live a half-century in peace. One was a mother who had lost a son in a war. And here were a sixteen- and a seventeen-year-old killed

119

at home by guns and knives. Is it any wonder people were shocked?

Between the four who had died of natural causes, they had lived 351 years and left behind 146 descendants. Craig Lane left behind his parents, two half-sisters, one half-brother and a grandfather and grandmother on each side of the family.

∞

"You wouldn't expect this in Peterborough."
"It was just a matter of time."
"We're not immune."
"How could this happen?"

∞

Any murder is an invitation for the hasty algebra of moralizing and mourning. If x, then y. If x is murder, then y is the cause: the breakdown of the family, the church or the criminal justice system; the spread of TV violence; junk food; white sugar; too many guns; too few guns; too much government; too little government; the rise of a secular culture since the Enlightenment. This is connect-a-dot sermonizing, draw a line from the tragedy to the societal ills of your choice and create your own picture.

Unlike the local newspapers, which respectfully registered the community's grief, the *Manchester Union Leader* was ready with a connect-a-dot editorial: "Violence in Our Town." Noting that turn-of-the-century Peterborough was an inspiration for Thornton Wilder's *Our Town*, the paper said that as Peterborough "and hundreds of other Our Towns" approach the next century "something terribly new and different is happening in them. Violent, senseless death and destruction are becoming, if not commonplace, then certainly not all that extraordinary."

"Don't brush this off as an isolated incident," the *Union Leader* said. There are too many murders, and "we can't allow them to continue." The paper advocated justice, punishment, stiff sentences, support for the police and an unceasing pursuit of the "answers to why all this is happening."

The editorial, which began with the murder in Peterborough and soon spiraled out to every New Hampshire town, concluded:

> But moreover and more important, we must find ways to educate our children to the dangers of drugs and to instill in them— and perhaps reawaken in ourselves—such basic values as respect for life and property.
>
> In a world awash with sexual promiscuity and perversion, where unborn babies are killed at the rate of millions a year, where the almighty dollar is worshipped with more fervor than the Almighty, this is no easy task. But it must be done. It must be done.

∞

The police continued with their investigation and urged "anyone with even what they think is a minute detail" to call the police station. They released a sketch of the suspect, and Wanted signs went up around town. Silently volunteers would stream into stores and hang up the face that stared straight out, impassive, a mute face staring from a clutter of announcements for Celtic music, yoga classes, workshops to find your personal myth, crystal workshops and word processing services. In one shop the wanted face hung like a threat over the crop of customers' Christmas snapshots, babies in red and green Santa suits.

∞

Spring came. Two women stood talking in a Peterborough shop about how you would be given credit just on sight and how the store owner would leave a package out for you after he closed and you'd pay him whenever you got to it.

"Only in Peterborough could you do that," said the first woman and went on with a list of the town's charms that made it evident she was newly arrived.

121

"Well, we have our murders now," said the second woman.

"Oh, of course it's not pure," said the first woman.

"No place is," said the second woman.

The Wanted posters began to disappear, replaced by a new one, bright yellow and green: "Wanted: Girl Scout Troop Leaders." The murderer was still at large.

⌒

The town had gone through the shock of its first murder—the stock story of shattered innocence. It was a grisly, random murder. And as the first murder in recent memory, it had hit the community hard.

Only it wasn't the first murder. Three and a half years prior to Craig Lane's murder, there had been a killing that passed with the briefest of mentions.

⌒

Until an otherwise fine June afternoon in 1985, there had been but one murder in Peterborough this century, and that had taken place fifty years before. On that June afternoon, Lorraine Manha, a house cleaner, was either leaving or entering a house (the accounts never agreed)—she was carrying a vacuum cleaner—when she was shot four times and left lying face down in the driveway. A red car was seen speeding away from the scene. Neighbors heard several shots but thought that it was just kids playing with cap guns.

Her estranged husband was the suspect. He had threatened her and tried to kill her once, and she had gone to the police. She told the police that he had said he would kill her if their divorce proceedings took place. A few weeks before her murder she had appeared in court for a divorce. She feared for her life, her brother said. Police did increase their patrols near her house, but after a while the patrols stopped. She moved out of her old house and altered her work schedule.

The killing of this "cleaning lady"—as one paper called her—received scant attention. There were no articles recording the shock of a town. No talk of community grief, family grief. No asking: How could this happen—to them, to us?

No one knew her history. No one knew her present. No one cared to ask. She was a domestic in a domestic dispute. Her obituary was short: She was born in Peterborough, graduated from Peterborough's high school in 1956 and was a self-employed housekeeper and mother of five.

There was only a sense that Peterborough's box score had been blemished: fifty years without a murder. As the *Ledger* reported in a small box:

> Murders are extremely rare in Peterborough. Several town officials this week said they could not remember the last time a murder happened here. An examination of town reports going back to the 1890s, most of which contain a list by the chief of police noting the different crimes that occurred during the year, shows the only other recorded homicide this century happened in 1936 or early 1937. [And that was a murder of someone from another town, the newspaper said. The body had been dropped off just inside Peterborough's border.]

A small item in the newspaper reported her funeral: The church service was guarded by police sharpshooters and plainsclothesmen. And it also said that the church had collected $3,000 for the family. But that was it. There was a curious distance to the reporting of a local tragedy.

In fact, one of the town's newspapers wrote an editorial about the shooting, titled "Terrorism at Home and Abroad." It linked the shooting with the act of a group of Shiite terrorists who had seized a TWA plane that same week. The murder around the corner was just as faceless, distant—the unknown behind the mask, the hand on the gun. The other paper said nothing. There were no letters to the editor about the murder in either paper.

∽

A week later, Lorraine Manha's husband, Nicholas Manha, drove head-on into a granite ledge at an "extreme rate of speed." There were no skid marks. The car's front end was entirely gone, and the car came to rest on top of the ledge, eleven feet off the ground. The fire department had to reach it with ladders. For six days he had eluded the police's "intensive manhunt."

One week a woman is gunned down. The next, her husband, the primary suspect, drives his car into a granite ledge. End of story. The "most violent crime in Peterborough's history" faded in two weeks. The scandal of the pig farmer who refused to muck out his piggery had a longer shelf life. The papers were filled with plans for Fourth of July picnics, photos of the high school graduates and the warm promise of June, when all life moves outdoors.

∽

Why the silence?

A family had come apart. To say there were warning signs is to put it mildly. He had broken into her house and shot at her three times as she lay in bed, one shot grazing her forehead. He had been in for psychiatric treatment at the veteran's hospital.

Was this a crime with a narrative: The war between men and women? Was the town averting its eyes from a dispute, from suffering that should have remained private? It was bad manners to have yourself murdered in fine summer daylight, by your own husband.

This was a violence easily cordoned off, attributed to marital distress. Perhaps it was even understandable. I remember a short debate at a New Ipswich Town Meeting about allocating $50 to the region's women's crisis center. One man rose to speak in its favor: "If I beat my wife up, I want to know there's a place for her to go."

This was a murder among "thems." Scanning the news, we daily sort the tragedies: That's not us, it's in another country; it's in the next state, county, town. That's not us; they were druggies, illegal aliens,

124

or just plain careless, luckless. And after all, he could have gunned her down anywhere. He could have waited until she was up over Temple Mountain, into the next town and ended her life there.

But soon the distinctions wear thin and the narrative line taut. I was talking once with friends from the city about the crack problem, and in their few city blocks is a parable: "It's not bad where we live," they said, "only over on 112th Street." "What's your address?," I asked. "109th Street." But that's how we survive; we draw lines, cut streets off our maps. Before long we have to draw the lines pretty tight around ourselves, make a narrative lifeboat, and our caring undergoes the same transformation to lifeboat ethics.

Thinking back over the town's reaction to the two murders, one resident said of Lorraine's murder: "Well, that was a domestic dispute. Two people who had it in for each other. He was not going to murder anyone else. He's not some lone murderer who comes through your town on a Sunday afternoon. It's creepy—this guy could come back."

∞

The broom: A week or so after Lorraine Manha was killed, I ran into a woman who had heard the gunshots. The evening of the murder, she had gone to a George Winston concert, New Age piano, quiet music that can turn an entire auditorium reflective, leaving each person on a desert island of his or her own thoughts.

"Did you like the concert?" I asked her idly. We were in line at a store. "I don't remember much about it," she said. "I couldn't stop thinking about that murder. I kept hearing the shots." She answered with a troubled look, her eyes not acknowledging the change the cashier had put in her hand. She just stood there, a lone mourner in a town refusing to mourn.

I think of the mourner and the unmourned sometimes when I pass that part of the road where two cars had collided. The man striding out with the big broom and the accident so quickly swept clean.

125

The Many Mitzvahs
of Myer Goldman

Here, in this world below, the death of Myer Goldman produced no monument, no historical marker to celebrate his memory. Except this: Fifteen years after his death, ask people about Myer Goldman, and they will smile and say his name, sometimes twice or more just for the joy of it. "Myer Goldman. *Myer Goldman.* It's been years since I've said that name—God, it feels good just to say it again. ... Oh, Myer. ... To see him going by in a car, or see him at a distance, or going to see him, I'd look forward to it. Always."

And then they will begin a story—only to stop—like people back from an exciting trip abroad, they want your attention: riches are about to be shared; this is no idle chat about the weather. "Would you like a cup of tea? Make yourself comfortable." And they tell.

In the stories they are twenty or thirty years younger—the world is younger—Myer Goldman is alive, and Peterborough, New Hampshire, is a small town in a still quiet New England.

Mary Garland and her husband came to the small towns north

126

of Mount Monadnock in 1956. At a time when people their age were touring model homes in Levittown, they were thinking of moving into a chronically depressed region. "My husband and I were considered total oddities. Young people didn't move into this area. Young people moved out." She remembers the first time she met Myer at his drugstore.

"We were in Peterborough on a Saturday night, and in those days stores were open on Saturday nights when the farmers came into town, and the Village Pharmacy was there—this Rexall drugstore. And we went in, and I'll never forget being absolutely bowled over by Handel's *Water Music*"—she laughs—"just blaring forth as we walked in the door. It just seemed like the most unlikely thing to greet one as you came into a Rexall in a little town in the sticks. It was really such a delight."

Delight at the unexpected, opening the door to the mundane and finding Myer. It struck many. Louise Talma remembers the first summer Myer and his wife, Florence, were running the drugstore, the summer of 1949. Talma, a distinguished composer and the recipient of many honors, was in residence at the MacDowell Colony, the artists' retreat in Peterborough. "I went into this new drugstore, and I was hearing Wanda Landowska playing Bach. And I thought, 'What kind of drugstore plays that?'"

Liz Prestopino is a painter, and she remembers with a painter's eye: "Myer always had these two [window] boxes of flowers that he put in, some of them were wild asters. And that was part of the picture: Myer standing up on the porch. He'd be out there with these flowers around him."

After Myer had died, and the drugstore moved out, the picture remained for her and other colonists: "The image was there—it's really amazing. You just expected to see Myer there. You'd drive by and think, 'Well, where's Myer? He's not standing on the porch. He supposed to be standing on the porch when you arrive in town.'"

But that is a rare picture: Myer standing still. He was always in motion, talking, kibitzing, holding forth. Rosellen Brown remembers him striding down the hill: "a tall, very good looking man with a shock of prematurely white hair, in his white druggist coat, really a wonderful looking man." And Merton Dyer, who ran the town's other drugstore, remembers passing the Village Pharmacy late on summer nights, 2 or 3 A.M.; the lights would be on, and Myer would be sitting out on the steps with the actors and crew who were unwinding from that evening's summer stock performance, talking and listening to music. And Myer would be up to open the store at 7 A.M.

Myer—or Mike, as he was known to many in town—loved to talk, and he always spoke his mind. Fritz Wetherbee remembers the first time Leonard Bernstein came into the store. "Lennie wanted cigarettes. Lennie was a chain smoker," says Fritz, at that time about a pack and a half a day. "Myer sat him down and gave him a lecture—a lecture! Myer Goldman was in the health business." After the 1964 surgeon general's report, the first to find smoking harmful, Myer stopped selling cigarettes—most likely the first pharmacy to do so in the country. If cigarettes killed, then it was wrong to sell them in a pharmacy, Myer believed. Never mind that everyone still smoked back then, that any social gathering meant standing in a room choked with smoke. "At that time everybody thought he was being extreme," says Merton Dyer. "He just recognized the problem earlier than most of us."

Sometimes people stalked out mad because they couldn't buy cigarettes. "He lost half his business," says Charlie LaRoche, Myer's best friend, who was with him every day for twenty years. "And I think he gave away more drugs to the sick than he sold."

Bernstein didn't forget the talking to. They struck up an acquaintanceship. Bernstein and a friend called for Myer in a Lincoln convertible, and Myer showed them Peterborough in a grand style. Later on, Bernstein left tickets for Myer at Lincoln Center. He admired Myer's principled stance. "He's a saintly man to do that. A saintly man."

∞

"How he ended up in Peterborough, I'll never know," his friends will stop to wonder at some point in the stories. "I can't imagine that

the early years were easy. They were the first Jews in Peterborough—
in the whole area. The first to brave being Jewish in Yankee country."

∞

In the first week of December 1948, Myer and his wife, Florence,
with one suitcase, drove up in a Volkswagen from Boston to look at
a drugstore that was for sale. "December 6 it was," says Florence,
"another Pearl Harbor."

They were joined in town by a doctor from Boston interested in
investing in the business, and his lawyer, who was to check on the
pharmacy's reputation in town.

"Myer's got his suitcase in his hand, and he's going to stay to see
what the store's doing," says Florence. But the owner "wouldn't let
Myer come in the store until he had the money in his hand. He said,
'You bring it up next week and you can have the key.' We should
have known something was wrong," says Florence, but neither she
nor Myer nor their partner knew anything about business. The
pharmacy owner refused even to show them the books. This did not
worry Myer. "Myer was always very enthusiastic. Nothing was gray
with Myer. He never knew character. People could impress him,"
says Florence. "And he always wanted to believe the best of people
instead of the worst."

The Village Pharmacy did have an excellent location. From the
stools at the soda fountain up front, you could look out and see the
movement of the whole community at the heart of Peterborough, the
intersection of Grove and Main streets, known through the generations as Robbe's, Cass's, Trufant's and Bishop's Corner. Next to the
pharmacy was the old tavern, a bookstore and a barbershop; across
the street was the A&P and the town's other drugstore. The American
Guernsey Cattle Club was one of the town's largest employers with
two hundred people, which made for a large lunch crowd. Everything came through town then: The bus stopped right at the door of
the Village Pharmacy, and the trains were still coming in at the depot
around the corner. This was long before a bypass was built for the

major road and long before the two shopping centers. All business centered on a compact town, and the town's Broadway and 42nd Street was the corner of Grove and Main.

They bought the business. Only later did they learn about the pharmacy's previous owner: "Everybody hated him," says Florence. "And they used to call him dirty Jew—he was a goy, but they called him dirty Jew because they hated him so much. And we didn't know that. ... "

Their first day, before Christmas, they took in $50. "There was no business. We had to build up that business. I'm not unhappy that we bought it, but we worked for seven years like Chinamen. Open seven days a week [to midnight in the summer]. Both of us and only one salary." They lived above the store with their two children, Stuart and Ann Sharon. They couldn't afford much. But: "From the day we opened the store, practically, he bought a Telefunken, a big, big radio." And the music began.

∞

The first years were difficult. The New England cold shoulder is famous. New Englanders abound in ways to label someone an outsider, to draw the line between us and them. Move into an old house, and you live your days under the name of the previous owner. It's the Standish house—even if the last Standish has been lying under the thick moss of the old burial ground for a hundred years. Have a summer place and not only are you "summer people," but the sin will be visited on your children and your children's children— even if, as frequently happens, they move up year-round. Summer people waist deep in snow. (*The History of Dublin, New Hampshire*—Dublin adjoins Peterborough—lists the men who served in World War I. Those who were summer residents are written up separately, with much less detail.) Move up from the city, from the flatlands along the Connecticut River, move from the hills, move *all the way* from Massachusetts and present yourself for labeling. The flatlander and newcomer all share the same sin: moving. In colonial times "undesirables" would be "warned out" of town, in the words of town laws, "to prevent such inconvenience as may come if every one be at liberty to receive into this town whom they please." Nothing goes on like that today, of course, but history does have a way of lingering. There may be more words in a New Englander's vocabulary for "outsider" than for the kinds of snow and rain and ice.

Two Jews from Lynn, Massachusetts, setting up shop on Main Street certainly qualified as outsiders. ("Of course they were complete foreigners when they came.") But to most in Peterborough, Judaism was merely theoretical—some ancient religion that had gone on before Christ and was in some way going on someplace. Before the Goldmans, there had been only one other Jewish family in town, the Cohens, who had a clothing store along about the turn of the century.

Catholicism was the threat, a clear and present danger; those people were breeders. "I saw this all the time," says Florence. "I'd mention names, someone having six or eight kids. Someone says to me, 'Catholic?' I says, 'No, Protestant.'"

There were plenty of ways to end up on the other side of the us-and-them divide. "They used to call us tradespeople. They looked down on people that ran stores. It was one of those things." Florence ignored that. She always spoke freely and was active in the many women's clubs that then comprised the town's social life. "As far as I was concerned—I had a college degree—I never felt that anybody was any better than I was."

Not that there weren't a few harsh words—once in school their son was called "a dirty Jew" by another child. "So I called the mother up, and the mother was very, very upset." When Myer and Florence finally bought a house in town, there was a comment about "letting those people in." And there was one expression that people used unthinkingly, something the Goldmans had never heard before: "Jewed them down."

"I had a friend who used to say that, so I just ignored it," says Florence. "That was part of her vocabulary. If she had thought about it, she wouldn't say it because she knew I was Jewish—I was a very good friend. You know what Myer would say to them? If they were French: 'You mean Frenched them down?' Something like that."

That was the only comment like that they heard spoken in the store. "If they didn't like us, they went elsewhere," she says. "When the Jewish holidays came, we closed the store, when we first came, because we had nobody to work, like for Yom Kippur and Rosh Hashanah. And I think they respected us more for keeping our Jewishness. I'm quite sure they did—people of any value."

Myer's Judaism unsettled many people, says Mary Garland. "He took a lot of people aback because he"—and here she lowers her voice to a jesting stage whisper—"*admitted it*." Later on, there were a few others "lurking around" who may have been Jewish, says Mary, "but it was absolutely, totally, completely, covered up." In the face of this, Myer "celebrated his Jewishness." He would do Passover services at the Episcopal church in Peterborough, Rosh Hashanah services at the Cathedral of the Pines and was a cantor at a synagogue in the nearby city of Keene.

"I think it was tough for some of the old folks—it was not just that he was Jewish. It was also that he was liberal and warm and fun and amusing and open and affectionate. He was no uptight New Englander at all," she says.

"I do remember one simply delicious time when our kids were little, when he just appeared at the door unannounced on the first night of Hanukkah, and had a bunch of candles and set them up and then went through a story and songs for our little kids. Such a sweet thing to do. They all loved it. They all adored him.

"He really opened up a lot of things for many people, for the very narrow-visioned people who had never, never encountered anyone who wasn't a Presbyterian or a Unitarian in their life. And it was also wonderful for some of the people who had been hiding the fact that they were Jewish, who took courage from his pride. And instead of living in fear and hypocrisy, were able to join in. I knew people who wouldn't even have admitted they knew what Hanukkah was, but once this was something that Mike did freely and openly, would have Hanukkah for their kids."

∞

Roland LaRoche, Charlie's brother, was a close friend, the kind of friend who would go with Myer to a pharmaceutical convention even though he wasn't in the business himself. "We were supposed to meet for dinner. He didn't show up in the dining room. I say, 'Gee, maybe something's happened to Mike.' I go back to our room. I get to the door, and I hear this moaning or this chanting. I say, 'Jesus!' I knock on the door, I say 'Mike, are you sick?'" He laughs now, but he did think Myer was in pain.

Myer was *dovening*, praying, and lost track of the time. "Boy, he'd got lost in the stuff," says Roland, who makes it clear he is an ex-Catholic and tired of all religions.

"I said once, 'Mike, how does it feel to be Jewish?'"

"And he said, *'Great.'*" Roland holds his shoulders square and smiles as he says that. *"'Great.'"*

∞

Still the distance between Christian and Jew remains. In other times in history it has been a distance marked by walls and weapons. But here in this land of a secular protestant religion, you trip across the difference, like tripping over a low curb you never saw coming. Among educated people it's not the anti-Semitic remark that wounds but rather just plain lack of knowing.

"Because he wore his Judaism on his sleeve," says Fritz, "he was always dealing with people saying to him, 'You're the most Christian person I know.' Things like that to be nice to him. 'You may be a Jew, but you're the most Christian person I know.' He got that—a lot of that. Well-meaning people who really liked him."

There is always a difference, and sometimes it's comic. Two friends were trying to find the word in Yiddish for Myer:

First friend: "What is the Jewish word—very sincere—?"

Second friend: "A *schmuck*—I don't know what that means."

First friend: "A *schmo*? A *schlemiel*?"

Those are not the words they're looking for, unless they mean to call their friend several garden varieties of jerk and fool.

First friend: "He was very sincere, but not a practical man."

Second friend: "There you go."

∞

"He was a Jew, of course he was interested in cultural things." That was what people said of Myer's support of writers, artists and musicians at the MacDowell Colony and of his help to the Peterborough Players, the summer theater. It's a stereotype made with the best of intentions and, in this case, one that is probably right. "He needed them as much as they needed him in the early years, when he had a rough time being accepted by the community," say friends. It was the only thing open. They weren't invited to join the country club, for example, but it was easy to invite fifteen colonists, the entire winter population, to dinner.

"Forty years ago, who were the colonists?" asks Florence. "A bunch of hoboes, bums, reds." That is how they were regarded, she says.

In a scrapbook, Florence has a photo of the front of the store, early 1950s, and in the window where you would expect to see the mandatory display of bedpans and crutches there are instead paintings.

"At that time ... most of the artists were starving. So there was this Japanese fellow. We put his pictures in the window. Sold them for him just like that. You could buy a watercolor at that time for fifteen dollars." They helped him out in other ways, gave him clothes, and one day found some paintings he had left at their door in gratitude.

The Goldmans looked after the colonists. If a colonist was broke but needed a dentist, Myer would make a few calls, arrange some bartering, some art for a filling. They took colonists out to dinner with them, often the most forlorn, outcast ones, people said. They took the colonists and their problems into their home. How much the Goldmans did can only be guessed at. In all the many recollections

134

of dozens and dozens of friends and neighbors, the same story never comes up twice.

"He had an intuition about the artists," says George Kendall, who was a director of the MacDowell Colony from 1952 to 1971. "I remember on one occasion his getting up early to drive an artist to a bus in Brattleboro—6 A.M. The fact that this particular artist was not very popular didn't enter into the picture at all. He did it because she needed help."

Myer was a fixture at the Peterborough Players' "strike night." Four or five times in a summer season the crew would have to strike the old sets to make way for the next play. At midnight Myer and Florence would show up with sandwiches, and they would all take a break.

"He did that quite unsolicited," says Bob Brown, whose wife managed the theater for twenty years. Early one morning, just after the pharmacy had opened, one of the players' apprentices came in and remarked on how they had worked all night and were really hungry. "In those days you just couldn't find food at midnight," says Bob. "The very next strike night, Saturday in those days, Mike showed up with food and it became tradition."

The word was out, in town and at the colony, that you had to go to Myer's. "You'd never know who you would run into," recall Bill and Liz Bauhan. "It was cosmopolitan but small town cosmopolitan." People were attracted to Myer, the way Myer had of talking to people, of being there, his "tremendous presence." "He was a big person behind that counter. He looked right at you, focused his attention, and you felt like you were his person."

"His store was like the village pub," says Mary Garland. "Colonists would come every day just to pick up a newspaper. Well, for God sakes, you can get a newspaper at the colony. But it would be just to come down, have a cup of coffee, see Mike, you know. The colonists were just absolutely devoted to him. He was father confessor and medical advisor and lovelorn advisor and comforter to hundreds and hundreds of people. He was just a very dear person."

⚭

It is part of the definition of a mitzvah that the good deed is done secretly and goes unreported in the general community. One does not stand before the TV camera to present a four-foot-long check. Most of what Myer did for people is only alluded to—how he would loan money to help someone get a business started, or bail out some troubled soul from jail, or how his store was sometimes an impromptu day care center with parents dropping their children off to play on the porch.

"He would hire people that nobody would touch, difficult kids or kids in trouble, and try to straighten them out," says Charlie LaRoche. He frequently had a troubled youth staying in the apartment over the pharmacy.

What may get lost in all this is that he was also an excellent pharmacist. Years before the public requested explicit information, he would carefully explain each prescription to his customers (or "patients," as Florence sometimes says).

"He'd correct the doctors when they made mistakes. When what they'd prescribe could possibly kill or maim somebody, and he'd call them up and say this isn't right," says Charlie. "Of course, the doctor wouldn't like it, so he made a lot of enemies by being frank and a man of his convictions."

⚭

While he was in high school and going to college, Jim Grant worked as a soda jerk in the Village Pharmacy. Myer helped pay for his college education. In later years, as principal of the elementary school in the town of Temple, Jim Grant won a following as a teacher who could reach the most troubled children.

"Mike was like a father to me," he says. "I was very close to the man."

"He was very unusual in his giving: He never expected anything in return. There were a lot of people who went through hard times.

He wouldn't bill them. And when he died, he had a lot of money out on the books from people that couldn't pay, and I guess didn't pay even after he died.

"His principles of life were guided by his religion. He would do no one harm. He would not involve himself in anything but fair practice. He had a sense of ethics that was unbelievable."

Jim likens Myer to the "community rabbi." "He was the wise man. There was always a table full of people—people would come to him for advice—kind of a soothsayer in some respects."

John Leonard is a critic and novelist who lives in New York City. He was in Peterborough in 1966, but he had no time to stop and chat with Myer at the drugstore. At the time, Leonard had married into the Morison family, which had a large apple orchard, Upland Farms, in Peterborough. "Everything was going wrong with the migrant workers," says Leonard. The family asked him to spend an apple-picking season there and figure out what was wrong.

"It was real rotten exploitation," says Leonard. "A bunch of Alabama bully boys, a black gestapo, who would pick up the pickers in school buses through the South. They'd bring all these bodies to Peterborough and put them in a shed, and they wouldn't let them go to town." The workers could cash their checks only at the company store.

Black migrant workers were certainly not welcome in town, as Leonard found out when he tried to end their isolation on the farm. "These guys would get their checks—their checks were from Upland Farms. They'd go down to town, and the banks wouldn't cash them, the gasoline stations wouldn't cash them. They kept claiming it was inadequate identification and all that, but these were checks handed out at Upland Farms. Goldman was the only one of the townspeople who would cash the checks of the black migrant pickers. He was the good liberal who understood what the problem was, and he helped out, and I was grateful for that."

∞

Florence is looking through a family photo album. "There's Thornton Wilder. He used to come to the house." Always greeted her with a kiss, she says. There are photos of the children playing around the drugstore, standing next to this composer or that artist. Pictures of the Goldmans as guests of a composer at Tanglewood, pictures of the colonists climbing Mount Monadnock, striking heroic mountaineering poses for the camera. Pasted to the black pages are Christmas cards and notes from all over the world.

A note from Alec Waugh in Denmark. "He came down to the store every single day at noon and had yogurt and tomato juice." A note from Louise Talma: "Greetings to all the Goldmans from Rome." A bill paid from a London hotel by Dorothy Heyward, who wrote the stage play of *Porgy* with her husband DuBose Heyward: "I am indeed sorry this bill should have gone so long unpaid. ... I have been quite sick since my summer in Peterborough and apparently my illness wiped out memory of my debt. Please forgive for the long delay. ... " A note from their kids at summer camp: "We went on a hike to the swamp and I fell in."

And notes of thanks, some for help in times of need: "Knowing you, breaking bread with you, talking with you in the intimacy of your home, are some of the warm, deeply moving experiences that I have taken away with me. I have related to my wife the entire story of our all too brief encounter, the readiness with which you have accorded me your mature understanding in moments of need. Your home and your store were a haven to me. ... "

And some for small favors: "Thank you and thank you for the lift from Keene, for your delicious dinner and breakfast, especially for the warm welcome. ... "

Thank you and thank you.

∞

A great heart, a generous soul may make no progress in the world, in the business world and in the great little American world of Me, Myself and I. You can apply Maslow's hierarchy of needs to the good soul, or any other psychological schema of the development of the self, and the good soul resists. You can scan his ledger books, and the good soul looks the fool. Why did he do all this? Did he need to do it? Did he curry acceptance? Maybe he just couldn't help himself. Such goodness baffles people. It is perhaps as baffling as evil. All the questions an evil act leaves in its wake can be asked of goodness: Why did this happen? Why did he do it?

One can look to biography. Myer grew up poor in Lynn, Massachusetts, a city just north of Boston. His parents were deaf mutes. His father died when he was four, leaving his mother to raise three children. His grandparents lived in the same building. Myer's mother worked all day at a factory. His grandmother did all the cooking. Florence lived around the corner, but, although her father was the Goldmans' doctor, she didn't know the family until she was engaged to Myer. "But I remember him talking that if his grandfather gave him a nickel to go to the movies it was wonderful. I mean they were really poor."

Myer was raised an Orthodox Jew. He followed the strict dietary laws; he had never eaten out of the house until college. His family counted as a relative Rabbi Moses Sofer, a famous seventeenth-century biblical scribe in Warsaw. There was music as well; his uncle Leon Goldman played viola with the People's Symphony Orchestra in Boston and was the music critic for the *Boston Herald Traveler*.

"'Myer,' as his grandmother would say, 'Myer is such a good boy because he was the middle one—the older one went off, the younger one went Joe College, you know younger kids, but Myer was the good one and would go to synagogue,'" explains Florence.

Fritz Wetherbee met Myer's mother after she had become diabetic and had to have her legs amputated. Fritz admits he was reluctant to meet a deaf mute in a wheelchair, a reluctance quickly dispelled. "She had a wonderful gleam in her eye. Terrific. I could see where Myer got it all. Just a wonderful lady. When you left you had to kiss her, you had to. You could see why he loved her."

Myer was proud of his mother and would not accept a description of her as crippled, as they would say back then, or handicapped, as they said later, or disabled. Fritz tells this story: "There used to be this guy who came around and he had ball-point pens. He'd come up and hand you the pen and a card; it said, 'I am a deaf mute. This is the only way I make my money. These pens are 25 cents'—this is back when ball-point pens cost a nickel—'give 25 cents or anything you care to give.' And he's coming through the store, and people are giving him a quarter. I look over, and here comes Mike Goldman. He comes over. He looks at the guy—he gives Mike a card. Mike rips it in half and begins talking with his hands. In sign language, Mike says, 'Listen you son of a bitch.' The guy starts backing out of the store. 'My parents worked—how dare you degrade. ...' That was an affront to his mother. It made his mother no better than a beggar. He knew the man could do something else."

∞

"'He was a saintly man,' I can see it in boldface," says Florence, remembering the headline on a letter to the editor at the time of Myer's funeral. But the subject turns to business—a pharmacy is a business, remember?—and her tone changes. "For someone to be a saint, somebody's got to be a devil. He could be as saintly as he wanted to, because he didn't have a care in the world."

There is a photo from 1950 showing the couple at work, filling prescriptions. Myer, resplendent in a bow tie, is smiling and talking. Florence, her head bent, is concentrating on the task at hand. "You see, there I am, the one working, and Myer is talking." And she has a good laugh on her youthful self.

After their rough introduction to the world of business, it was Florence who learned accounting, kept the books and did the billing. "It used to make me mad. I'd be sitting up in the kitchen, up to two o'clock in the morning doing bills, and he'd be sleeping already."

"Myer was a very good pharmacist, concerned about his patients," says Florence, but "he never made out a bill in his life. If it was up to him he'd never collect anything. He was everybody's daddy-uncle, and he let people use him. He was always giving stuff to the colonists for nothing. We've got tons of paintings here. And then I found out later we never really got them for nothing," she laughs heartily, "you know?"

"He was a philosopher. He could give people all kinds of lovely advice. But that was it. I used to say, 'You should have been a rabbi.' He wouldn't make any money at it ... but he wouldn't have any big pressure problems. And he could give advice. He'd never take advice for himself. But always philosophizing. I mean he never really was a down-to-earth person."

Myer had his own way of proceeding in the world. As Bob Brown saw it, "He'd act very quickly on emotion, but he tried hard to find an ethical grounding for what he did. I know at one point when his daughter Sharon had an automobile that showed up with some defect, I mentioned to him, 'Why don't you go ahead and sell it?' He said he certainly wouldn't sell a car that's defective: 'If it's not safe for my daughter to drive, it's not safe enough for anyone else to drive. I'm going to junk it.'"

He did not have the horse trader's love of commerce. Talking about business, Florence gets agitated. Once she was no longer working in the store with him, Myer stopped selling cigarettes, took out the soda fountain, closed on Sunday. "You throw out this, you throw out that," she says, and she goes right into a discussion of the bypass that diverted traffic from having to go down Main Street. "He would never concede that when they made the bypass it would cut down on business. I mean any dummy would know that!" You can hear the old arguments in her voice. And in that moment, you can see it from her perspective. *The Village Pharmacy is a business.* Not the social welfare agency, the Artists' Safe Harbor and Loan Company, the Peterborough Debating Society, or the Rexall Opera House.

Business, Myer Goldman didn't know from.

"I'm not saying anything against his growing up," says Florence, "but he thought he made it. He never made it financially. I mean he could never cope. And everyone thought he was rich."

∽

141

A painting here or there is a small expense. But then Myer, along with his friends, invested in a play. In that investment may be found the sum of Florence's frustration with Myer. Looking through the scrapbook, she finds a letter from the playwright. "Is this the five thousand-dollar letter?" she asks.

The play was *Birds of Summer* by Nick Kubly, who was a MacDowell colonist. Bob Brown was also an investor: "A lot of us went in for varying amounts. It never went on. It turned out to be essentially a con job by the man connected with the theater who said he'd line up production. But I'm sure it was no worse than lots of other times where you try to sell blue sky to promote a play and they manage to get it on and make money. Kubly was in no way involved with the scam. Many of us were friends of Nick: Hey, it would be nice if he had a successful play.

"I'll have to admit that although I invested a little, I never read it," Brown says, but a friend called it "the longest-running dirty joke ever. I think at one point there was supposed to be a woodpecker pecking away. That tied in with the activity taking place in bed.

"I got back three dollars. I was the only one, as far as I know, who ever got anything. I wrote the guy, I said, okay, you are broke, I can understand that, but you can afford a dollar a month. Start paying a dollar a month. I got about three letters.

"Mike ran the guy down, later, in New York. He said all he could do was feel very sorry for him. He said the place had practically no furniture. The guy was broke. I wouldn't be surprised if Mike gave him twenty dollars. That's just a hunch. But Mike came back very sympathetic to the fellow."

∞

Peter Pelletier worked in the pharmacy from his junior high school days on through college, when he was home for summers, about ten or twelve years. "For years I could tell you any aria from any opera. It was just osmosis. You heard it all those years whether you liked it or not—most people did not like hearing opera when they came into that drugstore."

He remembers how interesting it was, at first, working there, seeing people like composer Virgil Thomson, who came in every day when he was in residence at the colony. "Well, the world was different in 1957," says Peter. "It was a 'Leave It to Beaver' life. For any young person who had kind of an inclination toward some other life outside Peterborough, Mike's was a wonderful introduction to that. Because you couldn't go to New York, but there were a lot of New Yorkers who came through that store. It was easy to become sophisticated very quickly." In 1957 Peterborough, he says, that meant wearing a turtleneck shirt and reading D. H. Lawrence.

Myer's drugstore had its own clientele, and they were a minority in Peterborough. "I have tried to analyze the cultural composition of the people who used to come into that store," Peter says. "We really had two factions: the steady local people and this kind of fringe demimonde. An odd mix of people. I think for the most part, most working-class people in Peterborough traded at Clukays [later called Dyer]. Mike got welfare people, most of the nursing homes and the rich. And these summer people who needed a place to go."

But the Village Pharmacy did not suit most residents. They were uncomfortable with the music and Myer. "It was not out of his character to insult people if they didn't understand him. So in that regard, he could be very sarcastic, very intimidating.

"I was a great defender of his," says Peter. "It was often hard to work in that drugstore because people were critical of the atmosphere. I was very adolescent about it. I wouldn't let anyone else be critical, although I was."

Working behind the counter most of his growing up, Peter had a backstairs view of the Village Pharmacy. "Myer had one persona for the public and another for people who were close to him. I think he was a poseur—I mean I think he struck poses.

"I would never have gone to Myer for advice. I don't mean to be unflattering. I didn't think he was very wise. Not wise in the ways I was looking for. I thought in many ways he was very superficial. Often people would come in—and he did have this incredible ability

143

to focus his attention on people—and then they'd leave, and he'd ask me what their name was.

"All that had to do was happen more than once, and it changed your view. A lot of his relationships were of that caliber; people really felt that they were much more important to him than they were." That's often true of people with many friends, Peter says. "It may be trickery, but it might just be human nature."

"Myer was for many people what they wanted him to be," says Peter. He was a jokester to some, a wise man to others. "They just wanted some older kind of person who had a world view of things—or thought he had. And they had kind of an eccentric idea about want they wanted to do or be and someone who would accept them. I mean your parents are telling you that you should be a dentist or ought to be good at engineering and you wanted to be a playwright and Mike said, 'Yeah, that's a good idea. You ought to be a playwright.' Of course that's a very appealing kind of support." Myer also flattered the artistic aspirations of older people saddled with mundane occupations, Peter says.

"He just had this charade, kind of a sleight of hand characteristic. It's all right. He made a lot of people happy."

And he adds: "One thing that always impressed me, Mike would get this phenomenal number of Christmas cards. Like hundreds upon hundreds. A lot of those colonists didn't return; they'd come once for six weeks or whatever, and that would be the end of it. But they'd made this connection with Mike. So he'd get these wonderful cards, these handmade cards at Christmas. Always amazed me, the volume of cards he got, the people that would stay in touch with him. I know he didn't respond to those cards, so those people made that effort, kind of unilateral effort to stay in touch with him."

Roland LaRoche and his wife Barbara are debating Myer, as they must have often:

Roland: "Florence made him go to the store and work and work. And Mike would just do these things and she'd go crazy. Opposites."

Barbara: "His values are up here—"

Roland: "—Cloud 9."

Barbara: "A very kind heart."

Roland: "Of course, Barbara is very idealistic. He used to make me so mad because he's so impractical. I used to say, 'What the hell are you doing this for, Mike?' [He sounds like he is pleading with him even now.] 'You have a family too, Mike.'"

Barbara: "But we need impractical, warm, wonderful, loving people in this world. Sure Florence had a legitimate beef: You've got to pay the bills. You're giving to the people, what about your own kids? She had a legitimate beef."

Roland: "Once he had this guy who had problems—an alcoholic. He was an electrician. And his kids got sick, and Mike would give him this line of credit. Just anything he wanted. 'Mike,' I said, 'I saw him going to the liquor store the other day.' So Mike needed some electrical work done. So he hired him to do it. And the guy sent Mike a bill! And Mike paid it. That was really something. I said, 'Mike, why did you do that?' He said, 'Well, he needed the money.' I said, 'How about you, Mike? You have a family.' He was generous to a fault. He'd go overboard."

Barbara: "He was impulsive. He was impassioned about everything. Especially things that mattered—What does money matter? [She laughs.] Well, of course it does."

Roland: "He practically fed the colonists. And at times he had trouble paying his bills, let's face it."

∞

So what to do with the good soul in this world?

There is a Yiddish story Myer liked to tell that was known to probably every Jew of his generation. The story, by I. L. Peretz, is called "Bontshe the Silent," about a poor drudge who lives anonymously, "like some dull grain of sand," and is buried in an unmarked grave. "Here, in this world below," the story begins, "the death of Bontshe produced no impression whatever. ... Had a bus horse fallen down in the street, people would have displayed much more interest than they did in the case of this poor man."

But so uncomplaining has Bontshe been that he enters the gates of heaven, heralded by the trumpeting of the Messiah's ram's horn, the archangels flying about with excitement.

The Patriarch Abraham welcomes him at the gate of heaven: Shalom. Two angels wheel forward an armchair of gold and place upon Bontshe's head a golden crown set with precious stones.

Bontshe is frightened into silence. This must be a mistake. He is brought before the Supreme Tribunal. Never once, the president of the Tribunal is told, did Bontshe complain. Not when his mother worked him barefoot in the cold, not when his stepfather beat him, not when he staggered carrying heavy loads, dizzy from not having eaten for days.

The president of the Celestial Tribunal rules: Here stands a man broken by the world, not a limb intact, no corner of the soul untouched. Down in the world below they do not understand such things. "Everything here belongs to you; take whatever your heart desires."

"Really?" asks Bontshe.

"Yes, really," he is told. "All brightness, all splendor, it is yours."

"Really?" Bontshe asks again.

He is assured again.

"If this is so," Bontshe says, "I should like to have every morning a warm roll with butter."

The angels drop their heads, and the great court fills with laughter.

This a fable about the ultimate in humility. For who has not complained, who has not dwelled on his self-importance. And even in such a short fable one loses patience with Bontshe—people are always taking advantage of him; his own son throws him out of the house.

Bontshe the Silent hardly sounds like Myer the Kibitzer. And Myer would have rather thought himself a character in *Catch-22*, a favorite novel of his. But rethinking this story, one realizes that quite a few people are Bontshe-like in some part of their lives. There is this passage: "He never dared to raise his voice when asking for his pay. ... He was silent even when people haggled for his pay, knocked off something from it, or slipped a counterfeit coin into his hand. He was always silent!"

∞

"Which is not to say Mike was a saint," his friends will say after they've been talking about all of Myer's mitzvahs. "This is sounding as if he were nothing but a pure angel, which, of course, was not the case," says Mary Garland.

"He loved a raunchy joke," recalls a former customer. "Sometimes people would come in and say, 'Do you have cotton balls?' He'd say, 'What do you think I am? A rabbit?' *That* was Mike. Mike had all kinds of sides about him."

There was a certain quality to Myer, they say, and here they grope for the right word: boisterous, impish, given to excess, in Yiddish: a *tummler*, someone who likes to jump in and make a stir, a tumult. They give up trying to tag a word on Myer and tell another story.

"He could be infuriating. Unsolicited advice was his downfall," says Fritz. Fritz himself first met Myer when he was a young apprentice with the Peterborough Players. "He loved the theater, and if you appeared on the stage, Myer was there at every opening, and you got an individualized review of your performance. Myer didn't pull any punches—Myer made some enemies doing that on occasion. He had an opinion, and he loved to talk about it.

"Oh God, he would tell you what was wrong. On any subject. He would tell you what color you should paint your house, or how you should repair your car. I've seen him walk onto a job site and tell them they were doing it wrong."

Once Myer was standing at the window looking out over a construction site next door. The old 1834 tavern had been torn down for a new bank. Myer thought the foundation should line up with the other buildings alongside. "So he went down and asked who was in charge and chewed him out for not lining it up. Next thing we saw was Myer coming up the way, chased by a hardhat shaking his fist." Fritz laughs. "He was a buttinsky.

Myer was controversial and he enjoyed that. While to some, he was a fount of life, to others he was "an oddity, a real practicing, loud-mouth Jew." And "just an obnoxious male who always had to be at the center of everything." And inevitably in conservative New Hampshire: "I wouldn't go into that Communist bastard's shop."

The Village Pharmacy always ran a poor second to the other pharmacy in town, which was much busier and had more help but couldn't match Myer for art, music or politics. One time some people were greatly offended by Myer's choice of artwork for the pharmacy window: "Black-and-white photos of naked women—great big ones by some artist," says Betty Beale, who worked for years at the pharmacy. Myer met the town's consternation head-on. He and Betty pasted leaves on the photos in the appropriate places.

Myer was always in motion. He would work all day—seven days, 7 A.M. to 9 P.M. until the later years—and then go off to the high school gym some nights to play basketball, or go over to Charlie or Roland LaRoche's place to watch the fights on TV—not that the LaRoches were exactly boxing fans at all, but they had a TV and in came Myer to fill the room with talk and cigar smoke. He'd bring and eat a whole box of chocolates and a whole box of peanuts, says Charlie. Or he'd go to the American Legion to play cards.

"As I recall," says Bob Brown, "the story goes, some people quit going because Mike talked too much while they were playing cards." But even playing cards had an ethical dimension for Myer: "He felt the Legion was important in getting the GI Bill, so he owed them support. There again, what he did had some point of principle, some rationale."

Myer in motion. It is difficult to put a word to this: energy, moxie, the gift of gab, charisma, vibrancy, drive? It's not drive, the focused ambition of a man with his eye on the main chance; it's not directed at a point, but it's everywhere at once. This is just someone who loves life—a suspicious character to many. What Myer had is that indefinable spark—the spark of life. Friends will tell jokes, but it is the spark of life that they are remembering. And all the stories make the spark visible.

∞

After long years of living above the store, on the third floor in an apartment that was boiling hot in the summer, Myer and Florence bought a house. Their friends Charlie and Roland LaRoche had built it. The house had a splendid view. This was the first house Myer, at age forty, had ever lived in.

They held a party the summer after they moved in, a belated housewarming. "He was proud," says Louise Talma. "Finally he made good enough so he could buy a house. So proud." He held a ceremony for putting up the mezuzah, a small scroll bearing a passage from Deuteronomy, placed on the doorpost. "All his friends came. He was an established landholder. That was one of the happiest days of his life."

Myer and Florence lived in that house less than a year before they separated. They were married eighteen years. "It was the same as twenty-five years because we saw each other from the minute we woke up till we got to sleep," says Florence. The saint and devil roles had caught up with them. Myer moved out. They were divorced two years later.

It was the early 1960s. Florence says that Myer "ran around like the playboy of the golden west." And a friend, Rick Frede, remembers Myer in a small red sports car he bought, tooling around Dublin Lake with a young blonde, a colonist in her twenties, her hair flying. "He hit male menopause with a vengeance," says Frede. This was when Myer was forty-one or forty-two years old, the age his father was at his death. Forty-two was his worst year, Myer told Fritz.

There is another slant on that sports car story, though, another trick with memory and mirrors. Art Eldredge collects old cars and sold Myer that sports car, an Austin-Healey Bug-Eye Sprite, quite a little car for a big, heavy-set man like Myer. "He said, 'This would be great. I can lift my mother in there and drive her around.'"

With Florence gone, the "cafe-museum" and artist's salon atmosphere of the drugstore grew. Mike's enthusiasms were unchecked (if they ever were checked to begin with). The country was entering a time of strident disagreement and quickened tempers. Myer's passionate stances were magnified by the urgency of the late 1960s. He became incensed at the war in Vietnam. "If Mike had any drawback," says Rick Frede, "there were times when people would hesitate to go in for fear he would harangue them about his current obsessions. Almost berating people. He was outraged by anything that struck him as injustice. A couple of good, dear friends told him he was driving away business. I finally told him he was being overbearing."

His friend Bob Brown, a retired Air Force colonel, took the debate in stride: "He hated to be reminded of it, but the first year after we got involved in Vietnam he let his uniform out and marched in the Memorial Day Parade as a gesture of solidarity. Years after, he'd sound off about how we're so wrong in Vietnam. I'd say, 'Now Mike, you've got to remember you encouraged it when it first started. That's how it got going.' He'd try to deny it, yet he had to admit that, all right, my recollections were probably more accurate."

Myer let his hair grow, wore love beads and put a painting in the store window that said, "Make Love Not War." And came the 1968 primary, he declared his store a headquarters for Eugene McCarthy's presidential campaign. Photos of the pharmacy, decked out in McCarthy banners, were published nationally.

McCarthy recalls coming into Peterborough and seeing that banner, right at the intersection of Main and Grove streets. "He was a bright spot," McCarthy says. "Because you know they were pretty undemonstrative up there. To find the enthusiasm of Myer was a lift."

A lot of people in town felt that Myer overstepped his bounds by getting politically active. "Nobody wanted politics mixed with their prescriptions," says Peter Pelletier. "I think people would be willing to listen to some sermon on Prokofiev, but they didn't want to go in and listen to political propaganda."

Myer's political activities drew the wrath of the *Manchester Union Leader*, which ran articles about Myer wearing love beads and sheltering "hippie runaways" above the store. Myer, never shy of controversy, responded with a series of angry letters to the "Misleader," whose editor, William Loeb, Myer called "William Low-ebb."

"To those who were close to the *Manchester Union Leader*, he was a menace, an encourager of the rebellious young," says Bob Brown. "I have no doubt that some assumed he was handing out drugs. That was a minority, but the people who bought the pharmacy [after Myer] found there was a certain harvest of ill will along with the good will. There were people, who even after Mike was no longer there, would still not patronize the drugstore.

"I know that the time the *Union Leader* came out with a blast against him, several people came in and lifted their prescriptions that were on file and marched over to Dyer Drugs."

Florence thought her ex-husband was an overgrown Flower Child. "He'd be going, doing things. He didn't know what he wanted. He was searching. He was actually a Flower Man."

He may have alienated a portion of Peterborough, but toward the decade's end, he had what could be called a following. Part of Peterborough had finally caught up to Myer Goldman. There were a few Jewish families in the area by then, and many people shared Myer's views. Many of his closest friends are from this part of his life.

Myer remarried, to a woman twenty years younger and an Episcopalian, Diane Keegan. "Diane loved him right off," says Fritz. "When he was courting Diane, he took her to Lincoln Center to hear the New York Philharmonic, and they waited for Lennie Bernstein to come out afterward. Myer was sure Bernstein wouldn't recognize him. Lennie came out, looked across the lobby and went: 'Myer Goldman!'—came over and embraced him. Diane decided she was going to marry him right then and there." Fritz jokes, "Who knows a pharmacist? People walking by in New York saying, 'Who's that with Myer Goldman?' "

151

Diane doesn't remember it quite that way, but the spirit is right: They did take to each other immediately. They were married in Diane's hometown, in Ohio. "He had two kids right off and he named them Sam and Rebecca, which is what he wanted all along, of course, but didn't have license to do it because he was the only Jew in Peterborough and he didn't want to stick out." (Myer's father was Sam, and his maternal grandmother was Rebecca.) "For Myer's first children," says Fritz, "he and Florence had agreed on 'non-stick-out American names,' Stuart and Ann Sharon, which Myer felt a little guilty about."

So Myer, after more than twenty years in a protestant community, finally ran aground in the land of assimilation. His first two children, by a Jewish wife have fairly typical names; the next, by an Episcopalian, have more Jewish-sounding names. And more irony. His first daughter, Jewish, marries a born-again Christian. His second daughter, not Jewish by Jewish law, goes off to a fine college bearing the name Goldman. She discovers anti-Semitism and sets a course for Israel, where she meets and eventually marries a young orthodox rabbi. (One time Myer told Roland LaRoche: "My children will never marry Christians. I would never allow such a thing. My religion won't allow it.") Irony, what would life be without it? A world of ordinary, neon-lit, Muzak-playing drugstores, perhaps. When Myer's friends at his synagogue heard that he had married an Episcopalian, in Ohio, on a Saturday, they couldn't believe it. "How could he get married on a Saturday, the Sabbath?" they said.

With his second wife, Myer cut back the store hours. For the first time in his life, he had time to play, friends said. "Diane was the most unbelievably energetic person on the face of the earth," says Mary Garland. "Mike would work all day long and then come home at night and they would drive about two hours to Hanover to see a good concert. He had to be at work the next day. He would do things like this three times a week. Sometimes I think he was pretty well worn out by the busy schedule he had. But it was just wonderful, he really loved it. He enjoyed playing and would do things like canoeing or spending lovely long summer days. I don't think he ever had that as part of his life before." In particular, Mary remembers setting out with canoes full of children and food for a picnic at Willard Pond. "A delicious warm summer day with little kids."

With Diane, Myer learned to ski, took up pottery at the local arts center, went to see opera in Boston and almost every local music performance. "One summer we went to every single Monadnock Music concert," says Diane. "It got to be sort of a game." They traveled to Mexico and England. "I don't think Myer ever relaxed, because he wanted to see everything. So we always got up and did everything. When we went to London, we went to fourteen plays and concerts."

Myer had tutored a friend's son for his Bar Mitzvah, which was to take place in Israel. In appreciation, the family sent Myer and Diane to the Bar Mitzvah. "We had ten days in Israel, which he just adored. That was the high point of his life. He just loved it. He couldn't wait to go back."

Myer rejoiced in his new family. "He was a grandfather by the time he had his second family," says Fritz. "He'd be in the store with his kids and people would come in and say, 'Is this your grandson?' Oh, he laughed. He had white hair, come on. Then he'd have the chance to say, 'No, it's my son, it's my daughter'—and get the embarrassment from them. And that was good for him, too, that made him smile."

∞

There are moments of triumph in life, moments we wish others would remember. If there is one moment in Myer Goldman's life that could be taken as triumphal, it was the biggest Passover Seder Myer ever led. And everyone does remember it; they were there: sixty-five people in Art Eldredge's barn.

Myer remembered the big Seders back in Lynn. His grandparents had lived to their eighties and nineties, and for years he went home for a big Seder, thirty or forty people gathered around the usual odd collection of folding tables. Now Myer, who looked like his grandfather, sat at the head of the table.

A newspaper photo shows everyone jammed in, seated at a series of tables that snake through the barn (maybe a half-dozen Jews among them), all gathered "to help Mike celebrate Passover," the newspaper said. "All wore skull caps. All sang (or tried to sing) the joyous Hebrew songs which celebrate the deliverance from slavery. All learned. And Mike in turn, arose early Sunday morning to attend Easter Service."

Fritz was there. "A room full of Episcopalians in yarmulkes. And there in the spirit of ecumenism, Myer reclining at the head of the table. I mean, when he did it, he did it right.

"What a great lesson, and what a kind lesson. He took a bunch of people who loved him personally, and he brought them into something that demystified it for them, and as a result there was a great deal more understanding. There is nothing more joyous than a Seder, there's nothing more family or comfortable. If Myer gave the community anything, he gave them that realization: there's goodness here, too."

∞

"He looked good. He was jogging. Then he got cancer." That is the telegraphic way Myer's friends remember the last years. Myer was always brimming with life, so they may have missed, or forgotten over the years, that he was in pain. He would feel faint, but he'd go to the doctor, and they could not find anything wrong. One day he fainted in the drugstore, fell right over. This time they found colon cancer, and they were too late; it had spread to his liver. Fritz: "He said, 'What's the prognosis?' They said, 'Go home and put your affairs in order, you're going to die.' "

After a time, he sold the store. His friends rallied to his side. Out of the hospital, he and Diane spent a weekend in Maine with Fritz and his wife. The LaRoches took them on a cruise to Bermuda. He received a little recognition for his work: a round of applause at the last play at the Peterborough Players and at MacDowell Colony's medal day.

That spring Myer had what his friends realized would likely be his farewell Seder. There were fifty-five people partaking, but it was altogether different from the triumphal Seder in the barn, nine years earlier. Myer felt he didn't have the strength, so he had a friend conduct the Seder, Marvin Hoffman, Rosellen Brown's husband, a school principal who also taught Hebrew lessons. This Seder wasn't a community display, a joyous tumult. Only his friends came, recalled Rosellen Brown. It was a cold day late in March, and they were out on Rosellen's enclosed but unheated porch, although between the people and the kettles of chicken soup, the porch warmed. And it was sad.

The last autumn was painful. Myer was on chemotherapy. A box hung around his neck and loudly ticked as it dispensed the drug through a tube into his sternum. A clock ticking toxin.

Myer at least had time to attend more of the classical music performances he loved. But that "little square box made all this noise, tick, tick, tick—loud," says Fritz. "They're trying to play, and there's this guy in the front row going tick, tick, tick. People saying, 'What's that noise?' But I'll say this: it was the kind of thing he just laughed at. I mean, it hurt him, of course, but he saw the joke, and he laughed at it."

But the clock was ticking. He called Florence, and they spoke for one of the last times: "I remember his voice cracking. He didn't want to go in the hospital because he knew the next time he went in, he would not come out."

∞

Finally he was in the hospital down in Boston, nevertheless receiving a stream of visitors who claimed they just happened to be in town. Myer was very weak, and visitors were allowed to stay only five minutes. As Rick Frede was leaving, Myer reached out and formally shook his hand. "I thought that was strange," said Rick. "It was not until months later that I realized with great shock that he knew he was going to be dead." Myer was fifty-four.

⌒

In 1948, Myer Goldman had arrived in Peterborough with only a suitcase. In 1974, three hundred people crowded into the Unitarian Church for a memorial service. "Here was a person who came from someplace else to this community of Yankees," Peterborough native Elizabeth Thomas reflected years later. "And he wasn't a Yankee. It was like an angel come into our midst. He didn't try to be a Yankee. It was his Jewishness that made him better than the rest of us."

⌒

Nubanusit Lake is a place so beautiful that you want to believe the name is Indian for "blessed waters" or "tranquility." You can look it up in three or four dictionaries of American place names and come up with as many meanings. The best is "at the place of gently sloping banks." But that brings you only to the lake shore. After a time—summers and falls of canoeing, winter on its ice—the name itself is tranquility.

On a fall day, Diane and Fritz, his wife and his father set out in a small boat to spread Myer Goldman's ashes on the waters of Nubanusit.

It was Myer's will that he be cremated, contrary to Jewish law. Diane had brought the box to Fritz's house. "We took the wrapping off and opened the box, and inside the box was a second box, a gray box, and inside was this plastic bag. And I remember that the twist tie on the plastic bag was pink, fluorescent kind of pink, just pink, happy pink. And in the bag were ashes—ashes like you see from a wood stove or a coal stove—just ashes, that's all. You expected some kind of horror, but it was just ashes. You knew that this was Myer. This was him. There he is. I'd seen him a week before. And here he was.

"So we got in the boat. It was a beautiful fall day. There was color still left, it was a little beyond peak, it was raining, but it was just gorgeous color. It was kind of misting and cold."

They stopped the boat and said a few words. They dragged their hands through the water, releasing the ashes.

The waters of the Nubanusit flow out through Skatutakee Lake, Harrisville Pond, and into the Nubanusit Brook. The Nubanusit comes down at the MacDowell Dam and encircles Peterborough like a man's arm around the waist of his partner as they dance. "It flows right down beside all the things he loved," says Fritz. "He is a part of it all."

∞

The haunting of losing someone close is that he is dead so long. The shock of grief passes, and the calendar takes over. And so soon it is ten or fifteen years later. Another lifetime really. The dead stay dead so long. They become, at last, memories only, memories in a perishable memory house.

In a room, fifteen years later, Roland and Barbara LaRoche are talking about Myer. How he drove them crazy with *Fiddler on the Roof.* Myer had seen the musical "and from then on, every time you went into the store it was playing." How he would fill any room he would enter. Barbara is talking: "One of these warm, embracing personalities. He came in here and he was big, and it seemed he was tall—was he tall? and—" She is fighting back the tears. "We still miss him," she says. She cries. "I'd love it if he walked right through that door. You think I'm foolish—" and she sobs some more. We sit, her husband and I, and look out on an April snow squall, and think of it: Myer Goldman entering the room, filling it with his presence, turning on a boxing match on TV, lighting up a cigar, or playing an opera or holding forth about Mozart or Vietnam or cigarette smoking or telling the Passover Seder story. Holding forth, a torrent of life. But instead it is quiet. The snow is falling in large flakes, like those in a glass globe. A fantasy of snow in the second week of April. If I could, I would take that glass globe and shake it until the snow was falling on Peterborough 1948, falling on the corner of Grove and Main, as I enter what seems to be an average Rexall drugstore, opening the door on the music. … I would see for myself. But I look up at Barbara LaRoche and I can see. Here was a beloved man.

157

∞

In the end, when Myer was sick, Rick Frede remembers going into the drugstore and finding Merton Dyer, the pharmacist from the other drugstore in town. Dyer was never close with Myer, and politically they were poles apart. But he volunteered his time, a couple of hours three or four days a week, filling Myer's prescriptions. Rick didn't know Mert Dyer at all, yet Mert said to him: "No one will ever know how much Mike did for this town. He gave prescriptions for anyone in need. I'm just filling in for what he did."

"He loved people and he hurt for people," says Fritz. "He was one of those guys that if there was somebody in pain, he would feel it for them. It would break his heart, which is why people took advantage of him. If you're like that, it's going to happen. He was the safety net for a lot of people. When he went, a lot of people said, Jesus, if everything went wrong in life, if the bottom dropped out, if you were about to become a homeless person, Myer Goldman was there. They knew that if their Volkswagen broke down on the road in the middle of Kansas in a snowstorm in the middle of the night and they had met Myer Goldman for three days once back in 1957, they could call him and he'd send them money. A phone call away for thousands of people, not just one or two, not just family."

∞

> When a Jew performs a meritorious deed and then forgets it
> ... God holds it in remembrance; if on the other hand, ... having
> performed a mitzvah, the Jew continually alludes to it, God does
> not remember the deed.
>
> —Theodor H. Gaster,
> *Festival of the Jewish Year*

∞

How do we settle on the story of a life? A life of nearly twenty thousand days. And among those days there are a few moments, a few deeds that people take as emblems. Here, they say, this conversation, this off-hand comment, stands for those twenty thousand days. These emblematic stories become currency—told and retold, passed from hand to hand until they are worn smooth like old coins.

Where do we leave Myer Goldman fixed in our minds? Behind the counter filling prescriptions? The Telefunken blaring out arias? Myer the tummler in the comic opera of small-town life, the man who could hold an impassioned argument even in sign language.

"There isn't much to tell," says Louise Talma. "It was a day-to-day existence of always doing good things."

I—who never met Myer Goldman—like to think of him in the most unlikely of places, far from the close rooms of his orthodox Jewish childhood. He and his wife are sitting in a canoe loaded to the gunwales with food and wine and little children. In other canoes are friends and more little children, "a delicious warm summer day with little kids," as Mary Garland said. They are paddling out for the Indian campground on Willard Pond, a picnic armada. Once across the pond, they will spread a linen cloth for the picnic.

There is light everywhere—blue in the sky, glinting off the water, light and warmth that dim all memory of the dreary late New Hampshire winters. Such a summer's day in a lifetime of New Hampshire winters is as welcome as a warm roll with butter.

And somewhere, in the middle of the pond—wooded hills rising up around, paddles lapping at the water, children noisily gurgling away—Myer hears a loon call. It reminds him of a favorite aria. Yes, he thinks, I will play that Monday morning.

Part IV

ABSENCES

Absences

Sometimes you can judge a landscape by its absences. The animals missing from the pastures here in New Hampshire, the vanished herds of antelope and buffalo on the plains, and even in a city like London the absence of parking meters and "No Parking" signs.

In America we specialize in the landscape of absences. The central metaphor is also the central space in our geography: the Great Plains. It is a well-known story: To those determined to reach the gold rush fields of California, the plains were an emptiness labeled on maps as the Great American Desert. After that, when we saw that the land was fertile, we cleared away the buffalo and Indian, creating an absence as looming as a desert.

But that is "once upon a time" now. Take the daily landscape of many Americans: Look at what we have done to our cities in the last forty years. We have cleared them of people, buildings and trees and then wondered why they are so lifeless.

The trees died from chestnut blight and Dutch elm disease and paving and neglect. Small buildings on twisting streets were cleared for urban renewal. The people who lived and worked there were banished. In a country untouched by the last World War, great parts of our major cities look as if the Luftwaffe had been through.

Today in so many American cities, we have block after block of absences. And all variety of absences. We have the ruddy-muddy cinder parking lots under the interstate. We have the tall corporate towers deserted by 6 P.M. but all lit up like hollow men.

We have everywhere an absence of memory. Architects sometimes talk of building with context and continuity in mind, religious leaders call it tradition, social workers say it is a sense of community, but it is memory we have banished from our cities. In every building leveled and every neighborhood cleared, we say "We just don't want to hear about it any more." We have made our bargain. We have speed and power, but no place. Travel, but no destination. Convenience, but no ease.

Banish the birds and beavers, fell the tall trees, impound the waters and lay out the grid, drawing the lines that separate us from them, us from the great everything we sometimes call nature. What we have called, in different eras, settlement, progress and growth, is the creation of absences.

The Passing of
Tall Tree America

"In the spring the chestnut trees, loaded with masses of drooping white blooms, in pasture and woods gave promise of an abundant harvest. Gathering nuts was a pleasant fall pastime," reports *A History of Walpole, N. H.* "In October 1879 the crop of butternuts and chestnuts was especially abundant, and it was said that even a freight train stopped by Buffum's chestnut orchard to allow all but one of the brakemen to leave the train to gather chestnuts and on the return trip stopped to pick them up. By 1921 the chestnuts were falling prey to blight, as the elms are now being destroyed by Dutch elm disease."

They left behind great names—the Divine Elm, the Justice Elm, the Pride of the State, the Green Tree. In their dappled shade countless towns found repose, places like Elmhurst, Illinois; Elm Grove, Wisconsin; and New Haven, "City of Elms"—many were the American cities that claimed that title. Elms were the landscape of America.

The tall trees have vanished, but once they were the pride of the community. Maples, oaks, elms and pines grew one hundred to two hundred feet tall or more, taller than most church steeples. There was scarcely a town that didn't believe it had the tallest elm, the oldest oak, the most beautiful chestnuts, the grandest avenue of maples. All those cities claiming to be the Elm City, all those Maple, Oak and Walnut streets and so many other street names and places and town slogans and nicknames ... we would like to be remembered as a country of trees.

The trees are pictured on old postcards from before the Great War—the hand-colored one-penny cards that travelers sent home—the equivalent of today's phone calls. Quite often they would send pictures of trees, as if to say, "Yes, though I'm in New Haven, I'm still on earth."

The tall trees are there in a postcard from around 1905: "Noontime, Lancaster, Massachusetts." A farmer at his well with three plow horses, small figures in front of a row of great elms. A dirt road stretches away into the fields and on toward a hazy middle distance of more trees.

There are tall elms over the bandstand in Keene, New Hampshire's Central Square (c. 1920), on the Green in Taunton, Massachusetts (c. 1905) and on Court Square in Springfield, Massachusetts, horse-drawn wagons pass by on the cobblestone street (c. 1905). On the Boston Common, women in white dresses stroll under the trees of the "Long Walk" (c. 1910). Under the trees in Lewiston Park, Lewiston, Maine, men in their Sunday best sit reading the newspapers; children play nearby (c. 1910). On the armory grounds in Springfield, Massachusetts, soldiers stand tall by the cannons. The trees stand taller. It is 1910.

It is 1910, and Christ Church, Westerly, Rhode Island, stands wreathed in the bright green of new spring leaves, and spring blooms over Andover Street in Lowell, Massachusetts, over Main Street in Thomaston, Connecticut, and at Ward's Corner in West Haven, Connecticut.

Need one go on? Once in our cities and towns, there were great trees to walk under.

∞

At my last visit to Peterborough, in 1874, I found (after thirty-seven years' absence) that the heads of my old school-mates were turning gray, and that their faces were furrowed by time, and, sadder still, that which was the crowning glory of Peterborough (next to her sons and daughters) had nearly disappeared. Your noble forests were gone. Those hills which had been covered with grand trees had been stripped bare and naked. The beautiful groves, "God's first temple," had vanished.

        —A letter home from S. J. Todd of Beloit, Wisconsin,
            to Albert Smith, Peterborough, New Hampshire

∞

We have lost tall tree America more than once, and we are losing it today.

The tall trees went by waste and by need, by the board foot and by the ash heap. They went for masts for the Royal Navy, for railroad ties, for houses, for a few seasons' corn. They were an obstacle to be girdled, felled, burned, pulled out, piled up—a deformity holding the land back from farming, in a century-long frenzy to "make land."

The trees fell, and the heirs to the settlers found themselves in barren villages. Some towns around Boston were running out of wood even before the Revolution. Village improvement societies began setting out trees, and by the last decades of the nineteenth century the villages had achieved the form that has never left the American mind: trim white houses under towering elms, ancient oaks hung with children's swings and tree houses.

But then we lost that America, too. Came the motor age, the horse and the cobblestone street left the city, and our shade trees have never again been as long-lived.

The story of America's tall trees is a tunnel of mirrors: a loss wrapped in a loss, wrapped in a loss. ... Each generation feels—knows—that it alone has lost the true Eden.

The Paradise of Utility:
The Song of the Broad Axe

Sailing to America, the early settlers could begin to smell pine trees 180 nautical miles from landfall. The reports back to Europe are filled with trees. Europe had lost its great forests centuries earlier, and here was an El Dorado of wood, another version of New World gold. "All Europe is not able to make so great fires as New England," wrote one pamphleteer in the 1630s. In this new land, he explained, a poor servant is one with fifty acres and more wood "than many Noblemen in England. Here is a good living for those that love good fires."

A French naturalist, touring America after the Revolution, reported home that he "scarcely passed, for three miles together, through a track of unwooded or cleared land." An English diarist in 1818 recorded each new wonder: "Yesterday I measured a walnut tree almost seven feet in diameter" and, he continued, nearby were large sycamores and oaks. A French botanist studying the great forests of Ohio around 1800 reported a sycamore with a circumference of over forty feet. In North Carolina, and elsewhere, families moved into the hollows of aging sycamores.

The measurements were not taken solely in homage. They were the preparations of a hungry man getting ready for the kill. Walnuts and sycamores of enormous size may suggest a paradise to us, but in those measurements the Europeans read good fires, good lumber and, once cleared, good soil. The New World was a Paradise of Utility, and its creed was Whitman's "Song of the Broad Axe."

To our modern eyes looking back, the unbroken forest is the "fresh, green breast of the new world" in F. Scott Fitzgerald's phrase. It is all promise. To the pioneers it was a threat. The forests were as strange as another planet, "a hideous and desolate wilderness," Pilgrim William Bradford called it. To their ears, this New World even sounded odd: there were no horses or dogs.

In the earliest history of New Hampshire, whose first volume was published in 1784, the author, Jeremy Belknap, comments on "the gloomy appearance of an American forest" and "the silence which reigns through it. In a calm day, no sound is heard but that of running water, or perhaps the chirping of a squirrel, or the squalling of a jay. Singing birds do not frequent the thick woods; but in every opening, made by the hand of cultivation, their melody is delightful."

The settlers pushed back the gloom. "Every tree which is cut down in the forest, opens to the sun a new spot of earth, which with cultivation, will produce food for man and beast," wrote Belknap. "As the earth is opened to the sun, many wet places are dried, and brooks contracted, and as the land is more and more cleared, finally streams disappear."

In the town histories the sawmills are the first manmade structures to appear—they precede the churches. The first chapter is often the natural history: the town boundaries, the mountains and ponds. The trees receive a passing mention as the "prevailing arboreal products." No rhapsodies, no praise. The sawmill is the machine that sets a town's history in motion.

The colonists weren't free to cut all the trees. The king of England claimed all pine trees two feet in diameter or more for the Royal Navy. Agents of the king rode the territory looking for trees that could be felled for ship masts. These were marked with the King's Arrow— a four-foot-long inverted v. This claim was frequently ignored. In the Bay Colony at one time, the king's agents had marked 363 trees in Northampton. All but 37 disappeared. There are two New Hampshire "Pine Tree Riots" on record, in Exeter in 1734 and in Weare in 1772. Each time the king's agent was run out of town, a revolutionary spark like the Boston Tea Party.

The felling of a "mast tree" was like a scene from *Gulliver's Travels*, men with axes swinging at a tree the size of an early skyscraper. Straight roads were cut miles into the forest to retrieve a single tree. Many smaller trees were felled to "bed" the mast tree, to cushion its fall. There are accounts of one tree that took fifty-five yoke of oxen to move. That pine was 110 feet long and measured 3 feet in diameter at the *tip*. (Alas, it broke up going over the falls at Amoskeag, and the king's agent fled, saying he was a ruined man.) In Goffstown, New Hampshire, a mast was cut on the farm of George

A. Bell that "was so large that a yoke of 'seven-feet oxen' could be turned with ease upon its stump." The timber was so thick in some parts of Goffstown, that there was no room for a cut tree to fall.

In a few places the mast trees escaped cutting and lived on as landmarks on the horizon—pine trees fifteen feet in diameter, towering over their neighbors until lightning or hurricanes took them. Mostly, succeeding generations were left with forests of large stumps. The old-growth pines were so resistant to rot that their stumps would stand fifty years or more. "The pine stumps used as a fence beside the road part of the way from Parker's ... being the last witnesses of the primeval forest, speak in truthful terms of the gigantic trees they once supported," said the *History of the Town of Goffstown* in 1922. Other old-growth pines were so large that they had to be split with blasting powder before they could be milled.

To "make land" the pioneers cleared trees *en masse*, sometimes in chopping bees, sometimes by one man "driving": cutting through each tree two-thirds of the way, then felling a tree into them—down the lot would come like falling dominoes. One man could fell an acre of trees in a day by "driving." The fallen trees would be left to dry until conditions were ready for a "good burn," usually during the long days of June. The ash was sold as potash and charcoal.

Even after the burn, large logs were left. These were cut up, sometimes in a chopping bee, and the land was burnt once more. On this charred land, the settlers would plant Indian corn.

The fires frequently spread through the forest. The ash from one out-of-control fire in upstate New York blacked out most of northern New England, causing "The Dark Day" of May 19, 1780. At 10 A.M. that day "a peculiar darkness began to close down upon the earth and deepened until it became so intense that a person could not distinguish an object at any distance," reports *The History of Hillsborough, N. H.*, just one of many accounts of the day. "The birds sang their evening songs and flew to their nests in the woods; the domestic fowl hurried to their roosts; the cattle in their clearings made a rush for their stalls, while the sheep huddling together made piteous bleatings. Women and children, and men, too, were frightened, many believing the end of the world had come." The full moon did not rise that night, and many parents sat up, keeping a watch on their children, says the *History of Antrim, N. H.* The terror was not forgotten. Nearly a year later, at Antrim's town meeting, the town voted to observe May 19 as a day of fasting. There were other fires that darkened the sky. One fire in the dry summer of 1761 started in Lebanon, New Hampshire, near the Connecticut River, and burned until it reached the Atlantic Ocean at New Casco, Maine.

In his travels in the Maine woods in the 1850s, Henry David Thoreau witnessed the clearing of the forest. One trail brought Thoreau through "more than a hundred acres of heavy timber, which had just been felled and burnt over, and was still smoking. ... The trees lay at full length, four or five feet deep, and crossing each other in all directions, all black as charcoal, but perfectly sound within, still good for fuel or timber; soon they would be cut into lengths and burnt again. Here were thousands of cords, enough to keep the poor of Boston and New York amply warm for a winter, which only cumbered the ground and were in the settlers way. And the whole of the solid and interminable forest is doomed to be gradually devoured by fire, like shavings. ... "

Invited to supper by a frontiersman, Thoreau remembered the kitchen fire, "which would have roasted an ox; many whole logs, four feet long, were consumed to boil our tea-kettle. ..."

Throughout the new country, the pioneers squandered forests that would have made an English nobleman jealous. Typical of the pioneer attitude was the method for sugaring maple trees. Instead of tapping trees, they would "box" the trees with an axe, opening the tree to disease and, in time, death.

There were always more trees. And new industries were arising to consume them. Before steam engines burned coal, they used a vast quantity of wood. The railroads radiating from Concord, New Hampshire, consumed seventy thousand cords of wood a year in the early 1880s. (As a comparison, a good-sized home of the era burned no more than twenty cords in a winter.) To lay the tracks, chestnut trees were cut for railroad ties.

The railroad opened up new tracts to logging. "Yearly the lumberman presses deeper and deeper into the forest, into more unaccessible localities and farther and farther up steep mountain sides," wrote Dr. Peter L. Hoyt of Wentworth, New Hampshire, in the 1850s. "How long will the old forest growth last with the present yearly consumption is a question often asked."

Exceptionally large trees excited notice, much as large catches are reported in fishing communities. In January 1867, the brothers George and Charles Wright cut down a pine tree believed to be the "oldest inhabitant in town" and the largest tree in New Hampshire's Cheshire County—three hundred years by its rings. The pine stood 121 feet, and at 4 feet from the ground, it measured 18 1/2 feet in circumference. Hauled to Faulkner & Colony's mill in Keene as fourteen logs, the tree contained 9,000 feet of lumber. The Wrights received the considerable sum of $180.

On January 4, 1889, a Keene newspaper reported the felling of a pine tree that measured 4 feet in diameter at the butt and tapered to 23 1/2 inches at the tip. It took several teams of oxen to pull it out of the forest and three flat cars on the railroad to haul it. There are "more left that are larger," said the newspaper.

The North Country of New Hampshire had the largest logging operations. From the 1870s to the First World War, the Connecticut River drive was the biggest annual event in the North Country: "the greatest thing in their lives," as one memoir recalled the dangerous work of riding the logs in the chill March water. In the last year of the drive, 65 million feet of logs were floated.

In Maine, Thoreau noted in 1837 that there were 250 sawmills on the Penobscot above Bangor and many more on the Kennebec, Androscoggin, Saco, Passamaquoddy and other streams. "No wonder that we hear so often of vessels which are becalmed off our coast, being surrounded a week at a time by floating timber from the Maine woods. The mission of men there seems to be, like so many busy demons, to drive the forest all out of the country, from every solitary beaver-swamp and mountain-side, as soon as possible."

By the 1830s European visitors were sending home reports of a barren landscape, houses standing naked in a raw land and forests reduced to a wasteland of slash and stumps. Time and again they said the Americans were in all-out war against trees; each standing tree was an enemy.

In 1810, Tench Coxe had introduced the U.S. Census with a call to cut as many trees as possible. "Our forests cumber a rich soil ... and prevent its cultivation." To clear the land, Americans were called on to build iron works, requiring charcoal, and to make furniture and gunstocks of the walnut and wild cherry, cabinets of the maples, casks of the oak, and of the rest, potash and pearlash, "boards, joists, scantling, shingles, charcoal and ordinary fuel."

Seventy years later, the 1880 census contained a different message: "The American people must learn that a forest, whatever its extent and resources, can be exhausted in a surprisingly short space of time through total disregard in its treatment." The forests of New York could no longer be counted on for lumber; white oak, hickory, ash, elm and other woods were scarce. Pennsylvania had run out of pine to cut, and the hard woods were of poor quality. Ohio and Indiana had almost completely lost their forests and would soon have to import wood. The "entire exhaustion" of the great pine forests of Michigan, Wisconsin and Minnesota, said the 1880 census, "is certain." Another report, delivered just after America had celebrated its first one hundred years, said that Ohio, Indiana and southern Michigan "now have a greater percentage of treeless area than Austria and the North German Empire, which have been settled and cultivated for upward of a thousand years."

∞

For the pioneers of those raw settlements, the gloom had lifted. They had made their land. Houses were surrounded by larger and larger clearings. They could see the sun most of the day and see clear across the valley to their neighbor's house. The old forest was gone, recalled one Michigan settler, and "the light of civilization began to dawn upon us."

How all alone they had been. The forest threatened to swallow up this new America. Town histories recount the desperate searches for children lost in the woods, who died but a few rods from their houses, hearing their parents call out. The woods were full of ghosts and bouts with "His Satanic Majesty." Far from civilization "the silence masters" the pioneer, said one town history. "He sees in each shifting portent a mystery, and reads in each mystery a sign. He peoples the space with invisible images, and so sees unaccountable shapes in the realm of his vision."

They were proud to note the first piano in town, the first clocks; every first pushed back the "gloom," the darkness. Later they celebrated the arrival of the first train, electric light, phonograph, telephone and automobile. Already by the Civil War, with many towns scarcely eighty years old, New Hampshire had cleared half of its land, Connecticut 70 percent.

Once in a clearing, the old religion and superstitions die, the ghosts vanish and the mysteries of the forest recede. As *The History of Weare, N. H.* recorded in 1888: "Ghosts. They were plenty and hundreds of people within the memory of the present generation saw them. Now they have all gone away somewhere and forgotten to come back."

So civilization begins. In Peterborough, New Hampshire, the first settlers arrived between 1739 and 1744 and girdled the first trees. By Peterborough's centennial in 1839, the chief address of the day opened by reminding the townspeople of an utterly different landscape, one rich in moose, bears, deer, wolves, beavers and fish:

> A hundred years ago this whole valley, from mountain to mountain, from the extreme north to the extreme southern limit, was one unbroken forest. The light soil upon the banks of the Contoocook was covered with huge and lofty pines, while the rocky hills and rich loamy lands were shaded with maple, beech and birch, interspersed with ash, elm, hemlock, fir, oak, cherry, bass. ... Bogs and swamps were far more extensive ... and the

woods in many parts, on account of fallen timber and thick underbrush, were almost impassable.

The landscape of 1839 may have fallen from grace, but it would look like a land of bounty to the next generation, forty years later. In 1876, Peterborough's historian described the depleted landscape of a New England growing poor:

> When the first settlers commenced, the land was in its virgin state, and was very productive without much fertilizing or labor; the same is now worn out and nearly worthless.
>
> Many large, productive farms are now so run out that they have been abandoned, and others will be as soon as the present buildings grow tenantless.
>
> It is doubtful if the wood now grows in town as fast as it is consumed, even with a considerable use of hard coal. Almost all wild game has disappeared, having no place of shelter now. The brooks, the home of the trout, have so dried up, with the clearing of the forests, as to afford hardly any retreat for them. We should be thankful that the birds will still remain with us, and accept our planted trees as a substitute for the primeval forests.

How many times have men looked up from the plow and the axe to find that the genius of the place had vanished? Once again the exile from Eden, God silent amid a changed landscape—a manmade landscape, a manscape.

∞

Just a few years after Peterborough's historian described a town of piebald hills, the full force of the machine age entered the woods. With the coming of the portable steam-powered sawmills in the 1880s, stands of trees that had been bypassed were cut down.

The portable mills were locusts, "liable to consume all the trees for a mile or more, every one of them," said one observer in 1883. Worse, the mills destroyed ponds and streams with their sawdust. "Consider that for every thousand feet of lumber sawed, forty bushels of sawdust go into the stream," said the *New Hampshire Fish and Game Report* in 1889. The pools and eddies where fish spawned were "a foul mass of decomposing vegetable matter."

In the town of Washington, New Hampshire, the mills arrived in 1900, ruining many beloved fishing spots. One portable mill in Washington had sawed more lumber than the town's eight stationary mills had sawed twenty-five years earlier. People used to logging were startled by the rapaciousness of these new mills.

The tax laws of New Hampshire were the force sending the mills into the woods. All growing timber was taxable at full market value (until 1949). Private landowners could not afford to let trees stand. All the once-publicly held land was up for grabs as well. In 1867, the state had sold off the last of its timberlands, some 172,000 acres, at 14 1/2 cents an acre.

The land stripped, the streams left for dead, the mills moved on to the next town. In New Hampshire, more timber was cut in 1907 than in any previous year.

Newspapers published pleas to spare roadside shade trees, and around 1900 the town of Washington observed Arbor Day, planting shade trees on town property.

The Arc of Elegy

In the *History of the City of Nashua, N. H.* (1897), there is pictured on one page: "The willows," a dirt road passing through a willow grove, their boughs forming a nave over the road; and on the opposite page, the public buildings: county records, police station and city hall. Each tree was a civic monument, something to be proudly shown off, like fine china, in the town history. When a traveling photographer came to town, he was careful to portray the town's leading trees along with the leading citizens and fine houses. In the *History of Salem, N. H., 1735–1907,* one page has a photograph of "The Rock Maple in Currier Webster Pasture, 13 feet in circumference." On the facing page is an engraving of Eliphalet Coburn.

The trees have an ethereal quality in the old pictures: solid at the trunk, but at the crown ghost-like, more light than leaf. A trick of the camera and the need for a long exposure.

Other trees are accorded a biography in the town's history, like this account of a large elm in the *History of Claremont, N. H.* (1895):

> It was planted by John Hitchcock more than a hundred years ago, is still growing, sound and healthy. A few feet from the ground it is nineteen feet in circumference, very tall, of graceful shape, and its branches cover an area of fully one hundred feet in diameter. Mr. Hitchcock's children watched its growth with much interest as long as they lived, and his grandchildren pay frequent visits to it.

From the centennial year of 1876 to the 1930s, you can trace the great arc of the industrial revolution in the growing celebration of trees. With the fall of country life and the loss of the great eastern forest, trees are honored in poems and stories; people band together for the sole purpose of planting shade trees, and a national arbor day arises in the 1870s from the plains of Nebraska.

As the *History of Ashburnham, Mass.* said succinctly in 1886: "To subdue a forest was the mission of the early settlers of Ashburnham. The planting and care of shade trees is an impulse of succeeding generations."

We began to recast ourselves as a country of trees, the friendly towns in maple shade, the parks of elms—so many, many elm cities. The forest was dead. Long live the forest.

In the villages and cities, trees led a different life. In Keene, a large elm tree stood in the way of traffic on one of the city's busier streets. An old postcard shows West Street bowing around the Cooke Elm and continuing under an arch of trees. In 1867 Keene was indicted for allowing the elm to stand, creating a hazard. At town meeting, the citizens voted unanimously to "protect and defend" the tree. That was the same year that the largest tree in the county, a three-hundred-year-old pine, had been sawed into 9,000 feet of lumber at a mill just a few blocks away. That was also the year that New Hampshire sold the last of its timberlands.

The people of Keene hung on to the Cooke Elm for nearly fifty more years. The road was widened, trolleys ran by, but they refused to part with the elm—it was the subject of an impassioned debate in 1901. Finally, in 1914, when the city prepared to lay brick paving, the Cooke Elm—140 years old—was cut down. In the forest, a tree such as the Cooke Elm would have been just so many board feet.

The town trees were the sacred cows lounging near the slaughterhouse door. Taken one at a time, trees were honored; in a new village, a large tree was antiquity, older than the nation itself. Taken as a woodlot, they were harvested. The two views toward "arboreal products" were held concurrently.

In the *History of Lancaster, N. H.* (1889) there is a poem and photograph of "The Old Willow." The tree "stood in front of the Lancaster House and was the pride of the village. It was killed by the burning of that hotel Sept. 27 1878 and was cut down Jan. 27 1881. This was the last of a row of Lombardy Poplars and willows that Judge Richard C. Everett, the grandfather of Nellie W. Cross, had set out … about the year 1800." And there is a poem by Nellie W. Cross honoring her grandfather's tree:

Graceful willow, tall and stately,
    Queen of all our village trees,
Taking May's sweet bloom, sedately
    Swaying in the gentle breeze;
What a tale your leaves might flutter. …

The poem continues, bringing to mind the medieval European belief that trees sheltered the souls of one's ancestors. A few chapters later in the history, the Reverend George H. Tilton is lamenting the destruction of Lancaster's forest primeval "for mere greed of gain." But then the reverend says, "These primaeval pines grew to an enormous size, and if standing to-day would be worth a vast fortune to their owners." Utility & Loss. The Paradise of Utility, the sacred grove as lumberyard.

The *History of Charlestown, N. H.* (1876) praises the hometown:

178

> The places are few which are rendered more beautiful by their shade trees than the lower part of Main Street, in Charlestown, by its "Great Elms"; and these *magnificent* trees ... have not only added thousands of dollars to the value of its real estate, but which in addition have been *invaluable* in the comforts they have brought to more than two generations, who have walked or sat beneath their shade.

The double view again. Always the double view. God grant us paradise, but also a real estate assessor to put a value on it.

The History of Hillsborough looks back from 1921 to wistfully imagine the settlers deep in the New Hampshire forest of 1738. The river "tumbling, foaming, roaring in between and over huge bowlders, with the banks overhung with lichen-covered bushes bare of leaves but tasseled with white and yellow fringes of last summer's foliage, back from the banks' majestic pines and lordly oaks, graceful elms and wide spreading maples, little wonder if they stood with uncovered heads for sometime in silence."

This is a long way from the "gloomy appearance of the American forest" reported in the earliest *History of New-Hampshire*. Or is it? Much later in the Hillsborough history, after a short account of witches (basically old women who were under suspicion for living alone), the historian says: "There were other reputed witches in this vicinity. ...But it is not a pleasant phase of life, though this delusion ... exists today with the human race; always will, till man's mind is freed of the grossness of earth."

The grossness of the earth? Which is it? Majestic pines, lordly oaks, water roaring, a paradise, or the grossness of earth? Will we ever decide?

∞

Reading these town histories, one sees the rise of an elegiac voice. The elegies, a whisper in the 1880s, have by the eve of the First World War become a lament for everything that was once despised: the rank forest and the "savages." The elegies rise up in an arc that mirrors the rise of the industrial revolution.

179

As the laments grow, the golden era moves farther and farther back in time. The *History of Hudson, N. H.* (1913) pauses to imagine how the region appeared two-and-a-half centuries ago. A romance of Indian life is sketched.

> Upon the shady banks beneath the giant trees of the primeval forest … he reared the conical walls of his regal wigwam, watched the talking smoke of his council fires and … caught the salmon, shad, alewives and eels in almost countless numbers.
>
> Since then what a change the white man has wrought. The woodsman's ax, with the help of fire, long since leveled the beautiful original forest. The dams have stopped the migrations of the fish. …The game had mainly fled.
>
> Let us drop a tear of pity upon the ashes of this race whose representatives welcomed the Englishmen to their wild shore, and preserved them when famine was at their door:—those sons of the forest, though savages, possessing many of the most worthy and noble traits of character.

The imaginary scenes of the vanished New World grow in detail until there is an apparent hunger by some writers to will themselves back into the "forest primeval."

In the 1930s, the authors of the *History of the Town of Jaffrey, N. H.*, detail the great mast trees that were cut there and locate in the landscape a ruin worthy of their imagination; acres of large pine tree stumps, cut in deep winter snow, four or five feet feet from the ground: "The rough bark had fallen away and many of them had decayed to mere shells, whitened by sun and rain, suggesting gravestones of a departed titanic race." These tree stumps are their Tintern Abbey, the romantic ruin of a nobler era.

After ranging over the township, describing even a forest of stumps, the authors turn to a grove of memory in a passage full of longing:

> The last stronghold of the ancient forest in Jaffrey was the Town Farm Lot, No. 20 in the 3rd range of lots. … It should have been preserved as the redwood forests of California have been

preserved, as something more beautiful, if less ancient and sublime, than they. It should have been preserved as the old cathedrals of Europe have been preserved, as Nature's temple with architecture beyond comparison with the greatest works of man. It should have been preserved ... as an example of Nature's finest gift to the people of New England, unappreciated until too late, and now lost.

A few people remember the Town Farm Lot, but not one has the gift to describe it in its beauty and grandeur. It was a vast arboretum of one hundred acres bearing nearly every variety of tree and shrub common to its latitude ... with pines and spruces and hardwoods intermingled in Nature's way, with corridors, colonnades, chambers, and cloisters that no architect planned, opening one into another, by winding ways, each differing from the other, the product of ages when Nature was undisturbed and centuries of no account. ... There were openings in the roof through which the sunlight filtered down to illumine, one after another, the towering tree trunks and to play upon the forest floor. ... The air was sweet with pleasant odors, and always in summer there was the minstrelsy of insect and bird in harmony with the scene. And there was that without which no forest is at its best, a tiny brook, nowhere else so clean and cool as in New England, winding its way like a silver thread to guide the wanderer through its untracked labyrinth. ... It lived a charmed existence until 1899, when it was sold to a lumber company from Massachusetts, and was one of the first in Jaffrey to fall before the invasion of the portable sawmill. In a year this masterpiece of the ages was destroyed, leaving behind only a waste of bushes and briers.

The uses of elegy are many. To these laments we owe the village improvement societies—by 1870 there were two hundred in New England alone—and a national arbor day, which made the barren towns bloom. To plant a tree was a blessing upon the world, it was said.

The American elm was the queen of all the trees, "the glory of New England." America claimed the elm, planting cities and towns, parks and campuses with some 77 million of them. Pioneers packed potted elms into wagons on the westward trek. No American place was without its Elm Street. To mark the centennial, President Grant traveled to Lexington, Massachusetts—"The Birthplace of American Liberty"—and planted an elm on the Green.

The elm is a storybook tree, praised for its vase-like shape and the way rows of elms branch out, forming a cathedral nave over streets. "Nothing finer has been given us and nothing finer could be wished for," said one former dean of a forestry college.

And then in a lifetime, the achievements of so many village planting programs began to vanish. Dutch elm disease was striking down rows and rows of the old trees. In a wink, towns stood as barren under the sun as in the settlers' time.

No one understood this new disease. When Dutch elm first appeared in Holland in 1919, it was thought that the disease had been loosed upon Europe from the mustard gas of World War I. This theory was poor science, but as an allegory for evil it was perfect. From Flanders Field, from the Somme, from the trenches, the veterans were returning home, some disfigured for life. The evils of the war had come home, sifting and seeping into those once safe homes.

The trees were dying. The old order was dying. Farewell comfort in the shade, farewell trees that our mothers' mothers had known. The world was to be different. The long peace was ended. The next war wouldn't be hidden in the trenches. It would take the proud old trees and the houses beneath them and the families inside.

The Groves of Memory

The memory of trees is green and unfocused, an everywhere-at-once green from the days of summer youth. I have been touring the forests of the memory house. I have been walking in groves a century or more gone. The great trees of yesterday, do they grow greener in our memory? Are we talking about our own childhood when we talk of tall trees?

In *A History of Nelson, N. H.*, Dr. Alfred Morgan Struthers remembers a grove of tall evergreens:

> That was Nelson for me at my youngest. This was the dark, cool, friendly but awesome and impressive contact with Nelson I felt. This was where the men folks gathered boughs for the women making balsam pillows at Arcady. This was where, as youngsters, my brothers and I would go exploring, venturing so far from home and safety, investigating every quiet shadow, before scooting across moss and needles for some spruce gum. ... Then, about ten years ago, the trees, so vital to my woods, were removed and I had only my memory.

In another New Hampshire town, the memories of childhood helped save a tree. Around 1800, the Academy in New Ipswich, New Hampshire, bought the old Methodist Church and planned to move it up the road to add to their building. But there was one obstacle: an old oak tree would have to be cut down. "Mr. William Preston, with his reverence for the old landmark, felt that such a sacrilege should not be allowed and he at once purchased the tree ... giving it to the children of the district school nearby," says *The History of New Ipswich* (1852). "Some years ago an expert estimated the age of the tree to be more than 250 years, thus making it our oldest inhabitant.

"The Children's Oak! may its beauty continue for other centuries."

The sentiment that preserved the Children's Oak had become by the mid-nineteenth century a small commodity: memories of New England bygones. The essayist Oliver Wendell Holmes traveled the circuit, vending such memories.

Speaking in New York on "Country Life in New England," Holmes evokes an image of barefoot boys rambling on crooked paths across pastures, stealing apples from their favorite trees and then wandering through

> the woods where sweet fern breathed its fragrance and the bayberry repeated it. ... O, the remembrance of the early days

183

passed amidst these holy scenes!—of tumbling in long grass, and sucking of honeyed clover, and burrowing in mountainous haycocks and climbing elbowed trees; of waking to the clamor of twittering swallows, and sleeping at the curfew of purring crickets ... of the chestnut tree that dropped its burs at the first frost ... of the sweet music that is in the open air from the days when you hear the soft breathing of the cows as they crop the tender grass. ...

And on Holmes rhapsodizes through the fall and winter. "If you were born and bred among such sights and sounds as these, they will never die out of your remembrance," he says. The child of New England going forth, is fortified against the evils of the world. Nature "gives him lessons of beauty no counting-room can smother with its ledgers; it gives his soul a horizon no lines of warehouses can so wall in that he will not see its blue heavens through them ... let him tread the grass for fifteen summers, and then plod the pavement for forty years, and his dream will still be of running barefoot among the clover."

New England, in this view, is paradise and the city is exile. But this, too, is an Eden born of the broad axe. This is a pastoral, English conception of nature—nature with the proper manners for a Sunday tea. "Nature not wholly rough and uncultivated," Holmes writes, as it is on the frontier "with the unsightly ruins of forest ... but nature subdued and humanized, without being deprived of its greenness and fragrance."

Holmes, in his guise as the *Autocrat of the Breakfast-Table,* comes close to tree worship. "I want you to understand, in the first place, that I have a most intense, passionate fondness for trees in general, and have had several romantic attachments to certain trees in particular," he writes. "I have as many tree-wives as Brigham Young has human ones." He would journey for miles on the rumor of a great ancient tree. And he always brought his tape measure. "I always tremble for a celebrated tree when I approach it for the first time."

Holmes was particularly transfixed by the American elm—"a great green cloud swelling in the horizon." Before mighty elms he had bowed his head "and could without shame have knelt and kissed the turf at their feet. ... " Elms were the first signs of this green earth his "infant eyes" saw from his "birth chambers," he says.

"I wish somebody would get us up the following work: *Sylva Novanglica—Photographs of New England Elms and other Trees, taken upon the Same Scale of Magnitude.* ..." Thirty years later, a photographer granted his wish.

Typical Elms and Other Trees of Massachusetts is an oversized volume, slipcased. There are maybe forty trees portrayed, one to a page. The book itself is scarcely in this world. When they bring it forth each time at the Boston Public Library, a little more of it falls away in small, yellow flakes, the color of oak or beech leaves in autumn. There is an Oliver Wendell Holmes essay in the front, and the old autocrat's pages are torn most of the way through. The photos are crisp, black and white, and again there is the vagueness of light up in the crowns of the trees, the kind of light always shown in biblical illustrations of heaven. This "biography of distinguished trees" is a perfect memory house of tall tree America, a fading, decaying book of trees gone by.

Inspired and guided by the autocrat, a photographer canvassed the state for large trees, determined to photograph them all on a comparative scale. No less than seven times he was informed of an elm that was the largest in the state or even the nation.

This is a book of high elegy; each tree photographed is a funeral monument to the forests that once surrounded it. "The axe of the woodman has done its work so well that few are aware what stalwart proportions our native trees attain," writes the book's author, Lorin L. Dame. "Napoleon deflected his great military road across the Simplon to save an ancient cypress; we cut them down to straighten a country street," she writes in the preface.

The book opens with the Washington Elm in Cambridge, Massachusetts—"the most honored of American trees living or dead." The photograph shows the Washington Elm standing in the middle of a street, surrounded by a fence and fronted by a monument. Washington is a fabulous invalid: branches are broken off, others are braced. This is a tree you would not stand near on a windy day.

185

In its day, great claims were made for the age of the Washington Elm; the tree conferred the blessings of antiquity and continuity on the young republic. But, the book says, it was probably no older than two hundred years when photographed, having had its start in the 1670s. There were bigger trees and there were older trees, and there were even—it is implied—more beautiful trees. (So it is with most patriotic shrines—there are much better houses than Mount Vernon.)

But there are no trees that are more important. There is no doubt that Washington took command of the Continental Army under this very tree. A "venerable Mrs. Moore," who had lived in a house opposite the elm, was an eyewitness to the event and seventy-five years later, in 1848, was still "describing the glories of the occasion."

"Fathers who were eyewitnesses standing beneath this tree, have told the story to their sons, and those sons have not yet passed away. There is no possibility that we are paying our vows at a counterfeit shrine."

Tree worship merges neatly with ancestor worship: it is the tree that is ennobled and "honored by the presence of Washington." (Other trees in the volume have to make it on beauty alone, such as an elm in East Watertown, Massachusetts, "that has not had the good fortune to be associated with any stirring historical event, having passed, like most trees and men, an uneventful existence.") "When Washington drew his sword beneath the branches, the great elm, thus distinguished above its fellows, passed at once into history."

And so this elm was honored; people came to gather leaves and wood from this shrine; Longfellow wrote an inscription for a granite tablet in front of the tree. On the one hundredth anniversary of Washington assuming command, July 3, 1875, the tree was decorated with the American flag atop and "hung with a profusion of smaller flags. ... Never a tree received a more enthusiastic ovation."

Other trees in the book are also honored for their particular patriotic lessons: Under an elm at Rocky Nook in Hingham, men marching off to battle in the War of 1812 halted and "listened to a sermon on the duties of the hour. ... May we not, with the lively imagination of the ancient Greek believe that the tree—native

American in root and branch—was no indifferent spectator of the scene; that some occult influence emanating there from, fired the preacher with patriotic eloquence." (Why are we always dragging flora and fauna into our battles?)

For all the towering trees in full vigor, these photographs are still death masks. Each tree is nearing the end of its life. The American elm in particular is a fragile tree, a hothouse flower. Even Holmes has to admit that the great trees he had visited thirty years before—his many tree wives—have since died.

Writing in 1890, Lorin Dame is sure that there will be other great trees:

> Fifty years hence most of the elms figured in this volume, it is likely, will have become ... the wrecks and memorials of a stately past ... but there will never be a dearth of noble trees. Thrifty elms of seventy-five to a hundred years old, ranging from nine to fifteen feet in girth, are scattered in favorable situations over the State. These will, in turn, put on a mien of sovereignty and receive the homage of men.

A trip to see if any of these great elms, chestnuts and oaks have somehow survived would be a sorry journey indeed. I can't decide if it would be a journey marked for a modern sensibility of loss or a Victorian one of melancholy.

Perhaps one arbor day, the people of the Commonwealth of Massachusetts could replant each tree and leave instructions for the *Typical Elms of Massachusetts* to be photographed again in a century's time.

I open the book for one last look. Here is the Society Oak in Charlemont: "Under its shade the old men of to-day, when schoolboys sixty years ago, ate their dinner at noontide; and under the same sheltering branches those from the vicinity who are still living gather their families once a year. ... " I close the book, slide it into the slipcase and sweep the table clean.

∞

I close the book and journey to a forest that is part way between existence and memory. In the southwestern corner of New Hampshire are twenty acres of virgin hemlocks and white pine, a small patch of land living untouched, as if the Europeans had never arrived. There is one problem though; most of the trees are lying on the ground, blown down in the great hurricane of 1938.

I go to see the trees with a group of about twenty others. It is a hike of eight miles or so, part of it just bushwhacking up Chestnut Hill. Everyone has heard of this stand of trees, and I wonder what to expect. The tall pine cut in 1889—the one that took up three railroad flat cars—came from the same area.

Up and over the hill, some scrambling through a bog, and there are the trees; fifty years after the hurricane, they lie facing northwest, moss growing on them, some trunks going soft, caving into an outline of themselves, other trunks strong enough to walk on. You can still see where the roots pulled out of the earth. Amazing: Half a century later, and you can still see the violence of the storm.

There are three live trees left. We gather around one and stand looking up at a pine tree perhaps one hundred feet tall, maybe three times as tall as what stood around it. A tree untouched since the white men had been here. There it was. A keyhole glimpse of the "forest primeval." From the vast eastern forest down to three trees here and maybe a handful tucked in other spots of New England.

We talk about how the great pines were taken for ship masts, and we talk about Thoreau's three journeys into the Maine woods: "It was 1850, and he couldn't find an untouched, virgin stand of forest," our guide says.

As we hike out, I ask a man next to me what he thought of these tall trees. "Eh, I've seen bigger trees at Lake———," he said. I didn't catch the name. He had driven from a place about an hour and a half away to see these trees. It wasn't really worth the hike, he said. Those surviving trees were no more special than any of the other large pines we were walking past.

I think we had come to be awed. Instead, the site had the quiet dignity of a Japanese rock garden; here was the memory of a forest, more hints, more work for the imagination.

⌒

The forests of northern New England stretch from the Maine woods, across the North Country of New Hampshire, the Northeast Kingdom of Vermont and into the Adirondacks of New York State—26 million acres, almost all second-growth forest and most of the pure lakes and rivers remaining in the eastern United States. It has been logged for centuries, but modern avarice may make the past logging practices look like temperance.

One summer I follow U.S. Highway 1 to where it begins at the top of the country: Fort Kent, Maine, a small town right at the Canadian border. Its treeless Main Street is the first mile of U.S. 1, which runs south for another 2,208 miles to Key West, Florida. The nearest interstate falls short one hundred miles south of here, and the ice leaves the lakes and ponds in the first weeks of May. On the map of Aroostook County—a county larger than Connecticut and Rhode Island combined—most of the roads are the private property of logging companies. Logging is the biggest industry in the region. Up here when a logging truck roars past, it leaves a wake of pine scent you can smell for miles down the road.

Leroy Martin knows the Allagash Wilderness of the county well. As a boy he traveled the woods with his father. Three generations of his family have worked in the forest. Martin runs the Up North Company, lumber contractors, and employs forty people.

He stands in front of a floor-to-ceiling topographical map in his office, which shows the logging territory in fading greens, and says, "The forest is not what it used to be. When I was a boy with my father we used to come to the end of the road. Now they're all connected. The forest is shrinking."

And it is shrinking at a disturbing rate, he says. In the last few years foresters have been aggressively clear-cutting with a new generation of huge machinery. Everything is clear-cut, even the wood that is not marketable. In five years, an area nearly the size of Rhode Island has been clear-cut in the Maine woods. Selective cutting, taking only certain trees and returning in other years to select others, has all but ceased.

The loggers are in a race with spruce bud worm disease, Martin says, and it's "cut it or lose it." Landowners are afraid of losing timber to the disease, so they have contractors come in five to ten years earlier than what used to be standard practice.

His grandfather logged with horses; these days Martin uses skidders to drag the timber out of the woods, and delimbers—big machines that shear the branches off a tree. But these are not the biggest machines in the forest now. The big operators are using feller-bunchers, six-ton machines that grab a tree in their jaws and snap it off. If H. G. Wells had envisioned modern lumbering equipment for *The War of the Worlds*, it would have looked like this. After the land is clear-cut, they bring in stump crushers—big rollers that pound the stumps into the ground. One study of a clear-cut showed that half of the forest species had not recovered after eighty-seven years. Most land is cut every twenty-five to sixty-five years.

"Twenty ... twenty-five years ago, we thought we'd never run out of wood to cut," Martin says. They are facing a shortage of "high-grade trees": trees with trunks ten inches and up.

As I listen, I think of Thoreau's journey 130 years earlier and the rivers choked with logs five feet in diameter—unheard of today. Thoreau had come to the Maine woods looking for true wilderness. He found men working like demons to clear the forest. In the 1980s land-eating was going on faster and faster just to feed short-term debts.

"We certainly don't have a healthy forest," says Martin. "I can remember as a young boy walking through the forest, everything was green. We have a very sick forest. You wouldn't have to be a forester to see that. It's not green with life like it used to be."

∞

In those old postcards from the era before the Great War, the tall trees arch over Commonwealth Avenue in Boston, over all the Elm, Maple, Oak and Chestnut streets. But in the auto age the great trees gave way to blight and disease, pavement and neglect. And worse, we have forgotten that once our cities bloomed.

In Boston, landscape architect Frederick Law Olmsted laid out a chain of parks he called the Emerald Necklace. In 1890 one could walk, without leaving these parks, from the State House, across the common and public garden and out for miles to the Arnold Arboretum. The Emerald Necklace has long since come undone, part of it gone for roads and expressway ramps. The same story is repeated across the country. In Philadelphia, Detroit and Dayton in 1970, for example, more trees were cut down than were planted. In Atlanta, a city that celebrates its dogwood bloom, the metropolitan area loses fifty acres of trees a day, the *New York Times* reported in 1989. An environmental impact statement for a proposed highway didn't even consider the trees. In New York City, highway median strips are counted as part of the city's park and playground acreage.

It takes more than forty years for a shade tree to mature, but the average shade tree survives only ten years in the city. Our trees live in a Sahara of paving, locked into a small spot; their soil is compacted and becomes salty from dog urine and road salt. On some streets they are overheated and grow into stunted desert forms; on others they die from too much water trapped in their small bowl of earth. On still other streets they live in a constant windstorm, caught in the downdrafts from skyscrapers. They are poisoned by gas-line leaks and bus exhaust or knocked over by cars. The trees that survive are often dwarfed, reaching only a fraction of the size of a less stressed tree.

"The street tree is an endangered species," writes Anne Whiston Spirn in *The Granite Garden*. Dutch elm disease took cities by surprise, she says; "the current gradual, but inexorable, decline of urban trees is taking place over a longer period of time, but will eventually yield the same result."

Throughout the century the roster of tree epidemics has grown: chestnut blight, Dutch elm disease, maple decline, beech tree disease, a new palm tree illness, a new elm disease. The forests in the East, from Maine to Alabama, are showing a broad decline; several evergreen species are growing 20 to 30 percent more slowly than in the past. On Mount Mitchell in North Carolina, the highest peak on the East Coast, virtually no plant life is reproducing. There are stands of dead fir and red spruce trees. Heavy-metal concentrations are twenty-five times normal conditions. No one knows if the cause is ozone, acid rain, sulfur or nitrogen pollution, climatic change. …

Trees are the canaries in the mines.

∞

We have lost tall tree America more than once, and we are losing it today. In every American's lifetime, America is unmade anew.

Helen Butler, a native of Syracuse, New York, remembers when that city, in the 1950s, was covered by one-hundred-year-old elms: "They were just gorgeous. You would walk down streets—Oxford Street, I can always remember. And they have—they had—tulip trees and they were under the elms. And in blossom it would be a sight to go down that street. The elms made archways over the street and the sun would shine through and on a day that was very bright, especially in the fall when the leaves were beginning to turn yellow—you know and dry up and go—it was almost golden going through that street. Just to look down it, just like gold. Oh, many streets, many. …"

The Divine Elm. The Green Tree. The Justice Elm. We are left with the names. The Pride of the State. The Preston Elm. The Children's Oak. …

Just like gold. So many trees. Oh, so many.

The Shrinking of
the Grand Monadnoc

Thou Art All Grandeur!

From her home in the village of Ashburnham, Massachusetts, Elsie Kibling Miller had a clear view of Mount Monadnock, a dozen miles away. Sometime in 1850 she wrote:

> Monadnoc! proud in thy sublimity!
> On thee I gaze, as I have ever gazed,
> Till my heart swells with rapture and delight.

"Thee I love," she continued. "And ever shall while memory endures. .... Thou art all grandeur!"

From her home near the base of the mountain, in Jaffrey, New Hampshire, Mary Belle Fox wrote this poem, which was read at the town's centennial in 1873:

> Grand mayst thou seem to strangers' eyes,
> And strangers' tongues thy praises sing;
> We hold thee in our memories,
> And love thee like a human thing.

From Concord, Massachusetts, Henry David Thoreau looked out some thirty miles to Monadnock and the Peterborough Hills "and the great gap" just south of them: "Humble as these mountains are compared with some, yet at this distance I am convinced they answer the purpose of the Andes; and seen in the horizon, I know of nothing more grand and stupendous than this great mountain gate or pass. ..."

"Those grand and glorious mountains, how impossible to remember daily that they are there, and to live accordingly!" wrote Thoreau. "They are meant to be a perpetual reminder to us, pointing out the way."

The Grand Monadnoc beckoned. From its summit, you could see all six New England states. "Centre of awe, raised over all that man / Would fain enjoy ... ," wrote Thoreau's friend, William Ellery Channing. Timothy Dwight, first president of Yale, saw Monadnock from Mount Holyoke and pronounced it in 1796 "the richest prospect in New England, and not improbably in the United States." Nathaniel Hawthorne in his travels in western Massachusetts looked on Monadnock as "a sapphire cloud against the sky." Bostonians viewed Monadnock from the Bunker Hill Monument. For captains at sea, it was the first promise of landfall. And Ralph Waldo Emerson, in a long and celebrated poem of the era, *Monadnoc* (1847), gave the mountain a literary pedigree so that James Russell Lowell could call it "our most highbred of mountains," as if he were describing a proper Boston family.

In the time of first settlement around Monadnock, after the Revolution, it was too early for verse. In a "region of rocks and woods and wolves" the town of Jaffrey regarded the mountain within its borders as a hardship. It was "not habitable"; it was "waste land."

The last wolf in the region was slain in the winter of 1819–1820, and a wildness went out of the world. From their cleared fields and hard-won village greens, people now admired the Grand Monadnoc; it was sublime, it was "unhandselled." Monadnoc was the wilderness—at the right distance, powerful, but welcoming enough for a Sunday's berry picking. "It stirs the depths of man by its sublimity but does not oppress his sensibilities with terror or dread," said a later history of Jaffrey.

The mountain was a prized antique—an "antique brownish-gray Ararat color," said Thoreau. "The color of things that endure ... color of Egyptian ruins, of mummies and all antiquity. ...." From before the Civil War to after the Great War, local parsons and visiting poets looked to the mountain and wrote essentially the same poem: Faced with Monadnock, man is small, time is long:

The tallest monuments of human pride
Crumble away like anthills.
(1846, Rindge, New Hampshire)

His head is quite bald, and has been growing gray
Since Adam and Eve saw the light of the day.
(1852, Walpole, New Hampshire)

When Earth forgets that man was born,
Monadnoc still shall hail the morn,
His aged crags not yet outworn.
(1888, Lowell, Massachusetts)

Fore-elder, thou, of simpler, saner days,
When God meant prayer, and Fatherland meant praise.
(1895)

O lonely monarch! Solitary Throne! (1895)

Queen of the Air, thou spirit whispering Soft. (1905)

Speak to us, O, mountain vast. (1907)

Before there was in Egypt any sound ...
You loomed above ancestral evergreens ...

And when the last of us, if we know how,
See farther from ourselves than we do now,
Assured with other sight than heretofore
That we have done our mortal best and worst,—

Your calm will be the same as when the first
Assyrians went howling south to war.
(Edwin Arlington Robinson, 1921)

Centre of awe. Monadnock was vast. Rising just over three thousand feet, it would be lost in almost any mountainous country, a foothill, but here it stood alone. A small vastness. To the people living in its shadow, it contained the world. *Thou art all grandeur.* News came of grander places: Niagara Falls, even the White Mountains in the north—but it was the rare villager who would see them. In the early settlement days, a carriage journey from Boston to New Ipswich, New Hampshire, would take a wearying fourteen hours, departing Boston before first light at 4 A.M. and arriving in time for dinner, 6 P.M. The railroad arrived in 1847, bringing visitors like Thoreau, but the towns around Monadnock remained a place apart. (Today Boston is less than two hours by car, and in one school near Monadnock, when children made oaktag posters of foreign countries, one was of "Club Med.")

Monadnock was the villagers' companion. They watched the weather on "his mist-encircled brow." "In the soft beauty of a moonlit summer's evening, [I] was charmed with the pure light of the flaming, storied carbuncle." They wrote fables about the courtship of Wachusett Mountain by Mount Monadnock and at town centennials toasted "him" with ringing orations:

> His very name strikes a chord within me, that vibrates as to the sound of grand and solemn music. ... I have visited mountains more known to fame, I have stood on higher elevations; but from no point have I found the view so satisfactory—uniting so much of grandeur, beauty, variety and extent—as from the brow of old Monadnock. I hail him King of Mountains! May his shadow never be less!

∞

"That New Hampshire bluff," wrote Thoreau, "will longest haunt our dreams." He made four journeys to the mountain, one in August

1860, when he camped for a week near the summit, enthusiastically recording plants, rocks, insects, birds, quadrupeds and man.

Departing from the train in Troy, Thoreau and his friend Channing "crossed the immense rocky and springy pastures, containing at first raspberries but much more hardhack in flower reddening them from afar, where cattle and horses collected about us. ... Cattle young and old, with horns in all stages of growth; young heifers with budding horns; and horses with a weak sleepy-David look, though sleek and handsome. They gathered around us while we took shelter under a black spruce from the rain."

From the summit, they looked out on a peaceful land of pastures. "We heard no sound of man except the railroad whistle, and on Sunday, a church-bell." At sunset, they watched the valley below as "the labors of the day were brought to an end, the sheep began to bleat, the doors were closed, the lamps were lit. ... " On some evenings they would hear a cock "crow very shrilly" and the lowing of cows as Thoreau and his friend settled down for the night, under the shelter he had built of pine boughs.

At night they would have the mountain to themselves, but by day the summit belonged to picnickers and berry-picking parties. Going out before sunrise to gather blueberries, Thoreau was "surprised to hear the voices of people rushing up the mountain for berries in the wet. ..."

One afternoon he counted forty people at the summit and figured that "certainly more than one hundred ascended in a day."

When you got within thirty rods you saw them seated in a row along the gray parapets like inhabitants of a castle on a gala-day. ... They appeared to be chiefly mechanics and farmers' boys and girls from the neighboring towns. The young men sat in rows with their legs dangling over the precipice, squinting through spy-glasses and shouting and hallooing to each new party that issued from the woods below. Some were playing cards; others were trying to see their house or their neighbor's. Children were running about and playing as usual. Indeed, this peak in pleasant weather is the most trivial place in New England. ... Several were busily engraving their names on the rocks with cold chisels, whose incessant clink you heard, and they had but little leisure to look off. The mountain was not free of them from sunrise to sunset. ...

These Sunday picnickers left behind eggshells and chicken bones, bits of newspaper and the yarrow seeds they tracked up on their boots. But even so, Thoreau was able to find on Monadnock "parts of nature ... still peculiarly unhandselled and untracked," a terrain of solitude and mystery, "a place wild enough."

For a long time this was how people came to the mountain. Some came to write poetry, some to write their names, some to berry pick and a few to dance. "An old Concord farmer tells me that he ascended Monadnock once, and danced on the top," says Thoreau. "How did that happen? Why, he being up there, a party of young men and women came up, bringing boards and a fiddler; and, having laid down the boards, they made a level floor, on which they danced to the music of the fiddle."

Farmers began to take in a few guests, and the guests returned faithfully. The farmers fixed up the old ells on their houses, added on rooms, and the first small inns started around the mountain. Guests stayed for the summer. They gathered wild blueberries and mountain cranberries, climbed to the summit at sunrise and sunset, went picnicking, and laid out trails with romantic names like Fairy Spring, Dingle Dell and What Cheer Point. They wrote letters home praising the healthful mountain air and good, fresh, farm food and, after dinner, sat on the porch enjoying the prospect.

Two women, adventurously traveling on their own by horse and phaeton in 1873 found a Sunday repose: "The next day was Sunday, and a lovelier day never dawned. The peculiar Sunday quiet pervaded the very atmosphere, and we sat on the rocks reading, writing and musing all day, enjoying such a season of rest as one seldom experiences."

And so time passed in the nineteenth century. The country expanded, new wonders were found. What was Monadnock when compared with Yosemite? No longer "the richest prospect in the United States."

The Grand Monadnoc was part of a now vanished pantheon of the young nation's natural wonders: the sublime Hudson River, mighty Niagara Falls and the spectacular gorge of the Delaware Water Gap. The Hudson River is still beautiful but does not appear to be a chasm of light and mystery between the bluffs; Niagara Falls has been shrunk to a souvenir ashtray; and the Delaware Water Gap is now spanned by an ordinary bridge on Interstate 80. Few notice. What is the Delaware Water Gap when compared with the Grand Canyon?

New places beckoned. New England emptied out, houses fell into cellar holes, the forest overtook the pastures. Then New England filled up again. People returned, fixed some houses, built many new ones, and when they looked to Monadnock, they did not write poems.

After Berry Picking

America grew great and powerful. Her workers could jet or drive anywhere during their two-week vacations. They came to love the natural wonders—the ones in Kodachrome in the *National Geographic*.

In the Kodachrome age, Mount Monadnock shrank. It was Ararat brown, antiquity, sublime. The Grand Monadnoc shrank before the Rockies and the Caribbean islands. New England, too, shrank, from claiming to be the hub of the universe, the Athens of America, the storybearer of our history, to a region with just 5 percent of the U.S. population.

The new traveler wanted neon and chrome. He wanted to be here tonight and 250 miles farther the next day. The new vacation was about motion more than place: getting the maps, gassing up the car, going.

The inns and "mountain houses" around Monadnock began to close. The regulars were loyal, returning each summer well into their eighties. But it was a like a dying religion; there were few new converts. In another era, recalls Margery Shattuck, people were "happier to stay in one place than they are today." In the 1930s Shattuck had married into a family that ran a mountain inn.

The Shattuck Inn was typical of the small mountain hotels. The Shattucks were farmers who took in a few boarders as early as 1868. In the years after the railroad arrived in Jaffrey, they added an ell, then a third story to the house, bringing the capacity to seventy-five guests. Cottages added in the 1890s brought that number to a hundred. In the midst of adding another addition in 1909 there was a fire. The inn reopened the following year and two years later doubled in size, so the Shattucks could accommodate two hundred guests.

All the food was grown on the Shattuck farm, and it was said that Mrs. Shattuck would serve no vegetable over an hour old. The inn closed in 1952, early in the frozen-food era. For twenty years it served as a Catholic seminary and later as home to a group of charismatic Christians. Eventually the building fell apart.

In the mid-1980s along came two men who wanted to recreate the Shattuck Inn but on today's terms. The inn and its view of the mountain weren't enough. To attract guests they "needed more oomph," in the words of the managing partner, Ed Pittman.

That oomph was a golf course, swimming pool, tennis courts and 356 condominiums. The proposed Shattuck Inn Resort was far and away the largest project ever in the region, and it was taking place right near the entrance of the state park, in a landscape that had been declared a National Landmark. The condos and golf course abutted land that over one hundred years had been carefully marshaled and conserved. On a map, the four-hundred-acre project dwarfed its neighbor, historic Jaffrey Center. If completed as proposed, the resort would increase Jaffrey's population by nearly one-quarter. It was a development matched in scale only by a proposed mall in the city of Keene, bearing the unfortunate name of the Monadnock Mall.

It would be easy if Ed Pittman were a villain: the standard bulldozer-eager developer who gives progress pep talks at Rotary luncheons and finds romance in statistics about the number of cubic feet of earth he has moved. But no, Pittman says he is a "conservationist"—a conservationist who can spend hundreds of thousands of dollars dynamiting the land. One who can say, "A rose in the wrong place is a weed." He trained as a park ranger, and in the 1960s he was a no-compromise radical, he says, far ahead of the rest of the conservation movement.

These days he says: "I am not a preservationist only, like I used to be. I am a builder, but I don't believe it makes good sense to build unless we build in the correct relationship with what's around you, as we have tried to do here."

His partner and the project's financier, Richard Bryant, has had a "life-long love affair with the inn." Bryant's father met and married his wife there. The Bryants have owned land adjoining the Shattuck farm since 1913.

"Our economist sat right here at the table one day and looked at Richard and I: 'Hey, you guys, one thing I don't want you to do. I don't want you to fall in love with that big old building.' Richard looked at me, looked at him, said, 'You're too late. We already have.'"

"We have tried to maintain the inn in the same context that it had in 1909," says Pittman.

But 1909 was never like this. The condominiums would be clustered into "small New England villages" and screened from the road that approaches the park and from the mountain. The golf course would look like small pastures from the summit, Pittman claims, and from the road the only difference will be between cows and golfers. The Grand Monadnoc would first reveal itself to visitors through a clearing over the tennis courts.

When Pittman speaks before groups, he brings along a large drawing of the proposed resort; it's a beautiful wash of different greens. The trees are large, deep green strokes, the condo clusters discrete. Most of the wetlands have been preserved, and most of the space is open, as a golf course. Looking at this view can lull you to sleep: even the 350-car parking lot in front of the inn is green.

But listen longer to Pittman, and you recognize that old American creature, the pragmatist. He talks the peculiar frank language of utility. He points out the window to a "scraggly old pine tree." "From the golf course point of view, that tree's a weed because it drops needles on the green, but from the dining room it does an absolutely wonderful job of framing the sunset. I told the golf course architect that I won't even talk to him about cutting that tree down until he has eaten dinner at the Shattuck Inn and watched the sunset." Turning from the window, he says, "I'm realistic enough to know that the tree is not going to last forever, but I'd like to get ten years out of it."

Everything has its use. Preserved land creates value for someone, a cash crop waiting to be harvested. Our national parks, those Kodachrome wonders, are providing bumper crops to the developments that crowd right to the edge. Pittman admits that he benefits from the five thousand acres of conservation land next door. "I wish they were all around us," he says with a smile. In the end, all is commerce and commodity. There is no more unhandselled landscape.

Monadnock has a limited utility. The majority of "users of Mount Monadnock are from Boston. It really doesn't have a strong multi-day tourist draw to it," Pittman says. About 125,000 people "use" Monadnock yearly, day hikers who enter and leave the area without buying much more than a can of soda and a few gallons of gasoline. "Anybody who has a three-day weekend would go up to the White Mountains—including myself—and backpack to one of the AMC huts," he says. "Mount Monadnock doesn't have that for the wilderness enthusiasts. If they've got nine days to be away, they'll jump on a plane and go ski in Colorado."

Not enough oomph. "In the old days they came up on the train and stayed for two weeks and knew the Shattucks as people," says Pittman. "I would be delighted if we could restore the inn, put a deck around it and have a viable occupancy. But that doesn't happen. Today they've got to have something to do." In the modern "hospitality industry" you need activities for the "attitudinally affluent"—a complete resort. "For the people who come to stay, they might climb the mountain one day, go antiquing around the region one day, play golf one day. Maybe we could encourage them to stay longer than that." Particularly if the area changes to meet their expectations: the quaintness and convenience of antique shops in the postcard-perfect villages and an afternoon of shopping at the Monadnock Mall. The region lacks a big draw like

Santa's Playland, one businessman lamented in the *Keene Sentinel.* But to make up for it, there are "a lot of little things"—and first on his list of "little things" is Mount Monadnock.

"The shift from *accepting* tourists as guests to *catering* to them as consumers has changed the entire face of the land," says *Vacationscape: Designing Tourist Regions.* From guest to consumer, another twentieth-century journey.

Pittman is banking on the conversion of Mount Monadnock to a vacationscape. The day may be coming, he says, when people out west with nine days vacation will jump on a plane to New England. New Hampshire tourism is getting more and more inquiries from farther away. "I may be ten years early," he says, but one day "people from L.A. may be flying into New England for a vacation for a week at a time. Make New England a more viable and vibrant tourist industry. Because you're getting your long-term guests again like they had at the turn of the century."

Even then, in today's crowded entertainment market, Monadnock is a one-liner. "Late afternoon I'll quit work," says Pittman, and "watch the sunset on Mount Monadnock, and walk down and get a wonderful experience from it. I've only had to invest a few hours of my time, and I've got what Mount Monadnock has ... most of it."

∞

Charles Royce has spent forty-five years on Mount Monadnock, twelve years in charge of the Monadnock State Park, and he is not happy to see his mountain for sale. To him, Pittman and his partner are not conservationists but developers with a product to sell: the whole rural setting, condos with a view of Monadnock surrounded by thousands of acres of forested land: "That's a hell of a good selling point, that's for sure," Royce says.

In the drive for oomph, Monadnock's rural qualities will be overwhelmed. Oomph begets oomph. Like the old lady who swallowed the fly, there is no end. First a golf course is needed to sustain the inn, then condos for the golf course. Royce foresees further inroads: spraying pesticides to keep the blackflies off the golf course in May, and the use of all kinds of off-road vehicles like trail bikes, all-terrain vehicles. Recreation has changed. "It can keep on going. You could end up saying, yeah, you need a restaurant up on the side of Monadnock, too."

"There's still a lot of private land around the base of Monadnock that could be developed. It's impossible for the state and the forest society to acquire it all." Even on the higher slopes there are still some strips of land, fifty acres here, two hundred acres there "that could cause some problems in the future."

"You hope that the good judgment of the owners will protect the mountain … but that can't be guaranteed."

Tablet on Mount Monadnock
May it always remain as it is today, free and wild and beautiful, the unspoiled heritage of the past, a haven of refuge for those who seek its peace in years to come.

On a late November day, Ed Pittman has gathered several wagon loads of local people for a tour of the golf course under construction. We sit on bales of hay, some of us holding hors d'oeuvres or drinks from the buffet inside. With maps in hand we are given a tour of what nearly $5 million looks like when applied to four hundred acres. The large wheels of the farm tractors pulling us swim through mud, over newly made bridges and through entire man-made mountain passes of blasted granite, toppled trees. We are voyagers in an alien landscape. People turn the map this way and that and soon let it drop: mud and granite and in places some finished golf tees, small plateaus like Machu Picchu, the grass an unnaturally bright green—like the green of artificial turf in indoor stadiums.

We are pulled up the tenth fairway, great view of Monadnock; past the third tee, great view; at the bend of the first, great view. We jounce along for more than an hour like this, stopping for a rest by the third and fourth holes, which surround a beaver pond. We head off to the eighth hole. There are some existing buildings on the map. And there, in twilight, is the most beautiful farm I have ever seen in New Hampshire: farmhouse, barn, great rolling hills and, rising up in front of us, Mount Monadnock, a purple range in the day's last light. I have traveled halfway around the world to see landscapes less stunning. One old tree holds a child's tree house. The greens keeper will live here now. You tee off for the eighth hole in the barnyard.

As we pull away, I turn and look at the farm and think about the life that had been lived on that farm; I can see sheep on those hills, and I want to stay, even in the instant that I know hill farms like these have not paid their way since the turn of the century.

On the wagon, all the people are for the project: it's marvelous for the community, they say. They are awestruck by the planning and scale. "They can't stop him now," they say, and talk with admiration about the bulldozers and all the big machinery ($90 an hour just to run it). They can't wait to play golf, and talk about other courses: how it takes five hours to play, but now the demand is so great they are trying to get people through in four hours—no more walking from hole to hole. And to meet the golf demand, the National Golf Foundation says we have to build a new golf course a day for the next twelve years.

A golf course is open space, after all, the people on the wagon say. Better than having houses there. Well, after nearly $5 million dollars it is no longer "open space," as is claimed, but as artificial an object as an interstate cloverleaf. There is a great difference between a cow pasture and a manicured green. No open space I've seen around has had to be dynamited and bulldozed and has needed nine miles of erosion fence and fifteen thousand bales of hay to hold it in place during construction. It looks like an earthquake, someone said in the wagon, as we pulled past the piles of boulders and trees that could one day be Cutter Brook Village.

And no cow pasture needs, in the charming phrase of the National Golf Foundation, "a palette of chemicals." Anywhere from thirty to thirty-five different chemicals are used to maintain that Technicolor green. Many of the chemicals have not been tested for their effects on health and the environment, and there is incomplete data on all of them. In New York State, a single application of Diazinon on a golf course killed seven hundred Brant geese, 7 percent of the state's winter population. Diazinon is now banned.

On a golf course, the "grass becomes a chemical addict," says Susan Cooper, a staff ecologist with the National Coalition Against the Misuse of Pesticide. The grass is very stressed; it is kept so short that it is starving, Cooper says. She likens it to sending a malnourished person into a room of people with the flu; the grass can't fend for itself and needs a constant chemical fix. "The bottom line is that there is going to be ground water contamination," Cooper says, as well as pollution downstream.

I wanted to say to the people in the hay wagon, Don't you know, today you're getting the royal tour—hors d'oeuvres, wine—but once these condos go in, your town will lose a good measure of its sovereignty. You will be colonized: a second home colony. Your children will be cleaning toilets for these people.

Even if this resort has the potential of being a good condo project, why here at the foot of Mount Monadnock? How many Monadnocks do we have? In the New Hampshire manner, this mountain is a patchwork of private and public ownerships. All we need is for a steady trade wind to blow this way, some new economic formula, and Monadnock could be wreathed in condominiums. For the right price, we would bulldoze Monadnock: It's what people want, we would be told. You can't stop progress. You can't have your little fantasy land up here; people want to live on Monadnock. It's their economic right, and then the discussion would move onto matters of drainage and septic: Monadnock would be zoned for a montane septic system. ...

The "attitudinally affluent" today *need* Jacuzzis, golf and tennis and pools and cocktail lounges. That is oomph—for now. If tomorrow oomph is something else, the hospitality industry will change. Let's say America goes on a blueberry-picking binge: the *New England Journal of Medicine* publishes a study that says bending to pick berries is the best exercise of all, and berries picked off the bush reduce cholesterol and retard aging. In addition, it is hinted, they have mystical and financial powers. Blueberry fields would be planted everywhere, and the hospitality industry would find a way to create great indoor fields the size of football stadiums. The bushes would be controlled to ripen in a sequence so there would always be berries, and your very own condo-bushes would be timed to ripen the week of your vacation. That would be berry-picking today.

∞

Darkness rose from the hills, the driver turned on his tractor lights, and the farm was out of sight. Sheep farms are a long vanished landscape in the hill country of New England. The economics aren't there for them. And the economics aren't there for little mountain inns whose "product" was fresh air and fresh vegetables and a view from the porch. We don't live that way anymore. Now we need million-dollar dynamiting of the landscape, private condos on the green with all the amenities. It is after berry-picking time.

The charm of the towns around Monadnock has been a pre–Great War manner of summering: the same families returning to their summer homes, attending summer theater, or the summer lyceums, content to swim or canoe, content to sit on the summer porch with friends or with some old musty novel left behind by a guest the last summer Adlai Stevenson was a hot topic. That lingering way of summering has faded. It is a wonder it lasted as long as it did up here.

Bring on the new Monadnock Mall, bring on the golfers and condos. Welcome to the dreary convenience of progress. It is after berry picking now.

No doubt some night there will be a lecturer at the inn talking about Thoreau's mountain and how he slept under a tent of branches. It makes for a nice story, before one retires across the eighteenth fairway at dusk, the sprinklers gently watering the grass, a manufactured dew fall. Up behind the tenth tee is the inn, the windows all cozy with light, and off up the tenth fairway, Monadnock. Yes, the people will think, Thoreau was right. It is all so beautiful. Just as he said.

207

The Ice King's Walden

In the winter of 1846–47, Henry David Thoreau looked out from his cabin on the shore of Walden Pond one morning to find a scene of industry. A hundred men had arrived "with many car-loads of ungainly-looking farming tools, sleds, ploughs, drill-barrows, turf-knives, spades, saws, rakes, and each man was armed with a double-pointed pike-staff, such as is not described in the *New-England Farmer* or the *Cultivator*. ... "

They had come to harvest the ice. "They went to work at once, ploughing, harrowing, rolling, furrowing, in admirable order ... took off the only coat, ay, the skin itself of Walden Pond in the midst of a hard winter.

"They said that a gentleman farmer, who was behind the scenes, wanted to double his money, which, as I understood, amounted to half a million already. ... "

The men were working for Frederic Tudor, "the Ice King," the man who had pioneered the trade in ice. Tudor was far from being a gentleman farmer with a hobby of shipping ice. He had given twenty years of his life, his health and all his imagination to creating the ice trade.

Ice was his one true belief. He had envisioned the small ponds around Boston cooling the thirst of people half a world away. A dozen years before his men had arrived at Walden Pond, Tudor accomplished the first shipment of ice to Calcutta, a trip across the equator twice, the ship four months at sea.

Thoreau responded to the poetry in that undertaking in a celebrated passage from *Walden*:

> Thus it appears that the sweltering inhabitants of Charleston and New Orleans, of Madras and Bombay and Calcutta, drink at my well. In the morning I bathe my intellect in the stupendous and cosmological philosophy of the Bhagvat Geeta. ... I lay down the book and go to my well for water, and lo! there I meet the servant of the Bramin, priest of Brahma and Vishnu and Indra, who still sits in his temple on the Ganges reading the Vedas, or dwells at the root of a tree with his crust and water jug. I meet his servant come to draw water for his master, and our buckets as it were grate together in the same well. The pure Walden water is mingled with the sacred water of the Ganges.

For a few days that winter, Walden Pond was home to two competing views of success and wealth. America was then just seventy years old, a child among nations, and there was still the drama of choice; the republic was yet an invention in the making. The heroes of the Revolution had only recently passed from the scene, the Civil War was fifteen years off, and America could one day be anything.

To Thoreau, Walden was purity. "A lake is the landscape's most beautiful and expressive feature. It is the earth's eye: looking into which the beholder measures the depth of his own nature." To Tudor, a lake was also beautiful, but it was its utility that he admired. In his journal he wrote: "The frost covers the windows, the wheels creak, the boys run, winter rules, and $50,000 of ice floats for me upon Fresh Pond."

Tudor the Ice King and Thoreau the Transcendental Philosopher: Once upon a time, there was room enough for both in America.

Time is money, said one view.

Time is life, said the other.

On the shores of Walden two highly individualistic Americans created their Americas. Both men had chosen Walden to conduct business, and both men were inventors.

A History of Myself

Frederic Tudor was born into one of Boston's leading families in the years after the Revolution. His father, William, had inherited wealth, but it was not money that commanded respect. "William Tudor was first and foremost a gentleman," said one portrait, "by nature serene, dignified and considerate, concerned with things of the mind." William and his wife, Delia, had made the grand tour of Europe twice and at home entertained foreign guests. The children grew up tutored in French, music and drawing.

At one of the many social gatherings the Tudors hosted, the eldest son, William, put forth the idea that money could be made by harvesting ice and selling it in the Caribbean. A few wealthy Boston families had private ice houses and were cutting ice for their own use, but this ice would be cut for a profit. This was just one of William's many ideas. He was "full of plans," as he himself said, "but then, you know, it is not necessary to execute them."

Frederic seized on this idea—no one else took it seriously—and ever after claimed it as his alone; it was he, the Ice King, who had invented the ice trade. Many years later, when a close relative mentioned that it was William's idea, Frederic refused to speak to him ever again.

As his first act in his new business, he bought a leather-bound journal. On the cover he printed the year, 1805, and this motto: "He who gives back at the first repulse and without striking the second blow despairs of success has never been, is not, and never will be a hero in war, love or business." He came to call this his *Ice House Diary*. He was twenty-two and had found his life's calling.

Within a year he had his first shipment ready. He was sending 130 tons of ice to the West Indies: Martinique, Guadaloupe, Antigua, St. Croix, St. Thomas, St. Domingo, Barbados and Jamaica. That the West Indies had never asked for ice was of no consideration.

"No joke," reported a Boston newspaper, "a vessel has cleared at the Custom House for Martinique with a cargo of ice. We hope this will not prove a slippery speculation."

His venture, wrote Tudor, "excited the derision of the whole town as a mad project." (It was said that no ship would take on his cargo—Tudor had to buy his own ship.) His brother William thought he had disgraced the family by going into business. His three brothers had gone off to Harvard. Not Frederic. College was for loafers; it led to an unnatural over-refinement. At age thirteen, he had apprenticed himself at a store, and later he speculated on whatever was making money at the moment: flour, sugar, tea, pimento, nutmeg, candles, cotton, silk, claret. … "For minds highly excited and in great activity there is no Sunday," he later wrote in his diary.

The *Ice House Diary* and *Walden* are both autobiographies, each "A History of Myself," as Thoreau had titled an early version of *Walden*. They are particularly American autobiographies; each is the story of a self-made or self-willed man, each a profile of individualism. And both books are sermons, a classic American form. Thoreau's, of course, is a tract on how to be awake in this world. And Tudor's diary is a testament to ice and the idea of success itself.

On March 5, 1806, Tudor arrived in Martinique with his first shipment of ice. He had sent his brother William and a friend down to prepare the way, but the two had no mind for business and had only created skepticism. "On my arrival I found my brother had been exceedingly discouraged in the enterprise, every one assuring him no person would purchase any if it came," wrote Tudor.

Tudor was stuck with a ship full of melting ice. He faced the problem of all business pioneers: creating a market, creating a demand for something people didn't know they wanted. With a reformer's zeal, he spread the New England gospel of ice cream. He railed against the ignorance of these islanders:

It is difficult to conceive how determined to believe most of the people are here that ice will melt in spite of all precautions; and their methods of keeping it are laughable, to be sure. One carries it through the street to his house in sun noon day, puts it in a plate before his door, and complains that "il fond." Another puts it in a tub of water, a third by way of climax put his in salt! and all this notwithstanding they were directed in the hand bill what to do.

These people don't know how to live, he is saying. And that delivered in much the same tone, is also the message of *Walden*. ("The greater part of what my neighbors call good I believe in my soul to be bad ... ," and so on.)

Tudor shows them how to use ice. He insists that ice cream can be made in the West Indies. He writes one man an order for $40 of ice and tells him to have his cream ready, and he will come and freeze it. He makes the man ice cream, and it is a big success: the vendor received "for these creams the first night $300; after this he was as humble as a mushroom. ... "

By the middle of April, six weeks after his arrival, his cargo had melted. He lost at least one-third of his investment, and he returned home to try again. But he had written a chapter in the "history of luxury." A Martinique newspaper reported: "It will be a remarkable epoch in the history of luxury and enterprise that on the sixth of March ice creams have been eaten at Martinique probably for the first time since the settlement of the country and this too in a volcanic land lying 14 degrees north of the equator."

The Way to Wealth

"I have thought Walden Pond would be a good place for business," wrote Thoreau, "not solely on account of the railroad and the ice trade.

"My purpose in going to Walden Pond was not to live cheaply nor to live dearly there, but to transact some private business with the fewest obstacles. ... I have always endeavored to acquire strict business habits; they are indispensable to every man."

So here, at Walden Pond in the winter of 1846–47, were two business experiments. Thoreau's business was to live honestly, or as he said: "I went to the woods because I wished to live deliberately, to front only the essential facts of life, and see if I could not learn what it had to teach. … "

His business undertaking is well documented in the many ledger accounts in *Walden*: the cost of his house, the cost of his crop, his wages from day labor, how he obtained his clothes, the cost of rice and molasses—all very business-like records that Frederic Tudor could have easily surveyed. *Walden* is an annual report to any who would dare to be stockholders. "Follow your genius closely enough, and it will not fail to show you a fresh prospect every hour."

Compare Thoreau's accounting methods with Tudor's.

Thoreau's house:

Boards, ...$ 8 03 1/2,	mostly shanty boards
Refuse shingles for roof and sides, ...4 00	
Laths, ...1 25	
Two second-hand windows with glass, .2 43	
One thousand old brick, ...4 00	
Two casks of lime, ...2 40	That was high
Hair, ...0 31	More than I needed
Mantle-tree iron, ...0 15	
Nails, ...3 90	
Hinges and screws, ...0 14	
Latch, ...0 10	
Chalk, ...0 01	
Transportation, ...1 40	I carried a good part on my back
In all, ...$28 12 1/2	

And Tudor's figures in 1806 for his next shipment:

```
Cost of 32 cords of ice, which the next winter need
not be so much except for the first cargo or two ............ $162.05
23 loads of shavings ................................................................. 15.50
Carpenter preparing the hold ............................................... 25.50
Stevedore (too much) ............................................................. 40.00
Say for wharfage 50 cents a load ......................................... 16.00
                                                                                            $258.05
```

Thoreau is the more exacting ledger keeper. Tudor is off by a dollar, and this may well foreshadow his later travails.

Walden and the *Ice House Diary* are two works in that classic American genre: The Way to Wealth. Thoreau says we have only to awaken to this world to be wealthy. "Our life is frittered away by detail. … Simplicity, simplicity, simplicity! I say, let your affairs be as two or three, and not a hundred or a thousand. … Instead of three meals a day, if it be necessary, eat but one; instead of a hundred dishes, five. … "

"A man is rich in proportion to the number of things which he can afford to let alone." But if this were true for every one, who would leave the safety of home and risk life and limb at sea to bring ice cream to the people of the tropics? If all "traveled a good deal in Concord," the world, as we know it, would cease to spin. Appetite, in all its many forms, sets the world spinning.

"A man without money is like a body without a soul—a walking dead man," Frederic Tudor quoted approvingly. He set about getting a "soul."

Consider Tudor's life as a parable: "Once in Shawmut," the preacher would begin, "lived a man who set upon himself the task of shipping winter to the regions of eternal summer. And mightily did he labor, though his work did vanish in the noonday sun." And so forth and so on. "For the works of man are like ice in the tropics."

Tudor's next ice shipment arrived in Havana in 1807. There were heavy losses, but the future looked promising. Then came the Napoleonic Wars, and President Jefferson ordered a trade embargo. Tudor had to return home from Havana. Following this, he wrote later, "the business struggled against all manner of discouragement for twenty years."

Back home, his father lost the family fortune in a bad real estate speculation. Now Frederic had to bail out his father and employ his brothers, who had no talent for business.

Waiting to resume his trade, Tudor spent his time trying to perfect an ice house that could be shipped to tropical ports. The embargo lifted, and he headed back to Havana in 1810. He intended to request a monopoly in the ice trade from the government. (Tudor had brought this up three years earlier. At first, the governor's interpreter refused to even translate the request, thinking it crazy.) Tudor caught yellow fever and suffered through the early summer. He persisted, however, and won a six-year monopoly for Havana. No one else could bring ice in. One Philadelphia merchant was forced to dump his ice in the harbor.

He was meeting with a modest success, but it wasn't enough. He would use the money gained from one venture to start another venture, a shell game of debts and investments. He piled risk upon risk. Not satisfied to pay his debts from the first shipments, Tudor instead tried mining coal at Gay Head on Martha's Vineyard. He impetuously hopped from scheme to scheme, and his creditors were close behind. "Will you learn to lay the foundations before raising the roof?" a cousin implored him. More than once he was arrested and thrown into debtors' prison.

The War of 1812 stopped the ice trade once more. Tudor chased other schemes. He designed a new ship hull, had it patented and actually got it built. On the day of the ship's big debut, which had attracted much attention in Boston, he was arrested on the ship and taken to debtors' prison. The once-noble Tudor family—his brothers and even his father—began taking turns in the debtors' lock-up.

Tudor wrote in the *Ice House Diary*:

I complain of hard destiny and have I not reason? ... I have manfully maintained as long as I possibly could that "success is virtue." I say so still; but my heart tells me I don't believe it. Have I not been industrious? ... and have not all my undertakings in the eventful Ice business been attended by a villainous train of events. ... They have worried me. They have cured me of superfluous gaiety. They have made my head grey; but they have not driven me to despair.

Ten years after he had made his first ice shipment, Tudor returned to Havana in hopes of saving his business. The war was over, and he had one year left on his monopoly agreement. He left Boston "pursued by sheriffs to the very wharf."

He erected his ice house, and, watch in hand, he studied the rate of ice melt, experimenting with different types of insulation—straw, wood shavings and blankets. The old-style houses lost more than 60 percent of their ice; his new design lost less than 8 percent. The ice began to sell, and he gloated in his diary: "Drink, Spaniards and be cool, that I, who have suffered so much in the cause, may be able to go home and keep myself warm." (To which Thoreau might have responded: "If that was your need, then how much simpler to work up a few cords of wood.")

Tudor also experimented with preserving fruit. One experiment in shipping tropical fruits packed in hay and ice nearly set a boat on fire. This time he planned to ship fruit back from Havana. He borrowed $3,000 at the "modest interest" of 40 percent. The fruit spoiled, and Tudor piled up more debt.

He returned home, borrowed $300, gave "$50 to a thankless brother" and sneaked out of Boston. "Oh! hateful and debasing feelings to be in such a situation as to be obliged to leave one's home in anything like a clandestine manner. Had the vessel been delayed a *day*," he wrote, he would have been jailed.

He tried and failed to obtain a monopoly for ice in Charleston. ("It is apparent that I am considered by many persons a mere ice seller.") His ice house was almost removed in Havana, and his business neared bankruptcy.

"What signifies courage if it abandons us in our utmost need," he asked in the *Ice House Diary*. He struggled on and wrote his brother Harry: "I put my shoulder to the wheel and after many a hard struggle I have rolled my waggon on." His ice house in Havana was saved, he started to do business in Charleston and avoided bankruptcy once again. "I have so willed it, and you may depend upon it that a thorough determination will overcome difficulties."

"Through a wearisome march of 12 years I have got within grasp a most distinguished success." At the beginning of yellow fever season, Tudor sailed once more to Havana.

His father wrote to him: "Come home and let us all strive to restore former days, and if we can not be rich, leave it to those who are to be querulous and miserable."

Tudor responded: "There is nothing in my opinion debases a man's spirit like penury. Its tendency is to degrade the soul; reason and philosophy preach in vain."

To his brother-in-law, Robert Gardiner, he wrote: "I became satisfied in my mind of the absolute worthlessness of our existence here. ... 'Do good to thine enemy; love them that hate you.' I cannot take as a rule of life; neither do I believe it was intended by the founder of our religion to be literally carried into effect. ... "

As for "riches": "They are necessary to a full enjoyment of this life. Wealth adds luster to our virtues ... because it carries an unquestioned authority in the world and must make a good man better. ..."

And in a subsequent letter, he wrote Gardiner: "I hope you will not think me extravagant when I tell you it is my solemn resolution to accomplish a most brilliant success or perish in the attempt. That strong expression of the old Roman comes frequently to my mind, who when his friends would dissuade him from going to Rome on account of the danger, answered: 'It is necessary I should go to Rome; it is not necessary that I should live."

∞

"Why should we be in such desperate haste to succeed, and in such desperate enterprises?" asked Thoreau.

> Men think that it is essential that the *Nation* have commerce, and export ice, and talk through a telegraph, and ride thirty miles an hour. ... Why should we live with such hurry and waste of life?
> If the day and the night are such that you greet them with joy, and life emits a fragrance like flowers and sweet-scented herbs, is more elastic, more starry, more immortal,—that is your success.

∽

In July 1819, Frederic Tudor returned home from months in the south to find that his father had died the week before. "I can truly say that a part of my desire of success arose from the consideration of his hearty participation."

That fall, attempting to settle old debts, Tudor wrote to one creditor: "Sales are regular, progressive and certain, like the demand for bread at a Baker's. That I am inevitably and unavoidably rich."

Nine months later, he wrote: "I am without a dollar, having exhausted every means in my power. The distress I suffer is without alleviation, and coming upon me when in low state of health cuts me most deeply." The year 1820 was one of a severe economic depression, the first major banking crisis in U.S. history. His brother Harry was under two arrests for bad debts. Tudor tried to extend his ice trade to New Orleans: "I find a continual war with adverse circumstances is the only alternative I have if I would have at a future time a great success and for which I have suffered and am willing to suffer." In 1822, Frederic Tudor had a nervous collapse.

∽

"I have since learned that trade curses every thing it handles," wrote Thoreau.

> I found that the occupation of a day-laborer was the most independent of any. ... The laborer's day ends with the going down

of the sun, and he is then free to devote himself to his chosen pursuit, independent of his labor; but his employer, who speculates from month to month, has no respite from one end of the year to the other.

Cultivate poverty like a garden herb, like sage. Do not trouble yourself much to get new things, whether clothes or friends. ... Sell your clothes and keep your thoughts. ... Superfluous wealth can buy superfluities only. Money is not required to buy one necessary of the soul.

New Inventions

"A great idea is a useful invention, like an eyeglass or a new fuel," the poet Robert Bly wrote of Thoreau. "When an idea is an eyeglass, details otherwise fuzzy become sharp. ... Thoreau understands that we have the winged life inside us. ... When Thoreau set that idea to his eyes, he saw that most people around him were living meanly."

In *Walden*, Thoreau proposes an invention to measure the meanness and falsity of our lives. His device would work like a Nilometer, which was used to gauge the rise and fall of the Nile. His invention: "a Realometer, that future ages might know how deep a freshet of shams and appearances had gathered from time to time."

So when Tudor's men arrive at Walden Pond that winter, we are seeing a battle of inventions: Thoreau's "Realometer" versus the ice business.

Tudor's invention was not harvesting ice. That was already a common practice, though he held patents that improved the harvest, nor was it shipping ice, though he held patents for that, too. His invention was making people want ice they had never wanted and then *need* the ice. He took a luxury and turned it into a necessity. Tudor's great invention was the creation of a commodity—he made ice a "product."

The heart of Tudor's invention lay in this statement by Jacob Bigelow, a Harvard scientist. In 1829, Bigelow wrote: "The economy of the ancients consisted in diminishing their technical wants; ours in devising cheap means to gratify them."

Tudor is the modern salesman; he comes knocking at your door to create a want and then fill it. Had there been advertising as we know it in the 1820s and 1830s, Tudor would have advertised widely in ports that had never seen ice from New England ponds. Instead he sent along instructions with his representatives, like these on creating demand in Rio de Janeiro: "If you can make a commencement for introducing the habit of cold drinks *at the same price* as warm at the ordinary drinking places ... even if you *give* the ice ... you will do well. ... "

This was a marketing strategy Tudor had kept in mind since his first shipment to Martinique: "The object is to make the whole population use cold drinks instead of warm or tepid. ... A single conspicuous bar keeper ... selling steadily all his liquors cold without an increase in price, renders it absolutely necessary that the others come to it or lose their customers—they are compelled to do what they could in no other way be induced to undertake."

His man in Rio was also directed to construct an ice house, spread the ice cream gospel, introduce ice to the hospitals and then convince the Brazilian government that ice is a health necessity and have them remit all export duties on Tudor's departing ships in gratitude for this necessity.

In Charleston, South Carolina, he placed this notice in the newspaper: "The inhabitants are invited to call for ice in such quantities as shall enable the proprietor of the house to continue the present price which cannot be the case unless ice is used rather as a necessary of life than as a luxury."

Tudor had extended the idea of property—frozen pond water was now property. Other men joined in the ice trade, and competition to cut ice became so fierce that his assistant (and later competitor) pioneered the idea of buying a legal right to harvest the ice—even though a 1641 law respecting "Liberties in Common" said that all ponds over ten acres belonged to the people of Massachusetts. Ponds were not supposed to be property, but throughout the nineteenth century the American landscape was becoming a check-erboard of property rights: mineral rights, water rights, easements, tenant farms and boarding houses, gold claims and railroad right-of-ways. Tudor's ice trade, said one remembrance, imparted "a value to that which had no value before."

A new America was coming along. Thoreau saw it in the railroad that ran along Walden's western shore. With the arrival of the railroad, time became standardized—time was on the way to becoming property. Time was money, and land was money.

"To do things 'railroad fashion' is now the by-word," wrote Thoreau. "We live the steadier for it." He admired the power of commerce—"I am refreshed and expanded when the freight train rattles past me," he said, thinking of the salt fish, lumber, cattle and coconut husks racing from one place to the next. But Thoreau saw that a great machine had been set in motion. "We have constructed a fate, an *Atropos,* that never turns aside." In classical mythology, there were three fates; one spun out the thread of life, another fate measured it, and the last fate—Atropos—was the inflexible one that cut the thread of life. Atropos, said Thoreau, "let that be the name of your engine."

"This world is a place of business. What an infinite bustle!" Thoreau said in his lecture "Life Without Principle." "I am awakened almost every night by the panting of the locomotive. It interrupts my dreams. There is no sabbath. ... I cannot easily buy a blank-book to write thoughts in; they are commonly ruled for dollars and cents."

Frederic Tudor was one of those trying to hurry that new America along. To promote several proposed railroads in 1830, he brought the first steam locomotive to New England, a toy-sized engine that pulled a car carrying one person and ran on the sidewalk. "Steam will soon take the place of horses in ordinary stage coaches," wrote Tudor. "The times are surcharged with novel inventions and improvements of all kinds."

Tudor was all business—"I have, indeed, no leisure of mind," he wrote to his mother. In his business dealings he was described as "ruthless" and "militant, despotic and punitive." (In another era they might have asked: What makes Freddy run?) He was true to the motto on the cover of his *Ice House Diary*, to succeed in war and business, one had to strike back.

When competitors entered the ice trade, Tudor did everything to run them off. He tied up his ice harvesting methods with patents and even patented the use of sawdust to pack the ice. The designs were actually by Nathaniel Wyeth, who managed Tudor's ice company. Wyeth's improvements cut the cost of harvesting ice by two-thirds. Tudor took the patents as his own and controlled the rights. He engaged in price wars—undercutting his competition, selling his ice at a loss until they dropped out and he could again have a monopoly in port. He claimed ponds as his own "discovery" and put pressure on ice-cutting teams who dared to work for others, refusing to hire them or cutting their pay and calling in their debts.

"The last has been a year of battle … with a host of miscreant men and adverse circumstances. … All opposition has been met and overthrown. … If there are any unslain enemies, let them come out. … "

He was the Ice King, it was *his* ice trade. He was delighted to watch an "interferer's" ice melt on the dock in Savannah. Tudor had built ice houses there. He could drop his price until he had the market again to himself. He noted in his diary: "This interferer will get about $5.00 in all for what must have cost him at least $100. … This business is mine. I … have a right to rejoice in ill success attending others who would profit by my discovery without allowing me the credit of teaching them."

His efforts at trade were spurred on by a new concern in 1834—he had achieved a spectacular debt attempting to "monopolize" the coffee market. At first he made money, but the market fell, and he had to sell 7 1/2 million pounds of coffee at a loss. "I have lost in this speculation four times as much money as my grandfather (who died about forty years ago, noted as a rich man) was worth."

He had lost nearly a quarter of a million dollars. This loss, he wrote, "invigorated me." He expanded his business, putting into action something he had imagined twenty years earlier, something that others "thought too absurd to be entertained": shipping ice to Calcutta. A cargo of ice, cut from a pond and packed in sawdust, would have to be at sea four months or more, sailing sixteen thousand miles, crossing the equator twice.

In May 1833, he sent his first shipment to Calcutta: 180 tons of ice and some Baldwin apples. He told his captain: "As soon as you have arrived in latitude 12 degrees north, you will have carried ice as far south as it has ever been carried before, and your Ship becomes a discovery ship. ... "

Two-thirds of the cargo arrived. Calcutta was amazed. A crowd gathered at the docks to see the "crystal blocks of Yankee coldness." "If there be luxury, here it is," said a Calcutta newspaper. The overseas British population welcomed the ice. They paid fifty to seventy-five cents apiece for the apples. (Back in New England, a whole barrel of apples was worth no more than three dollars.)

In Bombay and Madras, the British communities paid for and built ice houses for Tudor. In Bombay, ice ships got the best berths in harbor and paid reduced duties. At Madras, ice was fifth on the duty-free list. The first items were bullion and coins, and precious stones and pearls.

The Calcutta ice trade was something of the moon landing of the East Indies trade. Tudor's reputation in Boston was restored. "Mr. Tudor and his ice came just in time to preserve Boston's East-India commerce from ruin. Our carrying trade between Calcutta and Europe had declined almost to extinction," wrote Samuel E. Morison in *The Maritime History of Massachusetts, 1783–1860.*

Tudor prospered and paid his debt. "Thus I have used 14 years of my life and accomplished the payment, at last,

of principal of debt	$210,094.20
Paid interest to close of 1848	70,060.39
	$280,154.59

"I began this trade in the youthful hopes attendant on the age of 22. I have followed it until I have a head with scarcely a hair which is not white." In January 1849, at the age of sixty-five, he was at last a free man.

∽

"Through want of enterprise and faith men are where they are, buying and selling, and spending their lives like serfs," wrote Thoreau.

∽

Frederic Tudor was a success. He had achieved the "delicious essence," as he called it, the flattery of others that he so desired. At the age of fifty he married a nineteen-year-old and spent his time at the grounds of his country estate in Nahant, Massachusetts, planting elms on that barren peninsula.

"Like almost everything else Mr. Tudor did, the setting out of elms was scoffed at—'no tree would grow on Nahant.' The Tudor elms now make one of the most handsome avenues of trees in New England," Morison wrote in 1921.

But Frederic Tudor had not turned into a Johnny Appleseed. His garden estate was true to his character: it went against the natural order. To protect his trees from the strong sea breezes, Tudor built windbreak walls, some as tall as twenty feet.

His other ventures were similar. In one, he tried to introduce salt water fish to Fresh Pond. "He gave a signal instance of how much could be done, by ingenuity, perseverance, and skill, in overcoming the most formidable obstacles of soil and climate, and obtaining a victory over Nature herself," said one remembrance.

The ice trade was established. Where once a single cargo would satisfy New Orleans, now Tudor shipped thirty cargoes. "In New Orleans a servile rebellion might be ... feared if deprived of the 50,000 tons of ice they receive annually from Boston," wrote Tudor.

By 1855 there were twelve companies shipping ice out of Boston on 520 ships—the city exported more tons of ice than anything else. Between 1836 and 1856 Boston shipped ice to every large port in the United States, South America and the Far East, including China, the Philippines and Australia. When a Persian prince met the U.S.

ambassador in London, he was full of praise for American ice; it helped to ease the fevers of the sick.

By shipping ice to those climates that most needed it, like India, New England's merchants were doing God's work. The ice trade had been divinely mandated, said *Hunt's Merchants' Magazine and Commercial Review* in 1855. "The Maker of all yearly matures ice enough for all his creatures, in all parts of the earth, and it only requires the swift ships of Commerce, that He seems to have foreseen and ordained, to furnish all earth's inhabitants with this necessary of life."

"Ice is important, even in promoting good morals," said the magazine. Temperance societies praised ice water. "How often do men in health drink ardent spirits as a beverage because they cannot procure good or only tepid water that ice would render palatable?"

Tudor had one-quarter of the entire ice trade. He owned ice houses in Havana, Jamaica, New Orleans, Charleston, Mobile, Calcutta, Madras, Bombay, Galle and Singapore.

The nation had been improved by the ice trade. "Railroads have been built (one of them solely for the transportation of ice); water on the shores of ponds is now *leased,* and is nearly as valuable, in convenient localities, as the land itself," wrote Tudor.

Ice cream, declared *Godey's Lady Book* in August 1850, was a necessity of life. To have a party without ice cream was as unthinkable as breakfast without bread.

Frederic Tudor was worth a million dollars.

Captain of a Huckleberry Party

Walden is a book that is nearly 150 years old and can still incite a white-hot resentment in people. They angrily call Thoreau's "life in the woods" a sham—he sometimes went home for dinner—and they ask, "Who is he to judge us?"

"We hate it when observers notice mean lives, because we are afraid we may be among those being watched," wrote Robert Bly. "Much of the hostility to Thoreau, which I remember feeling strongly in college—scribbled insults in the margins of my *Walden* remain as testimony—comes from the fear that we are being watched."

Even his friend Ralph Waldo Emerson lost patience with Thoreau. "Thoreau wants a little ambition in his mixture," Emerson said in 1849. "Instead of being the head of American engineers, he is captain of a huckleberry party."

For Tolstoy, Thoreau was one of "a bright constellation" of American writers who had "specially influenced him." In a letter published in the *North American Review,* he wondered why Americans didn't pay more attention to these voices and less to those "of financial and industrial millionaires or successful generals."

We tire of Thoreau. He is too demanding; he wants us to live like rejoicing priests finding our sacraments anew each day. He wants us to forego gossip and newspapers and fine houses and big barns and all the glittering prizes of the passing show. He is in the minds of many, an outcast, the boy-wild, someone who, as teachers used to say in grade school, "does not play well with others."

But we know Frederic Tudor only too well. He pulls himself up by his own bootstraps, he believes in pluck and luck, he says no guts, no glory, he says put your shoulder to the wheel and hook your wagon to a star. He makes big claims. He advertises himself. He says the last four letters in American are I can! He is the utilitarian supreme.

Frederic Tudor is such a modern American. His eye is on the main chance. He is the businessman on the shuttle flight listening to the self-improvement tape. He is all the salesmen on cable TV ready to show you how to get rich in real estate with *no money down.* He is the Dress-for-Success, One-Minute-Manager, Search-for-Excellence, over-mortgaged, over-extended, over-reaching American.

∞

Today Walden is crowded; its life as a natural pond is endangered—it is, in Thoreau's own pun, *Walled-in* Pond. It seems so domesticated, so trod upon, almost like a man-made reservoir. Walden is the closest swimming hole to Boston. In the hot summer of 1987, with more and more beaches closed from pollution, over four hundred thousand people used the pond. They are like any crowd at a beach, bringing radios, boomboxes, even portable televisions. Some Saturdays there have been twelve thousand at the pond at one time. (One Sunday crowd in 1935 reached twenty-five thousand.) In the past years Massachusetts, which runs Walden as a park, has been attempting to limit visitors to one thousand at a time. They have repaired the damage of the past, removing a concrete swimming pier, two concrete bathhouses and a concrete wall around a man-made beach. They are spending two million dollars to repair the badly eroded shoreline, in the process, some contend, creating more damage: paving parts of the shore with gravel and fieldstone.

There are no less than three replicas of Thoreau's cabin in Concord, the newest one right at the entrance to the parking lot for the pond. At this replica, there is sometimes a park ranger to explain Thoreau's works, and sometimes someone dressed as Thoreau. (The state of Massachusetts initially proposed to build it close to the original site—but to protect the cabin from vandals, they intended to surround it with a towering chain-link fence and floodlights.)

The year before Thoreau came to Walden the railroad was built on the western shore. In 1935, a highway, now four lanes, cut through the Walden Woods, within eight hundred feet of the site of Thoreau's cabin. The Walden Breezes Trailer Park across Walden Street opened in the 1920s, and the Concord town dump opened in the late 1950s next door. The town of Concord has approved an office park to be built on Brister's Hill, where Thoreau picked huckleberries. Condominiums were planned at one point for Bear Garden Hill, and there was talk of placing a power station in Walden Woods. Only a quarter of the Walden Woods, just 411 acres, survives. The National Trust for Historic Preservation has listed the woods as one of the nation's eleven most endangered historic sites.

Walden should have been Thoreau's monument, but it is Frederic Tudor's. His monuments are all around: railroad, highway, dump, office park, condominiums. What we have today is the Ice King's Walden.

On his graduation from Harvard in 1837, Thoreau took part in a commencement honors conference entitled "The Commercial Spirit of Modern Times." As he said in *Walden*: "This curious world we inhabit is more wonderful than convenient; more beautiful than it is useful; it is more to be admired and enjoyed than used."

But we know better.

The Pond in Winter

"White Pond and Walden are great crystals on the surface of the earth. Lakes of Light. If they were permanently congealed, and small enough to be clutched, they would, perchance, be carried off by slaves, like precious stones, to adorn the heads of emperors," wrote Thoreau. "But being liquid, and ample, and secured to us and our successors forever, we disregard them, and run after the diamond of Kohinoor. They are too pure to have a market value. ... How much more beautiful than our lives, how much more transparent than our characters, are they!" And he concluded the chapter of *Walden* titled "The Ponds": "Talk of heaven! ye disgrace earth."

Three years after *Walden* was published, Frederic Tudor and Timothy T. Sawyer wrote the "Report of the Committee of the Boston Board of Trade on the Subject of the Ice Trade." The report said:

> The trade founded on an article of no value, produces now a gross sale, at home and abroad, approaching a million of dollars, and calls into use other articles before worthless.
>
> The bodies of water in the vicinity now contributing ice have been held, and are taxed as the *property* of the abuttors, and have been growing in value as the trade advanced.

What was once worthless, wrote Tudor, is today worth millions.

"We have constructed a fate," wrote Thoreau, "that never turns aside."

Nothing but Remember

When it was over, when the wrecking cranes and the bulldozers had been through, when the copper and lead had gone for scrap and the bricks for landfill, all that remained were streets and streetlights, a city as flat as a child's game board. And then most of those streets were wiped from the map and two cities began to rise: the developer's city of luxury towers and the exile's city of memory. It has been thirty years, and today two cities occupy the same land: the one of bricks and steel, and the other a city of memory houses. One city is completed, and the other continues to build until today it is many cities.

There's DiMaggio's City.

"I remember old man DiMaggio sitting on his chair at the corner of Green and Staniford streets, nursing a bad leg and breathing gently through his bad lungs, mementoes of fragments and mustard gas incurred during World War I," recalls Joe Caruso. "Years later, just before [Boston's West End] was destroyed, the city erected a memento to the old man's only son, a boy killed on the beach at Anzio during World War II, Jimmy DiMaggio. ... The city named it James DiMaggio Square and then tore it down."

There's the Cool Kids' City. Richard Lourie remembers when he would skip school and wander the streets. "The West End was the best place I had ever been. Its winding dark brick streets seemed full of mystery and adventure without being mean and dangerous. ... Women called down from small third-floor windows in languages I had never heard before. There were the smells of a dozen 'old countries' in the hallways and the streets."

There's the City of Childhood. Vincent LoPresti has a vivid memory of that city—a memory from the time he was called Sonny, and all the world he knew was the twisting streets of the West End. LoPresti remembers the cranes with wrecking balls coming up his street: "Watching a house demolished—you knew the parents, grandparents and the kids, knew the families, knew the kitchens— it's like watching a person with cancer die. It's hopeless, knowing there's nothing you can do."

Nothing but remember.

∞

Barbara LoVuolo has a photo in her wedding album, 1963. The world she knew was also the West End. In the background, the photo shows the West End as it appeared on her wedding day: a forty-eight-acre vacant lot in the heart of Boston, a wedding on the edge of a wasteland.

LoVuolo and thousands of others remember the lost neighborhood, and when they meet, their talk is filled with a vanished geography of streets no longer on city maps, delis and bakeries long closed and a web of family names, associated even now with their old addresses. Do you remember? they ask one another. *Do you remember?*

The West End they knew was a poor neighborhood of Italians, Jews, Poles, Greeks, Russians, Irish, Ukrainians and Albanians, just down the slope from Beacon Hill. On the eve of its destruction in 1958, the West End was 47 percent Italian, 10 percent Jewish and 10 percent Polish. The remaining third filled out the neighborhood's twenty-three nationalities. "Growing up," says LoPresti, "it was strange to hear an old person speak English."

To these new immigrants the West End was home. The Boston Housing Authority called it a slum "detrimental to the safety, health, morals and welfare of the inhabitants." The housing authority portrayed the West End as a den of the ten plagues—among them, rats, vermin, tuberculosis, juvenile delinquency, "social disorganiza-tion" and narrow streets, a street plan unchanged since the 1840s.

"Sooner or later the old parts of a city wear out," said a 1954 housing authority pamphlet. It is not enough to replace just a few buildings, said the authority, "the lots are too small, the streets are too narrow and crooked, the whole layout is out of date." A "new and modern plan" was needed. ("Family life is generous with warmth, and community life is rich with vitality," said a social worker in a 1960 television documentary on the West End. "These areas, however, are often substandard. ... ")

To many Bostonians, the West End was a strange and depressing place. They read in its foreign manners a criminal threat. "The West End today is definitely a slum area," *Boston Herald* columnist Bill Cunningham wrote in 1957. "In fact it always has been," he said, claiming that the area was a haven for vice in 1900 and "since has slowly slid toward the worse." The neighborhood was a "cesspool" that needed "cleaning out."

Grandpa's City

"Grandpa was a kind, friendly man. He would sit in his favorite chair in front of his house with his cat Martha by his side from morning till night, greeting friends, neighbors and strangers with a handshake and a smile. He was known as the 'mayor' of Brighton Street," remembers his grandson, Joseph LoPiccolo.

In the summer, Grandpa would walk over to the park, where he'd meet his friends, play Bocce or Motta (a card game) or "they would just sit and enjoy the sun and reminisce about their boyhood days in Italy. On rainy days Grandpa would stroll up Leverett Street to Charlie Papa's Cafe for a cold beer, wander over to Gagi's pool room to watch the young guys play pool and sit and chat for hours with Sonny LoPresti's grandfather." Other times he would stop by the Italian American Club, or at Barney Sheff's Deli for a glass of wine, and then go to Angelo's Barber Shop or Baldi's Barber Shop, two favorite gathering spots.

Like his neighbors in the pre-refrigerator era, he made the daily rounds for his shopping. "Every morning he would be first in line at Nicolosi's Bakery to buy several loaves of delicious hot Scala bread. ... Grandpa would buy watermelon from the Watermelon Man who would travel the streets with a horse and wagon yelling 'Watermello.' ... Fridays came the Crab Man with fresh crabs and fish, yelling 'gowedy.'

"Everyday he would make a run to Spring Street, where Jackie the Bookie took his bets in the hallway. Grandpa would always play thirty-five numbers, a penny a number.

"Each September a hundred cases of grapes would be delivered to his house. I would help him carry them into the cellar ... and the wine making would begin. ... The aroma of it would filter throughout the building for many months. ... " In the fall, a truckload of coal was delivered to keep the potbelly stove in the basement going. In the winter, Grandpa would put orange peels on the hot kitchen stove, the aroma filling the house.

Then the eviction orders came. "Everybody had to move. Grandpa was devastated. At his age he could not understand what was happening, why his house, his friends, his neighborhood, his life was being taken from him. Is this America? Is this the United States, the land of the free? ... "

"It was such a sad day when we moved Grandpa to the projects in East Boston. Soon afterward his health began to fail. He could not get used to his new surroundings. He was lost, depressed, shattered. Then it was off to the Don Orione Nursing Home. Grandpa would just sit and cry all day. He missed his home, the West End. He had this empty feeling ... shortly thereafter he died."

Sick City

The language of urban renewal was cancer language. Cities were sick. Slums were cancer. And so—the cancer had to be removed. In a television documentary of the era, a Boston banker says: "There's only one way you can cure a place like the West End, and that is to wipe it out. It's a cancer in the long run on the community. This may seem ruthless, but this is an aspect of urban renewal.

"I am quite certain that under the present set up, the rights of people are being respected as much as possible, but it's silly to say that when you're having a major municipal hysterectomy like this that everybody's going to come out exactly the same. You just aren't. Some people are going to be hurt and their rights, in my opinion, will not be entirely respected, but when you're moving thousands of people around, you are really doing it for the good of the whole. And the people of Boston will benefit enormously from this."

In one scene in the documentary, a bulldozer is working away. The camera pulls back to focus on the ruin of a large clock, the hands gone, a hole in its face where noon or midnight would fall.

∞

To urban planners, the West End was ugly down to the numbers. Overall, buildings covered 72 percent of the land, and on some blocks, 90 percent. The modern-city ideal was 33 percent, the high rises standing amid green parks. "We wanted a suburban feeling right downtown," said Jerome Rappaport, the developer who built new luxury towers on the cleared land.

The city's leaders were desperate to lure suburbanites back to the city. Boston was languishing. In the 1950s the population of the suburbs outside Boston jumped 50 percent, and suburban employment increased 22 percent. Boston's population shrank 13 percent, and its employment fell nearly 8 percent. There had been virtually no new construction downtown since the 1920s. "Boston proper did not really recover from the Depression until the 1960s," says John H. Mollenkopf in *The Contested City.*

Fortune magazine, profiling Boston in 1964, described a city that was trying to shake itself free from "a half century of sliding." The waterfront was dead. The innovative spirit that had shipped ice and silk to the world was gone. Boston was now considered to be at the edge of a market. It had the lowest median family income of seven major metropolitan areas. The city was an economic backwater. (It had been thirty years since *Fortune's* last major article on Boston.) The interior of city hall was "painted two shades of the oily eye-ease green associated with run-down optometrists' shops," said *Fortune*. This "sick city" was "being turned into a laboratory demonstration of urban renewal techniques."

Boston's citizens were told that nothing less than the city's future was at stake. "If the West End can be switched from dilapidation to delight … it may be the trail-blazing spark which could revitalize Boston," said the *Boston Globe* in December 1959.

To reject this plan, said the head of the Boston Redevelopment Authority, would "constitute a body blow to Boston's attempts to revitalize itself economically and socially through urban renewal." "An imposing array" of the city's civic, professional and business leaders concurred. They "jubilantly" praised this "swank high rental development with a New Yorkish skyline," said the *Globe*.

In the face of this, the West Enders were not organized. They were unwilling to believe that an entire neighborhood could be taken from them. This perception was reinforced by the decade-long bureaucratic process: announcements would be made, nothing would happen and years would pass.

Finally, when the government told them to move, these formerly displaced immigrants moved. "In Russia, where my family came from, you could expect to be deprived of your home and your personal rights," said one young West Ender at the time. "But in a democracy, can there also be displaced persons?" They were promised places in the new towers, but they weren't told that rents would be four to five times higher than what they had been paying.

In 1958, after seven years of preparation, the city began leveling the neighborhood. Ten thousand people were dispersed. It was the opening act for urban renewal in America.

The city is decaying, said one television documentary, "but finally the nation is arising to rescue its unhappy Main Streets." It was a fate that could not be turned aside.

Quick-Take City

They set out to "cure" the West End. In April 1958, using the "quick take" laws, the Boston Redevelopment Authority assumed ownership of all the homes and businesses in the West End. Landlords and tenants now had to bring their rent checks to city hall. Demolition would begin in eight weeks. The landlords were placed in a financial squeeze by the city: they couldn't collect the rent, yet they had to pay their mortgages. With wrecking crews working nearby and their old neighborhood falling around them, the building owners were unable to move: They had received no money from the city for their property and did not know when it would come. After months of this life, they would desperately accept almost any settlement.

By the summer of 1959 only a few families were left, like the Vendittis. Mary Foti Venditti's parents came from Sicily to the United States and eventually to the West End. She grew up in the West End, was married there, and in time she and her husband bought a house on Poplar Street.

"We had six spacious rooms, which we fixed up at considerable expense. But we did not mind, as this was to be—or so we thought—our permanent home," she says. "Also, we had some income from the other apartments, which came in handy. Our children were doing nicely. There were a lot of things going for the youngsters then.

"Comes the housing authority one day and tells us that we have to vacate our home, our property was being taken by eminent domain. And what is eminent domain? I did not know. When my husband came home from work, I asked; he did not know either. How could anyone come into your home and take—steal—your property? We were confused and a little frightened.

235

"One day this fat man came to us with an offer which was far below assessment. How could they do this? We were paying taxes way above what they were offering. We refused the offer. In the meantime, Duane [John J. Duane Building Wrecking Company] was leveling houses left and right. They wanted to get the job done as quickly as possible. We stuck to our guns. We refused to sign until we got a decent price. Duane would harass us. He would bang the wrecking ball against our house to scare us. Ours was about [the last house] left standing. Some of the children would think the place empty and throw rocks at our windows. I was worried our children would get hit. We signed our home away.

"When the fat man came with the documents, he promised to find us a place to live. But that was a lie. A few days later he called and said the sheriff was in the house. I quickly left, hurried home. When I got home, I found this fat man sitting down with a gun and an attack dog. Two men were taking out our furniture. I asked fatty what was going on, and he said, 'We are taking the furniture to the storage.' My son wanted to get at the fat man, but what chance did a seventeen year old have against a slimy, fat goon with a gun and an attack dog? I tried to calm my son.

"When my daughter came home from school and saw the mess, she started to cry. 'Where are we going, and what happened to all my clothes?' I was frightened, but I did not want to show it. I did not want to traumatize the children. ... And that was the summer of '59."

In time the Vendittis found a house in Arlington—"a lovely town, nice people," she says, "but unlike the West End, where my husband, after a hard day's work on construction, would stop at the bar room on Leverett Street for a glass of beer and socialize a bit with his friends before supper, and after that sit outside and chat with the friendly passersby.

"My husband, being a gentle soul, took it much worse than I did. He was a good, hard-working man, a good father and devoted husband, but he was never the same after this travesty. After a while he could not hold a job for long. And then it was one hospital after another. It really hit him bad. ... "

236

Sociologists' City

Sorrow was news to the social scientists of the 1950s. They set about quantifying it. Two years after the demolition, sociologist Marc Fried asked: "How did you feel when you saw or heard that the building you had lived in was torn down?"

People told Fried:

"I felt like my heart was taken out of me."

"I felt as though I had lost everything."

"I felt like taking the gas pipe."

"I lost all the friends I knew."

"I always felt I had to go home to the West End, and even now I feel like crying when I pass by."

"Something of me went with the West End."

"I used to stare at the spot where the building stood."

"I was sick to my stomach."

"If I knew the people were coming back to the West End, I would pick up this little house and put it back on my corner."

In response to one survey question, 54 percent of the women and 46 percent of the men reported "severely depressed or disturbed reactions."

"These figures go beyond any expectation," wrote Fried. The urban renewal experts believed that being removed from your home was an upsetting but quickly passing experience. Fried reported: "Relocation was a crisis with potential danger to mental health for many people." Some residents, of course, were glad to be gone. They had found the neighborhood too congested, with too many barrooms. But among those who identified the West End as home, 81 percent grieved and two years after exile showed all the signs "strikingly similar to mourning for a lost person."

People were "grieving for a lost home," said Fried. They had "feelings of painful loss, the continued longing, the general depressive tone, frequent symptoms of psychological, or social or somatic distress ... the sense of helplessness, occasional expressions of both direct and displaced anger, and tendencies to idealize the lost place."

"Why," the study asked, "should the loss of a place, even a very important place, be so critical for the individual's sense of continuity; and why should grief at such loss be so widespread a phenomenon?

"In fact, we might say that a *sense of spatial identity* is fundamental to human functioning."

The sociologists wanted to know how these "slum residents" had created an "interlocking set of social networks ... so profoundly at variance with typical middle-class orientations." In short, why did these people like living in these dirty little streets?

The West Enders were studied in papers with titles like "Some Sources of Residential Satisfaction in an Urban Slum" and "Personal Identity in an Urban Slum," and in books like Herbert J. Gans's *The Urban Villagers*.

"A closer examination of slum areas may even provide some concrete information regarding ... the physical and spatial arrangements typical of slum areas and slum housing, which offer considerable gratification to the residents," wrote Marc Fried.

That the West Enders lived so differently than the middle class made the neighborhood confusing to outsiders. The middle-class neighborhood was one of boundaries, layers of privacy and propriety: you made appointments to see people; you didn't just drop in. You said hello to people on the streets, but you did not hang around for all hours on the street corner. The West End was aswarm with life on the streets and in the hallways.

"If you did anything wrong in the streets, rest assured by the time your mother came home she would know about it," recalls Charlotte Krim. "Ten people on the street would tell her. In fact, if you had visitors, they'd let you know. They'd want to know if you had boyfriends. A date?—forget it—because they wanted to know where everybody went."

"Social life has an almost uninterrupted flow between apartment and street," observed sociologist Edward J. Ryan. "Children are sent into the street to play, women lean out the windows to watch and take part in street activity, women go 'out on the street' to talk with friends, men and boys meet on corners at night, and families sit on the steps and talk with their neighbors at night when the weather is warm. ... "

"Certainly, most middle-class observers are overwhelmed at the degree to which the residents of any working-class district and, most particularly, the residents of slums are 'at home' in the street," wrote Marc Fried and Peggy Gleicher. Hanging out on the corner was an important part of life in the West End.

In a study of personal identity, Edward J. Ryan found that West Enders chose friendship over getting ahead. The West Enders were "asked to state which they would prefer to be, an auto mechanic who had many friends and who was contented, or a general manager who was to become a leading businessman but who had little time for fun. "Sixty-four percent chose the auto mechanic. What had the business-man sacrificed? the sociologist was asked time and again. Did he lose friends? Was he happy?

Ryan asked them to list "major components of good social standing." Education and occupation were named first, as would be expected, but "having a lot of friends" was a close third, ahead of income, influence and ethnic group—the last in determining standing.

They valued their "hanging group"—for men, the old gang that gathered at the corner to pass the time ("street corner society," William Foote Whyte called it), and for women, the coffee klatsch where they talked about "personal difficulties." (Today such talk is corralled into structured support groups and therapy sessions or broadcast as talk shows.)

This friendliness is what made the West End a neighborhood, they told Ryan, and it was what they missed when they were relocated: no more dropping in, no more street corner chats and no more looking out for one another, no matter the ethnic group. One Polish woman told Ryan how for several months she had paid the electric bill for her out-of-work neighbors by taking the bill out of the mailbox before the neighbors saw it.

"In conversation with West Enders it was rare to learn of either past jobs or occupational aspirations. Rather, the meaningful past was a sequence of good times and memories of places where the gang got together and of events that happened there. Tales of the past enshrined feeling in relation to others," wrote Ryan.

And Fried and Gleicher wrote: "This view of an area as home and the significance of local people and local places are so profoundly at variance with typical middle-class orientations that it is difficult to appreciate the intensity of meaning, the basic sense of identity involved in living in the particular area."

⌒⌒

After Prague's old ghetto was torn down, around 1900, Franz Kafka wrote:

> They are still alive in us, the dark corners, the mysterious alleys, blind windows, dirty courtyards, noisy taverns and secretive inns. We walk about the broad streets of the new town, but our steps and looks are uncertain. We tremble inwardly as we used to do in the old miserable lanes. Our hearts know nothing yet of any clearance. The unsanitary ghetto is much more real to us than our new, hygienic surroundings. We walk about as in a dream, and are ourselves only a ghost of past times.

Wonderland

Every warm Thursday night for a decade, Joseph LoPiccolo used to go to a bench by a Mobil Station to meet friends; a couple of years ago that station was razed. "My kids can't understand what I keep going back to: 'There's no West End—what are you doing?'"

In a famous Ray Bradbury story, *Fahrenheit 451,* all books are destroyed by the state, but people keep the legacy alive. Each person memorizes a book. They become that book. In America, we have not destroyed books, but we have destroyed cities, and now people walk around who are the West End in Boston or the Bronx in 1940.

Nearly thirty years after the West End vanished, there was a neighborhood reunion in 1986. It was planned for seven hundred people. Word spread and twelve hundred showed up, overfilling the Wonderland Ballroom in Revere, Massachusetts. People had to be turned away. Old West Enders came from Arizona, Texas, California. "Many of these people hadn't seen each other for thirty years. All they wanted to do was reminisce and see what had happened to who," says Vincent LoPresti, who helped organized the reunion. They wanted to find childhood friends, people who, when they had last been seen, were known as Babe, Spud, Yoyo, Beebo and Sparky.

For Mary Carnazzi, the reunion was "like a dream, because for thirty years I had no past." And now here were people she had not seen in a lifetime. For Delores Sannicadro, seeing the old neighborhood reborn for one evening helped to "heal that empty feeling" that "everyone of us has. We can't bring our children or grandchildren to show them where we grew up."

"Every person there had a big smile," said Barbara LoVuolo, another organizer. "The thought that raced through my mind was: I wish the whole world could feel this way all the time."

Another West Ender, who had lived for years in Israel, remembered how the earth of the Holy Land was treasured as sacred, people taking it back home with them. So while she was in Boston for the reunion, she and a friend found an unbuilt parcel of land "in back of the Winchell School at the location where Sharlene Trugman's grandmother had a small variety store." She knows it sounds crazy, but she feels better when she sees this bottled earth back home in her living room in Texas.

Other reunions followed, with thousands of former residents. There have also been smaller reunions. Nearly two hundred former residents of Wall Street have all sat down to dinner together. West Enders have gathered for family picnics at their old summer camp, Camp Gannett, and at the Suffolk Downs racetrack for West End Day.

Some West Enders did not need to have a reunion. The West End Bowling League has been together for fifty years, led by Tony Comperchio, seventy-four years old and an original member of the league. Others in the league have been bowling for thirty years. And there is a woman's club, the "Lucky 10." These ten women have been meeting every week for forty years.

Another West End institution that survived the breakup of the neighborhood is the West End House, the boys club that ran dances and basketball games and sent children to camp each summer. Although the West End House has moved across town, almost all its support comes from old West Enders. When the West End House celebrated its eighty-fifth anniversary in 1991, more than one thousand West Enders showed up. It is the only boys club in the country supported solely by alumni.

Many had read about the reunion plans in a newsletter, *The West Ender*. The newsletter has grown from one sheet mailed to 120 people in 1982 to a mailing list of nearly three thousand and issues running to twenty-five pages, filled mostly with letters asking: Do you remember? The Ceruolo family of eleven members? Baldi's Barber Shop? When Charles Street was paved in wooden blocks? And do you remember the sound the horses made when the militia came down Charles Street to the state prison on the Sacco and Vanzetti case?

Walk with me down Spring Street and Sprague Street, down North Russell and Eaton, the letters ask. Walk with me down all the vanished streets of childhood. In the newsletters, this is what they say to each other:

> You can think back and still see Charlie Papa behind the bar with his gigantic smile while telling all his jokes.

> We bought slush in envelopes at the corner store, taffy apples in the fall, and hot chestnuts in the winter from a man with a cart. On July 4th everyone would go up on the roof to watch the fireworks.

> On a hot summer night, my mother would send me to Klaman's Delicatessen for a glass of seltzer—two cents plain.

> I remember the warm evenings when all the neighbors sat on the front stoop talking ... drinking lemonade and tonics. ... The children would be watched while playing games in the street.

I remember Lazaro's for coffee, Andy's Pizzeria (my first beer), Moe Rush's drug store, Earl (Weasel) Bartholomew, Louis Kessen's radio repair shop, Sarkisian's grocery, Minnie White's, Joe & Nemo's ... Hurwitz Bakery: the aroma of the bakery was a sharp contrast to that which emanated from Waldman's stable on the corner of North Russell and Parkman Street.

I remember the parrot in the first-floor window that would swear all day on Green Street; the bar called the Bucket of Blood, the "doers"—the peddlers up early to stand at their pushcarts doing the same thing over and over—and the "action boys" shooting craps; Sally Keefe swinging her tassels at the Old Howard, she could swing them each a different direction. She was an artist.

They put themselves back on the map:

To me, a young kid, Klaman's Corner was the hub of the hub of the universe. It was over the radio behind the counter on that Sunday afternoon that I heard about the attack on Pearl Harbor.

My husband they called Ham and Eggs, or Hammy—he worked with Schnipper in his fruit store before he went into the service. Now he is retired, but he still loves the West End and goes back to see if any of his friends are around.

... and I was the child born in 1912 ...

... and we were happy ...

And they ask:

Do you remember the "Musical Waggenheims" (Sally, Nathan, Max, Goldie & Rose) had a spread in the Rotogravure of the old *Herald Traveler?*

Do you remember South Russell Street from 206 Cambridge Street to 35 Myrtle Street and no side streets, which made it great for coasting ... the balloon man, swimming in the Charles, the

Community Boat House, Charles Park before it was covered over by a highway, the oak tree at middle entrance to the park? I think every West Ender must have climbed that tree. The Saturday night dances at the Peabody House and the clubs from West End and Peabody House: Clovers, Rattlers, Embers, Rangers. Where are you? Call! Call!

What happened to the Parkers from Everett Street and the Cataldos, Raymonds, the DiGeatanos, Hutchins, Smiths, these people with big families ... or Richie Kohen? I used to trade bicycle parts for his pigeons in the early thirties. He always made out: The birds flew back to him. Or Dick the Bookie? Every time he walked at a fast gait (which he always did), he sounded like jingle bells.

Do you remember the woman on the fourth floor of a building calling out the window: "Hey, Mike, bring up a fifteen-cent piece of ice."

Who knew this family and that. Who knows me: Am a young senior citizen—let me hear from someone who knew me.

The letters conclude:

Tears come to my eyes. I can't explain to my wife: we were poor but rich ... a poor man's Camelot. ... The neighborhood existed in a now forgotten time. A drug-free world where the poor could still be proud. We never locked a door.

We were really one big family. Whenever I happen to meet an old West Ender, the feeling is the same as meeting a long lost brother or sister; I cannot tell you how much I miss that feeling.

The West End still lives in our hearts.

I could go on but sadness keeps creeping in. ...

Thanks for letting me remember.

"Memory is a kind of accomplishment," wrote the poet William Carlos Williams, "a sort of renewal."

∽

In Italo Calvino's magical novel *Invisible Cities*, Marco Polo describes to Kublai Kahn the numerous cities he has seen in his travels. One city is Ersilia. "In Ersilia, to establish the relationships that sustain the city's life, the inhabitants stretch strings from the corners of the houses, white or black or gray or black-and-white according to whether they mark a relationship of blood, of trade, authority, agency. When the strings become so numerous that you can no longer pass among them, the inhabitants leave: the houses are dismantled; only the strings and their supports remain."

In one newsletter, a West Ender writes: "I hope more young generation letters come in so I can broaden my memories." *Broaden* my memories. They are still walking the streets, still stretching the different colored string from invisible house to invisible house. In memory, the West End is a tapestry made visible.

City of Yoyo, Fat Schnipper & Tabachnik

"Johnny Hoar and Yoyo had a mutual agreement one day in Baldi's Barber Shop to have their heads shaved, no reason, just a dare," recalls Tony Oddo. "A few days later Yul Brynner won the Academy Award for *The King and I.* Johnny borrowed a trophy from Charlie Papa, and the guys drove through downtown Boston in a Cadillac convertible. He sat up in the back with the top down, waving to the people, holding his trophy in the other hand. My sister's girlfriend Shirley came running into my house; she was so excited: she had seen Yul Brynner downtown."

Tony Oddo also remembers going as a kid to Schnipper's fruit store on Spring Street: "He had a little Italian guy named Dominic that worked for him. All Schnipper did was sit on a milk case and yell

245

orders to Dominic. I used to stare in wonder at this huge man with his incredible bulk hanging over the sides of the milk case. Remember how they used to build those milk cases years ago with the steel rods and the hardwood frames with the steel braces. They could support the weight of a car, a truck or even Normie Schnipper.

"If you went into his store, he would say, 'Wachawant.'

'I want a head of lettuce, Schnipper.'

'Heada lettuce Dominic,' he would yell. 'Watelse ya want.'

'A pound of tomatoes.'

'Pounda tomatoes Dominic.'

'What else.'

'A dozen oranges.'

'Dozen oranges Dominic.'

"And it would go on like that until Dominic (via Schnipper) filled your order. Schnipper would ring up the sale on the register and then have a snack. Five hot dogs, a pound of corned beef eaten by hand without bread, a pint of coleslaw, a couple half sour pickles, three or four apples and two cantaloupe halves filled with ice cream would usually hold him till lunch.

"My brother Chubby ran an errand for Schnipper once to get his custom-made suit at Burns and Martin Fat Man's Shop. I will say that when Schnipper wasn't working, he was impeccably dressed in the latest style, and for a man his size, he looked very neat. Anyway, my brother Chubby and his friend decided to try the suit for a laugh before they delivered it to Schnipper. I swear this is true. They each climbed into a leg apiece, zipped up the fly, put an arm apiece into the jacket, held on to each other while they buttoned the jacket and laughed so much they fell down."

Tabachnik or Kabachink—no one knew where he came from or just how crazy he was, but he was seen throughout the West End picking through trash barrels or leading an invisible army or singing in the streets.

"I knew him from my childhood in the mid-1930s, when I was about thirteen. I knew a neighborhood character when I saw one, and he was a character," recalls Frank Lavine.

"He must have been between forty to fifty years old at the time, a bit under six feet tall, unshaven with short hair. He was built like a weight lifter and strong as an ox. He was the original street person: wore cast-off clothing, a rope tied around his waist and torn shoes. He was a barrel picker, but he carried himself proudly as he walked down the street, almost always with a paper bag tied with a string slung over his shoulder like a knapsack.

"He was supposed to have come from a wealthy family, was well educated, and he spoke English, Yiddish, Hebrew, Russian, Polish, Italian, French and German. He'd been in and out of mental institutions all the time that I knew him and was pointed out as an example of someone who went crazy because he read too much, a caution to those of us that thought we were bookish intellectuals. Today he probably would be diagnosed as a manic-depressive personality. He had probably studied for the concert stage. He could read and composed music. He carried manuscripts with him and often sat on a curb and composed. He had a beautiful voice. I would say it was of operatic quality. I heard him sing arias for food or coins many times. Other times he would carry a broken violin, guitar or other string instrument that he attempted to play, usually without success. This was when the kids would really bug him.

"Many of the old-timers like my father would feed him. I remember feeling very proud when my father would sit him in a doorway, then go up and bring down some black bread, sliced onion and pickled herring. We would watch him eat, because feeding someone like him was considered a good deed. It was my under-standing that he also had a weekly tab at the Causeway Cafeteria. This was left to him in the will of a rich West Ender that had felt sorry for him. I saw him there from time to time.

"There were many small synagogues in the West End. Almost every town and village from Poland or Russia had its own shul. The larger synagogues could afford to pay an expensive out-of-town

247

cantor for the High Holy days. But the small places were always short of money, and they would try and contract with him to sing the service for Rosh Hashanah and Yom Kippur. It was a gamble as to whether he would or wouldn't show up on the day he was supposed to. People would come from all over to see and hear him.

"The small place was always packed and the tension would build as the time came for him to appear. The back door would open, and he would enter dressed in splendid, clean white robes, wearing a gold embroidered hat, with a prayer shawl over his shoulders. He strode down the aisle like a king, walked up the few stairs to the platform in the center of the shul and began chanting the service. An unbelievable transformation had taken place. This man who the day before probably had been fishing through barrels and had chased and swore at kids for calling him names was singing with the voice of an angel."

∞

A group of women were talking around a kitchen table back in the 1950s, back in the West End. They were talking about a woman they no longer saw too much. That woman, they said, "had married outside" the West End.

City of Anger

Eleanor Wojciechowski watched with her mother, Anna, as a crane crushed the roof of St. Mary's Polish Church. "That little church inconspicuously sandwiched between houses, which represented the lifeblood for so many and which existed because of the sacrifices of all those Polish families who gave their first very hard earned dollars to the church—*their church*. In silence my mother stood watching, then shook her head and after a while turned slowly to leave. I looked up and saw tears streaming down her face. Did anyone care what impact this had on my mother, who saw her first home and her first church in America reduced to rubble?"

248

∽

Boston is a city of monuments. Tourists spend hours following the mile-and-a-half-long Freedom Trail from one shrine of patriotism to the next. Far from the Freedom Trail, there is a memorial for the lost West End. Along Storrow Drive is a sign that says: "If you lived here ... you'd be home now." The sign advertises the luxury Charles River Park towers, and to motorists knotted in traffic it just seems like your average ridiculous real estate boast.

That sign taunts the old West Enders—they *were* home before being evicted. The more one reads that sign, the more mocking it becomes. Tony Oddo has even titled a fictional account of his old neighborhood "If You Lived Here You'd Be Home Right Now." Oddo's manuscript is "dedicated to the people of the West End of Boston who, after thirty years, are still waiting to come home."

In the original plan, the West End was to have been removed for new low- and moderate-income housing: 1,175 low-income apartments, 200 middle-income and 640 high-income. A young developer, Jerome Rappaport proposed an opposite scheme: 2,270 units of luxury housing and 150 low-income units for the elderly. Rappaport had helped the mayor get elected. He had put in the second highest bid for the land. The highest bidder withdrew. The land was condemned and bought with federal money at $7.40 a square foot, revalued at a $1.40 a square foot. It was leased to Rappaport for a yearly rental at approximately 6 percent of the lower value.

"The important thing is that the area is cleaned of slums and middle-income apartments are provided that are taxable," Rappaport said in 1956. And years later, he justified his approach: To attract the wealthy that had fled Boston, he tried to build "a suburban oasis in an urban city."

The West Enders were promised the first choice of the new housing, and, they were told, they would have to pay only a small increase in rent. But apartments ranged from $125 (for a studio) to $325 a month at a time when most West Enders were paying around $50 a month.

The West End was a graphic example of the poor "subsidizing its own removal for the benefit of the wealthy," wrote Herbert J. Gans in a 1965 critique of the failures of urban renewal. The West End, like so many neighborhoods cleared for urban renewal, was chosen not because it was the worst slum, but because it was the best location for luxury housing.

Urban renewal was not for the benefit of the slum dweller. "Only one-half of one percent of all federal expenditures for urban renewal between 1949 and 1964 was spent on relocation of families and individuals," wrote Gans. The basic error is that urban renewal is "still a method for eliminating the slums in order to 'renew' the city, rather than a program for properly rehousing slum-dwellers."

Jane Jacobs, author of the 1961 classic *The Death and Life of Great American Cities*, says, looking back now: "You know, there was a lot of nonsense talked about how you were doing them a favor by throwing them out, that they really hated it, that it was not the kind of place to bring up children."

The West Enders lost their homes for a lie.

"The first question out of West Enders' mouths when they met in the early sixties was 'Have you heard anything about going back?' Of course we never did," neighbors recalled.

∞

The articles in *The West Ender* are laced with a bitter sorrow:

"A lot of us lost relatives in the Second World War, but our sacrifices meant nothing—instead of German totalitarianism, we ended up with a benign totalitarianism that would let us roam where we want to, but if [the government] wants our property or services, we have no choice in giving them up. ... You are only free in America if you have plenty of money."

The editor of the newsletter, James Campano, has been unrelenting in his attack on Rappaport and Charles River Park. Campano has talked of filing a class action suit. He has spent his afternoons with a few others picketing Rappaport's offices. The West End deal was, he says, "a reverse Robin Hood." "What a swindle. An invasion for the good of the people," he says. "They did it to us and they just walked away laughing."

"Half of Charles River Park's ground area is comprised of parking lots," Campano writes in one issue. "That means at least half of West End people were displaced for cars. ... Why couldn't the city take the lots by eminent domain and replace them with low-cost housing for West Enders?"

At times the newsletter reads like the Nuremberg war trials for urban renewal. But Campano says, "Let me put it this way: in certain quarters I'm considered a moderate."

West Enders are still angry at hearing their old neighborhood called a slum. "I never knew that I lived in a slum until *outsiders* told me that I had," said one. And another said: "Slum? Every Saturday before going out to play, the stairs had to be scrubbed, the sidewalk had to be swept and washed."

Slums, according to the sociologists, are communities that have ceased to work. They are areas with large transient populations. In a survey done by the Council of Churches in 1949, fewer than one in four West End residents "expressed a definite desire to leave." More than half had been born there or had been living there for almost twenty years.

The Boston Housing Authority recorded 80 percent of the housing as substandard, but another survey showed that 41 percent of the West Enders were living in good housing. Other studies found "some marked discrepancies" with the official data. (And a lawsuit challenged the tuberculosis statistics.)

And now thirty years later, narrow streets and ethnics are desirable. High-rise towers set in green parks are lamentable. Now, sometimes, the developers describe Charles River Park as a West End neighborhood. When the towers went up, they wouldn't dare use that slum name. The same newspapers that called the West End a "dirty slum," "a breeding ground for criminals" and a "cesspool" now praise the vanished neighborhood's ethnic diversity and close families. The politicians now say a terrible wrong has been committed.

"We remember the old West End as one of the finest, most integrated and stable neighborhoods in America, and it was destroyed," said Massachusetts governor Michael Dukakis in 1986. And as with all displaced tribes, there remains the small hope of a homecoming, or in the technical language, "priority for relocation after displacement by public action."

One small parcel of land has not been developed. The West Enders formed a Community Development Corporation and took a 10 percent interest in a housing project that would set aside some of the apartments for West Enders who wanted to return. The developers heard from more than four hundred families who wanted to return.

It was, however, just one of four proposals being considered for the site by the Boston Redevelopment Authority. The ownership of the land itself was contested—Jerome Rappaport believed that he still owned the land. The redevelopment authority thought his time to build had lapsed. Rappaport and the authority fought it out in court for years.

All of which left James Campano out on the sidewalk one winter day talking to a reporter from *Boston* magazine. They were standing in front of the empty lot where the proposed apartment building, the one Campano called his "dream," would have been. The building was going to have a glass-enclosed rooftop garden. Campano looked through the chain-link fence and thought about his West End friends returned to that garden under glass. He could see them all gathered there, laughing and talking, wrote *Boston* magazine: "He could practically feel the sun on his skin as he sipped his coffee in the atrium on a winter afternoon. 'I'm going to miss that atrium,' he said. 'I would have killed for that.'"

Campano pressed on. The Boston Redevelopment Authority won its court case. A building plan was chosen that will include a small West End museum.

◎

In January 1956, the Boston Housing Authority distributed a pamphlet called "West End Progress Report." The pamphlet was a series of questions and answers. One of these was:

What shall I do meanwhile if I am a tenant?
    The best advice we can give you is to "sit tight." There is no cause for worry.
    Every resident of the area will be re-housed in good housing. You are protected by laws which require that every family which now lives in the area must be relocated into "decent, safe and sanitary" housing.

City of Homecoming Denied

On a day that is not a day in a war, your neighborhood is leveled. The wrecking crew comes right down your street, right toward your building, your apartment, your kitchen and your bedroom. And then that's it. Your life as you know it is over. You are evicted. And for thirty years no one outside the old neighborhood wants to hear about it. Two cities start to rise, the luxury towers and the exiles' city of memory.

There is the City of William Bill (Ace) Regan. He says, "When I watch old movies and I see people coming back to their old hometown and how great it was to walk down Main Street and see the barbershop and the theater, bowling alley and drugstore, I think when I came back from the service in April 1960 and saw just a pile of bricks."

There's the City of Vic DeMarco. "My eyes fill with tears when I think of my old hometown," he says. "The West End, to me, was much more than buildings and land; it was a family and just like when a close ... member passes on, the hurt lasts a very long time. It seems to me my hurt has been continuous from 1958 when my mother, sister and I were forced to leave."

There's Joe Caruso's City: "I remember all the pretty girls, the volatile, lively men. I was in love with Fay Yaffa; it was a one-sided affair, I never told her. She lived on McLean Street, and I'd walk up and down the street looking for dragons to conquer. I was in love with Antoinette ... I forgot her last name. She lived on the corner of Green and Staniford streets. ... I think, in the end, I was in love with the West End ... and the smell of hot bread wafting through the narrow, blessed streets."

And there is the City of the Peddlers at Their Pushcarts. In one issue of *The West Ender*, there is this unsigned letter:

"I got your newsletter and see all the names, and it flushes out all the memories. God, how I wish I could turn back the clock and sell them all that fish again from the blue pushcart with that bell ringing to tell you we were coming—all except Tootsie Oddo who would buy ten pounds of squid and demand that I clean it and cut it up. (Heaven help me if I refused.)

"I still dream of the West End and the streets and buildings, seeing them so clear as if I were really there now and so disappointed when I awake—because who wants to leave the West End?"

Modern Times:
An Epilogue

The Clock Starts

"Esq. Stiles can remember when (1786 or thereabout) there were but four time-pieces in town," reported the *History of Temple, N. H.* in 1860.

Now start the clock, set it in motion, until every person is linked to a clock, and each clock to a machine. By the time Temple had written its history, there were entire cities in New England that ran by the clock, great mills, a web of belts and gears and looms that married each person, each motion of a hand, to the central machine.

"Of course, the system is yet in its infancy, but the wheels of revolution are moving rapidly," said one New Englander in 1863. "The hum of machinery is heard on every hand, old things are passing away, and all things are becoming new."

On Pigeon Hill

In the town of Lincoln, Massachusetts, thick flocks of pigeons in migration would stop to roost on a hill shaded by great oaks, "the

255

branches bending under the weight of their numbers." Pigeon Hill it was called in the years when America was a colony and nearby Boston a large town. Only the name remains.

In his *Letters from an American Farmer* (1782), J. Hector St. John Crèvecoeur described the netting of pigeons: "We catch them with a net extended on the ground, to which they are allured by what we call *tame wild pigeons*, made blind, and fastened to a long string; his short flights, and his repeated calls, never fail to bring them down. The greatest number I ever catched was fourteen dozen, though much larger quantities have often been trapped. I have frequently seen them at the market so cheap, that for a penny you might have as many as you could carry away. ..." Crèvecoeur was describing an America in its infancy.

The flocks of pigeons diminished, and Lincoln, and other towns, routinely voted at its town meetings "to kill Birds as usual."

Horsepower

Around the turn of the century, Abbie Phelps and her husband ran the general store in New Ipswich, New Hampshire. "We bought crackers by the barrel at first—later they came in pasteboard cartons," she recalled. "They were splendid goods, fresh and crisp, made in the nearby town of Winchendon and brought to the door in a huge horse-drawn wagon. Our salt pork came in barrels too, white, thick, sweet pork the like of which one cannot find today." Cheese came in large round wheels, molasses in hogshead barrels, the cod fish arrived whole, and the grain and meal and coffee in sacks. The coffee beans were ground by hand, "some job in itself," just to keep the town supplied. Everything had to be measured out and done up in paper bags, and in the later years, delivered.

Phelps's maroon grocery wagon was a well-known sight in the village. "You never saw a horse with a finer, cleaner harness on, brass buckles all polished beautifully. Wilbur Phelps took a pride in that team," recalled a neighbor.

Around the store's barrel stove, the "cracker barrel jury" assembled on chairs and sacks of grain and barrels. They spat tobacco into the sand under the stove as they "worked out the affairs of the town, country, state and nation" and reviewed all who came in to get marriage licenses and dog licenses or to pay taxes to Phelps, who was also town treasurer and clerk.

The cracker barrel was fast becoming a nostalgic set piece when Abbie Phelps wrote her recollections in 1939. Grocery stores, owned by chains, were opening in the larger towns. "The modern way is much to our advantage," she said of these glittering new stores. "You go into one of them even in mid-winter and find green vegetables and fruits that we of the old days were lucky if we could get in mid-summer, and the whole place is attractive and calculated to give one an appetite."

Still, something had gone out of the world: "For years all trucking was done by our two horses and our big wagon, and the nearest freight depot was three miles away. No black roads and the spring muds were sometimes something awful.

"At the last of our being in the store, we had a small auto truck which made it much easier. However, I heard my husband make this comment: 'When I had the horses, I'd get a good start for Fitchburg, get down there and put the team up in a stable to rest and get their dinner. I then went around to the wholesale places, had a good visit with all the men, saw the latest things on the market and had a good time. Then I'd get my own dinner, get the team and gather up my load and go home.

"'After I got the truck, I hurried down to the wholesalers, exchanged a few hurried words, bought what I needed, hurriedly loaded it up, hurried home and kept on hurrying after I got there. No friendly visit with the men, no good time, nothing but hurry as fast as I could.'"

The Last Forty Years

"Looking back, it just seems so almost like an *Our Town* dream world. Just forty years ago it was when we first came to town, it was half the size—if that. And everybody knew everybody else in town."

—Barbara LaRoche remembering
Peterborough, New Hampshire

"Look what's happening to our world. It's falling apart. People are being killed, planes are being hijacked. Something is dying everywhere I look."

—Michael Hart, fourth grader
at the Peterborough Elementary School.

Forty years separate those two views, and those forty years have brought modern times to New England. Little by little the world is remade, and then one day, when an old friend is gone or a tree cut down, or just one day when some ordinary errand is deflected, we feel that *now* the world is different.

To me so much of what has changed in American life is symbolized by a milk box I saw on a house from the 1920s. The box was built into the wall by the kitchen door. The milkman opened the outside door and left milk, eggs and butter. The housewife in the kitchen opened the inside door and removed the delivery. The two doors when opened together seemed like a grand entrance to a doll house.

But then the milkman ceased to deliver, the local dairy farm was sold for a housing tract, and break-ins began to occur in the neighborhood. The milk box was nailed shut, inside and out. A lock, and then a second lock with a deadbolt, appeared on the kitchen door. A light on a timer stood watch over the door. The rest of the house was sealed up, the summer porch glassed in, then abandoned, as the inhabitants retreated farther into the house. There is an antenna on the roof now, air conditioners in the windows behind a palisade of shrubbery that was once ornamental.

The car sits locked in the garage, waiting to get away down the road "beyond the troubles of this century," in the words of a 1951 Ford ad. The rest of the ad says: "Today the American Road has no end: The road that went no where now goes everywhere. … The wheels move endlessly, always moving, always forward—and always lengthening the American Road. On that road the nation is ... constantly headed for finer tomorrows. The American Road is paved with hope."

There were always getaways in American history: immigrate, migrate, head west, settle and sell, mine and move, hit the road. We believed in the road. But no one outruns history.

At one town meeting in my town, we were talking about garbage, how it was piling up. "This mountain we are building," someone said in a moment of offhand poetry. Others talked of the "waste stream," all the things we throw out daily. It used to be that you buried the trash and paid someone to haul away the bulky junk, old refrigerators and sofas. No more. "Pretty soon," said a selectman, "there aren't going to be any more 'aways.'"

⌒⌒

I have a friend who is building a house of memory. He collects chairs, tables, plastic radios—row upon row of radios—toasters, cocktail shakers, waffle irons, kiddie cars, gasoline pumps. ... Not a few people—including his wife—think he has collected quite a jumble. But it's not the objects so much, as the twentieth century itself he is collecting. All these things—streamlined toasters and seltzer makers—were tokens of promise. This is the great consumer utopia he is sheltering, "the highest standard of living in the world!"

Occasionally I go along with him when he goes collecting, though usually not until I have sufficiently forgotten the last trip. I am haunted by these trips. Things have a life, too. They flow on and on, coming to rest here, then there, but always flowing on. The world is a shipwreck on the land. We die trailing clouds of junk.

Sometimes we'll look at an entire attic of old chairs—rows and rows of them, lined up like soldiers fading away into the dark recesses. How many chairs? A thousand, two thousand? How many breakfasts and Sunday dinners, meals over good news and bad, meals eaten in a sullen silence? Some of those chairs have enough character to cast a play.

One time we went to an old warehouse in a small town in the Massachusetts outback. It was an old mill town where the pace of commerce had slowed to that of slurred speech. On the Saturday afternoon we were there, the only stores open were two liquor stores, a bar, and a small grocery. The barbershop (which was closed) had only one barber chair where there was space for three. That one chair so oddly sitting by itself in the middle of the floor made it seem like an arena for some kind of ritual sacrifice.

The warehouse was filled, three floors, with all the paraphernalia of middle-class life, say 1945 to the first oil crisis: jukeboxes, Coke signs, soda fountain stools, early TVs and radios, bicycles, kiddie car rides, even those speakers you hung on your car at the drive-in movies that made John Wayne sound like he was going through a puberty voice change. Here was the America that wore big hats, chain-smoked cigarettes, drove big, fat-finned cars and ate red meat on all days except Fridays in some quarters.

The warehouse was like a jumbled version of the Ford Museum, a museum of bygone consumerism. Things were arranged in so many layers of memory, like life in the rain forest: things were on the floor—you stumbled over them when you were looking up; things hung on posts, hung on rafters and, higher still, disappeared into the darkness in a dream-like way. It was all dream-like, so many cultural icons with powerful associations, all loose and adrift. Here lies the bobbysoxer and Coca-Cola America, Cold War America, the America where a family of four could live well on one paycheck. It was as if America had ended, and we were walking through the warehouse taking inventory. Here lies a thousand, thousand Saturday night dates. Farewell and farewell.

The colors on those Coke machines and signs were odd, as well. The machines and signs were rusted and weathered, but they still maintained the lurid colors of the 1940s and 1950s advertising that ran on the back of *National Geographic*. Red, red lips and rosy cheeks. Nothing in life was really that color—nothing but the promised good life.

I walked about in a daze in this building where men and women had once manufactured things. Up front, four or five people were talking. They were in their early fifties, is my guess. Only later did the force of what they said hit me.

"I don't know what the kids are going to do today."

"You know Mary's daughter, her and her husband both work— they're at it all the time, and they can't afford a house."

"I remember I bought those ten acres for twenty-five hundred dollars. That was in '62. And good land it was. ... Can't do that today. ..."

At last we left the warehouse. We stopped in the grocery store before we left town. It had been done up like a big-city supermarket, but a long time ago, maybe in the 1940s, judging by the Art Deco– style lettering over the freezer. The lettering and the rest of the interior looked like it belonged hanging from the rafters in the warehouse across the street. There was one checkout line with a short belt that hadn't worked in years. A line collected, four people holding a few odd items. We waited, shuffled from foot to foot. The young man at the register seemed almost overwhelmed by his task. This was stress; you could see it in his face. Time had slowed. Los Angeles is filled with people who fled towns like these.

∽

In the Renaissance, learned men rehearsed their memory by imagining a house. In each room they placed something to be remembered. Then they could walk through and retrieve the memory. To remember was to put everything in its proper place. Where is the memory house big enough to contain the last forty years?

Watching the Apocalypses Go By

We are gathered, eight of us, around a table of beautiful food, a festive meal with candles, a small arsenal of plates and knives and glasses at each place. Each of us is in fine health. We are plagued by none of the persistent pains that the average colonial American knew in his lifetime, nor do we suffer the wants of most of humanity. It is Christmas time, that steeplechase of nostalgia for adults.

We join our hands and silently say grace. Platters of vegetables are passed around, magnificent reds and greens, cool yellows, colors nowhere to be found deep in a New Hampshire December, but brought to us here by train and truck, by the hands of others. We feel a little bit guilty about that, and as New Englanders, native or immigrant, offer that guilt as our praise.

We talk: neighbors, weather, more neighbors, then food and the news (the last two are linked these days). And then, as so often happens, the conversation slides into elegy and apocalypse. The host says economist Lester Thurow has written that in twenty years the United States could have one of the lowest standards of living in the world. This brings us to this season's national obsession: the Japanese. Conversations about America seem to come in the compare-and-contrast mode; we are always looking at the greener pastures of some other society. In the late 1960s, people talked about Sweden; these days it's Japan. We sit and talk about robot technology on the assembly line. Most of us have read something about it, and we sally forth, experts all. The Japanese, of course, use robot technology much better than we do. Their robots produce more than our robots. Our host tells us that a U.S. company was astounded by this and sent a group over to study the Japanese factory. Their robots spent less time broken. They were shepherded by trained engineers; our robots were watched over by untrained wage-slaves who couldn't fix them, and so the assembly line would stop.

The assembly line stopping, I think, brings to mind in modern Americans, visions of a lost harvest. We go on to the next topic: the poisons in our food.

"Soak all fruit in Clorox," says someone.

"But the spray, it's inside," says someone else.

Everywhere people feel they are being poisoned. Once nourishing sights—sky, rain, earth, food—now pose a threat.

These poison discussions are shadowed by the elegiac recollections of childhood: the food *then*, the holidays *then*, the families *then*. The past has order; the present an apprehensive edge to it.

Is it fear that the machine will stop?—or that it won't? We can't make up our minds.

There is in so many conversations, in so much one reads, an "underlying sense of impending loss," as one book critic wrote. People can't define it, but they know they long for something across a divide.

Vacation plans in the late eighties: two friends are discussing renting a house in Hampton Bays, New York:

"It has a pool, so if any AIDS-infected needles wash up on the beaches, we'll be okay."

"Yeah, but if there is a water shortage, the pool is no good."

What was it John Cheever said about driving through the "melancholy spectacle" of stores sprawled along the highway? "He thought it a landscape, a people—and he counted himself among them—who had lost the sense of a harvest."

We look to the past in anger and sorrow and express our loss with elegy and jeremiad—the two chief products of twentieth-century memory. Both are lamentations at the grave of the world we once knew. Elegy asks: Where are the green trees we knew in our youth? Jeremiad decries: Our sins have killed the green trees.

We know elegy as nostalgia and jeremiad as the dire speeches warning of the decline and destruction of America. The jeremiad, historian Sacvan Bercovitch has shown, is a classic American form of political discourse. We have strayed far from our high ideals, says the speaker, and we are damned unless we rediscover those ideals.

The Puritans imported the jeremiad in their quest for a New Jerusalem. Six years off the boat, one minister could berate the Puritans for their wicked ways: "We never looked for such days in

New-England. ... [Are] all your promises forgotten?" The first American bestseller—1662—was Michael Wigglesworth's poem, *The Day of Doom*, 224 stanzas of hellfire and damnation, which many children were required to memorize. (At the last judgment, unbaptized infants are assigned to the "easiest room in hell.") Parts of the ballad were reprinted in grammar school primers throughout the eighteenth century.

With the depopulation of New England in the years after the Civil War, elegy and jeremiad were used in tandem to mourn New England. Each cellar hole where once a house had been and the stone walls defining the fields were viewed as the "silent memories of a dead race" as the *Atlantic Monthly* said in 1879. The "immutable relics of the hill country ... built with ceaseless energy—work comparable only to the building of the pyramids." Mourning New England was a small industry. Oliver Wendell Holmes toured cities dispensing elegiac recollections of country life, and people sat down to write popular memoirs of girlhoods and boyhoods with titles like *New England Bygones*—a title that could stand for almost every book ever written about New England.

These days we know the jeremiad as the bestseller that tells us we no longer have cultural literacy, or that we produce shoddy products, or that we are a nation of illiterate dope-heads merrily spending our way toward an abyss of deficit and anarchy and cholesterol. We have lost our way, say these modern-day preachers, and we must return to their definition of our fundamental beliefs. We must return to "the republican simplicity of those who have gone before us." We are wasting our wealth on too many fancy goods, "an extravagance which enervates and impoverishes our population," said New Hampshire governor Benjamin Pierce addressing the state legislature in 1829, during an era of simplicity that modern Americans would approach only warily on an Outward Bound expedition, and then only when equipped to the teeth.

Elegy may be our natural outlook. As adults we look back on childhood; society looks back on some always shifting, golden era; Western religion looks back on Eden. The first books of the Hebrew

Bible took shape in exile in Babylon and are, in part, an elegy to the lost Jerusalem.

I open my evening paper and read, there in the weekend entertainment section, a remembrance of making maple syrup at home, boiling the sap day and night in the kitchen, back when you could leave your door open without fear of thieves.

Now the maples the writer used to tap are dying. "These trees are big," he says. "One has an eleven-foot waistline. We think it was planted just before Thomas Jefferson wrote the Declaration of Independence." The big maple has been reduced to one branch; branches fall off the other maples so frequently that people don't dare walk past them.

The writer surveys the rest of the scene. "What happened to the whippoorwills who used to serenade us in the summer dusk? I haven't heard one in years. ... It's been a dozen years since I last saw a red fox, the one that ran along the top of the stone wall. ... The last mink I saw near our brook was ten years ago and the last otter in the Sugar River was eighteen years ago. ... Bobolinks used to bound in the pasture up the road. ... All this saddens me ... a disturbing feeling they don't like me and my kind."

More elegy: Friends back from the Dominican Republic give us the naturalist's report of the beach. There's the seaweed line, the driftwood line, and high up near where beach meets jungle: the plastic line. On a Caribbean beach, there are shower slippers, Clorox bottles, drink bottles. Everywhere plastic as if from a shipwreck. Fifty years ago many of these plastics didn't exist.

In all the elegies we are saying goodbye—to the elms, to the old neighborhood. Goodbye and goodbye again. We stand as if on a beach, the waters of the old ways fast receding, the sand under our feet giving way. Something new is coming, and we know not what.

∞

Once, America was promises. America is a poem in our eyes, said Emerson. In our eyes today, America is a ledger sheet. There is this

265

advertisement for improved seeds in *American Forests:* "It grows well in the ledger books, too. Our improved seed offers you a potential 500% return on your investment. So for every $10 you put into our seed, you'll get back $50 in return. Not bad."

Not bad, but why not more return? Once when I was picking up a New England housing magazine, the young woman behind the counter said to me: "I love that magazine. There's a house in there—the bargain of the month—a house and 120 acres of land by the Canadian border. You know, I hate to say this, but you could make a lot of money. There's a hundred wooded acres there. Go in and log the woods and then strip the top soil. And you would still have a fine vacation home. It wouldn't really matter."

⌒

The biblical question: For what shall it profit man, if he shall gain the whole world, and lose his own soul?

The modern question: For what shall it profit a man if he loses his soul *and* loses the world?

⌒

Everything is up for grabs; everything living or dead is a possession-in-waiting. In the Southwest, old Indian sites, undisturbed for centuries, are raided. In the deserts, rare cactuses are uprooted. In national parks, trees are stolen. In New England, there is a trade in tombstones stolen from old burial grounds. And so many old weather vanes have been stolen from barns that, says one antique dealer, "It's at a point where anytime I see one, I go up and tell the owners to take it down. I think almost all of them are gone."

Tradition, cultural memory, has become a trinket, a living room ornament. We have overrun ourselves with ourselves.

⌒

Poster in the office of Century 21 Real Estate: The earth seen from space, the blue marble. And under the photo: "Earth. Represented by Century 21."

I wanted to leave this quote by Simone Weil on the real estate office door: "From where will a renewal come to us, to us who have devastated the whole earthly globe? Only from the past if we love it."

∞

A man in Washington State has been searching for quiet. He has been looking for the last places where you can hear the earth as it once was for an eternity, before the machine. He is on a preservation mission. He first scouts air traffic maps to find the spaces in between routes. Then he goes off into the woods or marshes with his tape recorder. In seven years of searching in Washington State, he has found only twenty sites of peace.

Everywhere the clock, now set in motion, ticks away. The clock that once started so quietly as a few timepieces in a village, is now, as they said in the nineteenth century, an "infernal machine," a bomb. There are, according to the United Nations, more than three tons of TNT for every man, woman and child on earth. This is the way we lose the world.

∞

We are mourners at our own funeral. As Walter Benjamin wrote, "Self-alienation has reached such a degree that it can experience its own destruction as an aesthetic pleasure of the first order." Or to put it in a more American light, we are like Tom Sawyer and Huck Finn secretly watching their own funeral from the gallery. We want the joy of hearing ourselves eulogized. There's a thrill at our own power. We're so clever that we can end it all.

We dine out on lamentations, jeremiads, the somebody-done-somebody-wrong song on a cosmic level. To say it first, to be the bearer of the bad news, is to exempt ourselves.

267

Today we sit and watch the apocalypses go by. Doom and decline are another form of entertainment. A fireworks show. Oooh, that's awful—ohhh, that's worse. Will the end come by firestorm or ice or riot or grasshoppers or virus?

Still we resist our own best scares.

If we say that worse is to come, a small voice tells us that we can endure.

If we ask "where is it now, the glory and the dream?" a small voice in us answers, "The sun shines today also." There must be glory around.

If we are told for the hundredth time of how the pioneers found trees big enough to live in, of how there were parrots in the Carolinas and clams the size of plates in New York harbor and plenty without end, who can blame us if we turn on the old-timer telling the glory tales and ask: Are we to greet this dawn as a devalued dawn, a morning less worthy than one thirty or eighty years ago, less worthy than the sun that shone on the tall trees and the founding fathers?

We know that millions are starving, that untold animals are going extinct, and still we must rise each day, so we hide behind elegies and jeremiads. We take refuge in the soft focus of nostalgia, little homilies of reassurance that we can clip and fold into our wallets, a snugly warm world. We are released from any individual responsibility by the jeremiad—all problems are pitched at the same level of cosmic damnation, all solutions are to be found in a return to some bygone day when fundamental beliefs were in flower. We are freed from judging problems, as well as from trying as citizens to solve them.

When we seek to remember, we get nostalgia, or we get a swept clean and sturdy history, as in the way Johnny Appleseed is remembered and the way Kerouac's words are set into granite. We choose our ancestors.

Elegy and jeremiad have become a trap. We have yet to learn how to face the past. We are always looking back in anger and sorrow. We are caught between the jeremiad and the elegy, between calling for an angry God to punish us and reading the roster of all the squandered Edens. In all, we are mourning the loss of what made the world habitable, what made it home.

A story that was in the newspapers a while ago comes to mind:

> Glenmont, NY—Seven deer apparently frightened by hunters, jumped off a state Thruway bridge and plunged 35 feet to a highway below.

In the last paragraph of the story, the police sergeant said the deer were panicked. "They apparently lost all sense of where they were." The story hits home to me: They lost all sense of where they were. Whether it's killing pigeons or hunting deer, building big mills or big roads, progress is the creation of absences.

∞

At another dinner we have again talked about a few ecological disasters but mostly about the changes that will have to be made at our town's dump.

Where the conversation would usually trail off with someone saying, "*Well. I don't know what will happen,*" instead a friend says that we need to change our idea of what constitutes plenty.

Exactly. Behind all these lamentations is the loss of plenty—but plenty of two kinds. The classic cornucopia overflowing with the harvest, abundance without end, and the manufactured cornucopia filled with sleek inventions.

In the years of settlement, plenty meant having enough to eat. But that changed with the rise of machine-made wealth, and we became confused about what we needed and what we wanted. In the 1920s plenty might have meant a new radio, in 1959 a new car with fins, in the greedy 1980s, a class of people in this country defined plenty as a string of time-share condos on ski slopes and seashores.

Since the modern era began, we have been trading the classic cornucopia for the clever one. Only we never admitted it was a trade. All along we thought that we could have both. Somewhere in there, plenty came to mean excess, ever higher standards of material comfort.

The restored definition of plenty would mean clean water and sky, poison-free soil. But would we let go of our man-made cornucopia to grasp it?

∾

One Saturday afternoon in November we climb Monadnock. There is a spareness to the land in November; you can see the bones of the countryside. On the way down we stop at "Fassett's Mountain House," a ruin of boulders that was once an inn and a stable in the 1850s. We sit on the foundation walls and drink tea hot from a Thermos. The air is crisp with autumn clarity. We sit and watch the sunset as it touches a few clouds.

I think: What if this is the time before?

We are always talking about how good life was back then, back before x and y. And this may be the time before—here and now.

In another season, my wife and I are returning from an exhausting and disturbing journey. She is driving. I drift to sleep listening to some Chopin waltzes on the radio. By the motion of the car, I can tell where we are as we head toward Temple Mountain. I lean the seat way back and occasionally lift my lids a little. I am looking up toward the tree tops, an unusual perspective. I watch the landscape pass by as if I have never seen it before, as if I were watching a film fifty years hence, looking back, saying, "What a green and wonderful land."

Willing oneself into nostalgia for the present can, at times, make one see the beauty of what is near at hand. The world is still here for us.

The Eternal Present

As the modern era began, a town history could unfalteringly state its guiding belief:

"A town exists in history. Take away the memory of the past, and what remains? Only a name. Take away the example of the recorded wisdom of the past, and what ray of light would be left for our guidance? What could we do but wander in the maze of perpetual childhood?"

Once we were so sure that the past had something to teach us. Americans gathered up Washington's camp bed and bark from the tree under which he took command, and fringe from Lincoln's funeral car, and hardtack and muskets and hats and drums, and banked it all in little memory houses, the historical societies in so many towns that hold those relics like deposits against a rainy day.

Americans were eager for history. Europe had history; America had a rawness and a possibility. "Time will take away some of the monotony which comes from the absence of historical associations," wrote the Englishman James Bryce in his classic *The American Commonwealth* (1895). "No people could be more ready than are the Americans to cherish such associations. Their country has a short past, but they willingly revere and preserve all the memories the past has bequeathed to them."

Eighty years later, after two world wars and several lesser wars and military adventures, after riots and massacres, marches and reforms, after, at last, America had traded in its raw possibilities for a history, a well-respected professor contemplated history's lessons. What would he teach his American history students when they returned to Harvard in the fall?

Our history is irrelevant, David Herbert Donald wrote in the *New York Times*. "What undergraduates want from their history teachers is an understanding of how the American past relates to the present and the future. But if I teach what I believe to be the truth, I can only share with them my sense of the irrelevance of history and of the bleakness of the new era we are entering."

America had been "The People of Plenty," in historian David M. Potter's phrase. When we met a problem, a case of social inequity, we did not restructure society; we made the pie larger. "Now the age of abundance has ended. The people of plenty have become the people of paucity," wrote Donald in 1977. The lessons of the past do not apply.

"What, then, can a historian tell undergraduates that might help them in this new and unprecedented age? Perhaps my most useful function would be to disenthrall them from the spell of history, to help them see the irrelevance of the past."

271

ॐ

Take away the memory of the past, and what remains? the town history asked. The maze of perpetual childhood, was its answer.

I have an old friend who is a social worker, and each year we meet, at Thanksgiving or Christmas, and each year she has a new distressing outpost on the frontiers of domestic violence. One year it was a little different. She was counseling people who had struck their heads in auto accidents. They often walked away without a scratch. But these patients had no memory. She told me of one patient. From the moment he put his key in the door to the next moment, he couldn't remember what key this was, what door this was, or why he was standing there. He stood there dumbfounded, unsure of where he was going and where he had been. These patients live in the eternal present. They are a people living without a history.

The rest of us are much more fortunate. But we forget, too. One study of memory measured what an ordinary person remembers by monitoring a daily diary. After six years, one-third of all events noted in the diary had vanished from memory.

At the end of this century of extermination and extinction, we are like the head-trauma victims. Moment follows moment, event after event, but there is no memory. We live in the eternal present and occupy ourselves with an accelerating succession of novelty and fads, and tragedies as novelty, and political crises as fads. Time collapses in on itself, one airline hijacking is confused with another, and, to many younger citizens, all history is one event.

We have journeyed a long way, once ever so optimistically, and find ourselves far removed from the grist-mill and swimming hole, from the horse cart and elm-lined Main Street. We try nostalgia, elegy, jeremiad. All our efforts at recollection, and somewhere the past itself, are in the memory house.

ॐ

The curator of a modern memory house was talking about his museum's purpose, and oddly enough he was saying something very old-fashioned about the guiding light of the past, but he brought to it the urgency of a rescue mission. The Newark Museum had just completed its expansion when Samuel L. Miller, the museum director, spoke of his hope that the museum would preserve a sense of "beauty and order" in the ruined landscape of that New Jersey city. "There's a whole generation of kids growing up who have no idea of what the world is supposed to look like," Miller said. "They see decayed cities, littered streets, malled-over meadows. I want the museum to show them that there's a standard of excellence against which things can be measured."

I think of the test tube of Edison's dying breath in the Ford Museum. And here in Newark is more bottled breath from some fast-receding civilization that is, in fact, our own. In the modern memory house we want to save the dying breath of tomorrow—our children's.

You Have Seen Their Faces

There was a man I loved to visit. I could have listened to him tell me stories for hours. He lived in the house he grew up in. He told me once how his sisters' rooms upstairs got so hot in the summer, but they would run down to the swimming hole and come back and slip under the sheets—real cool. The swimming hole was fed by a spring. Some years back, the state widened the road and built a new bridge. They plugged that spring with a cement slab.

He has since died, but his words, deeds and children remain.

I often pass his house. His house is two hundred years old, shaded by a maple tree probably as old, and still the house seems to be keeping the tree company. Then I drive on, over that small bridge that smothered the spring.

When I am away from this corner of New Hampshire, down among the landscape of haste—parking lot and highway, mall and

273

condo—I look into the faces of my countrymen and I think of the plugged spring.

And I hear a refrain in my mind: *You Have Seen Their Faces.* That is the title of a Depression-era book by Erskine Caldwell and Margaret Bourke-White. It is a book of haunting photos of the sharecropping South, yet here in prosperity, I hear that title as a refrain.

I was reading a book once by an expert on pedestrian planning in the cities, and that refrain came to mind. The book was full of graphs and charts and plans to make everything efficiently wonderful. It stunned me. I flipped through page after page of photos of New Yorkers crossing the streets, surging up sidewalks. No one—not one—looked happy. Not one smile in the entire book. You have seen their faces.

I take those faces as a commentary on the quality of modern life. And I am afraid that a few wider sidewalks and other touted improvements will not restore any joy, any jollity to our cities.

I conducted a similar survey once myself, unintentionally. I wound up riding in the back of a pickup truck from New Jersey across Staten Island and through Brooklyn on the fabled Belt Parkway. I was sitting facing back the way we had come, looking into the windshields of the cars behind and alongside us, an unlikely point of view. And again no one was happy. People seemed annoyed, fretful, joyless. And I thought, these are my fellow countrymen.

Why are we so anxious? What are we waiting for—an apocalypse that will, at least, free us from daily routine? There is little joy in their faces, just burden, the burdens of daily worry, the burdens of expectation.

"We do not properly live in these days," said transcendentalist J. S. Dwight, "but everywhere, with patent inventions and complex arrangements, are getting ready to live. The end is lost in the means, life is smothered in appliances."

I see their faces, and I think of that spring where children once swam in summer twilight. A spring stopped from flowing, its cool waters dammed with hundreds of pounds of cement, such a lost spring is a monument to modern times.

Partings

LA SALLE CLAIMS AMERICA

At the mouth of the Mississippi, La Salle and his party pulled their canoes ashore to claim the Louisiana territory for France. After planting a column bearing the arms of France, La Salle "proclaimed in a loud voice":

In the name of the most high, mighty, invincible, and victorious Prince, Louis the Great, by the grace of God King of France and of Navarre, Fourteenth of that name, I, this ninth day of April, one thousand six hundred and eighty-two, in virtue of the commission of his Majesty, which I hold in my hand, and which may be seen by all whom it may concern, have taken, and do now take, in the name of his Majesty and of his successors to the crown, possession of this country of Louisiana, the seas, harbors, ports adjacent straits, and all the nations, peoples, provinces, cities, towns, villages, mines, minerals, fisheries, streams, and rivers. ... I hereby take to witness those who hear me, and demand an act of the notary here present.

275

"On that day," wrote the historian Francis Parkman, "the realm of France received on parchment a stupendous accession. The fertile plains of Texas; the vast basin of the Mississippi, from its frozen northern springs to the sultry borders of the Gulf; from the woody ridges of the Alleghanies to the bare peaks of the Rocky Mountains,—a region of savannahs and forests, sun-cracked deserts, and grassy prairies, watered by a thousand rivers, ranged by a thousand warlike tribes, passed beneath the sceptre of the Sultan of Versailles; and all by virtue of a feeble human voice, inaudible at half a mile."

BENEDICTION

William Mulholland, Los Angeles' chief engineer, tapped the Owens River to bring water 250 miles to the city. At the opening of the aqueduct in 1913, as the water rushed in, he made this speech to the assembled land speculators: "There it is—take it."

SHOT AN EAGLE ...

In the late 1930s Abbie Phelps set down some recollections of village life in New Ipswich, New Hampshire, in the 1880s:

> Now as we round the little turn in the road we come upon the village church (Methodist) the social center of the village, and of which affectionate memories are held by many. Strawberry Festivals, Oyster Suppers, Christmas Trees, Prize Speaking Contests, Village Improvement Societies, besides the Church service and Sunday School. After each social affair the doors each side of the pulpit and leading into the Engine Hall were opened. Old Water Witch Engine was drawn outside and all the old fashioned dances were enjoyed to the music of the organ or violin. An eagle adorned the hall, which was shot up the river by W. E. Preston, when he was 13 years old. ...

THE LEAVES, LIKE GOLD
(OR: THE ELMS—YOU SHOULD HAVE SEEN THEM)

Helen Butler, like many in her native city of Syracuse, New York, remembers when the elms, with their noble presence, sheltered every street.

"They were just gorgeous. You would walk down streets— Oxford Street, I can always remember, that's here in the city, and they have—they had—tulip trees and they were under the elms. And in blossom it would be a sight to go down that street.

"The elms made archways over the street and the sun would shine through and on a day that was very bright, especially in the fall when the leaves were beginning to turn yellow—you know and dry up and go—it was almost golden going through that street. Just to look down it, just like gold. Oh many streets, many. ... "

A BLUE FISH WAGON

Letter to *The West Ender*, the newsletter of a vanished Boston neighborhood:

> I got your newsletter and see all the names, and it flushes out all the memories. God, how I wish I could turn back the clock and sell them all that fish again from the blue pushcart with that bell ringing to tell you we were coming—all except Tootsie Oddo who would buy ten pounds of squid and demand that I clean it and cut it up. (Heaven help me if I refused.)
>
> I still dream of the West End and the streets and buildings seeing them so clear as if I were really there now and so disappointed when I awake—because who wants to leave the West End?

THE TREES, AT 180 NAUTICAL MILES; YOU COULD SMELL THEM

Sailing to America, the early settlers could begin to smell pine trees 180 nautical miles from landfall. Or was it anticipation?

Acknowledgments

The memory of a few lives animated the writing of *In The Memory House*. They were people I didn't know very well, or didn't even know at all, but whose lives, like good poems, had a certain rhythm, a beautiful pattern. I am indebted to these people, in particular Willard Richardson and Myer Goldman.

For their help, I thank these librarians and archivists: Pat Briggs, Judy Garabrant, Alan Rumrill and Sylvia Durfee.

For sharing their memories of Myer Goldman, I thank, in particular, Mary Garland and Fritz Wetherbee, and Bill Bauhan, Bob Brown, Rick Frede, George Kendall, Diane Goldman, Florence Goldman, Jim Grant, Charlie, Roland and Barbara LaRoche, John Leonard, Eugene McCarthy, Pete Pelletier and Goldie Silverman.

For preserving and honoring the memory of Boston's old West End, I offer my admiration and thanks to the editors of *The West Ender*, James Campano and Joseph LoPiccolo, and to all the people of that vanished neighborhood.

For their advice and insight, I thank Willard Williams, Jim Naughton, Lea and Gretchen Poisson. I must thank Christopher Hogwood for offering his continuing insights into the appetites of this world. And also to Tess for providing a paradigm of grace and speed.

For reading the manuscript and suggesting changes, I thank Elizabeth Marshall Thomas and Steve Thomas, Janice Gordon, Dan Chartrand and Joni Praded (may she one day see the light and appreciate Thoreau).

Thanks to my editor at Fulcrum, Carmel A. Huestis, and to Jill Mason for her careful copyediting.

Many thanks to my agent, Christina Ward.

Finally, my deepest thanks to my wife, Sy Montgomery, the best editor I have ever had.